THE SOVEREIGN ALL-CREATING MIND
THE MOTHERLY BUDDHA

SUNY Series in Buddhist Studies
Kenneth K. Inada, Editor

THE SOVEREIGN ALL-CREATING MIND
THE MOTHERLY BUDDHA

A Translation of the *Kun byed rgyal po'i mdo*

*

E. K. Neumaier-Dargyay

State University of New York Press

Published by
State University of New York Press, Albany

Printed in the United States of America

For information, address State University of New York Press, State University Plaza, Albany, N.Y., 12246

Production by Diane Ganeles
Marketing by Dana E. Yanulavich

Library of Congress Cataloging-in-Publication Data

Tripiṭaka. Sūtrapiṭaka. Tantra.
Sarvadharmamahāśāntibodhicittakulayarāja. English.
The Sovereign all-creating mind—the motherly Buddha : a translation of the Kun byed rgyal po'i mdo / [translated by] E.K. Neumaier-Dargyay.
p. cm. — (SUNY series in Buddhist studies)
Translation of: Sarvadharmamahāśāntibodhicittakulayarāja, from the Tibetan, Kun byed rgyal po'i mdo.
Includes bibliographical references and index.
ISBN 0-7914-0895-7 (alk. paper). — ISBN 0-7914-0896-5 (pbk. alk. paper)
I. Neumaier-Dargyay, E. K. (Eva K.), 1937- II. Title.
III. Series.
BQ2180.S2522.E56 1992
294.3'85—dc20 91-2500
CIP

10 9 8 7 6 5 4 3 2 1

To all who have taught me

CONTENTS

ABBREVIATIONS

Bh	Royal Bhutanese edition of the rNying ma'i rgyud 'bum
KBG	Kun byed rgyal po
Kh	Khyentse edition of the rNying ma'i rgyud 'bum
Khych	Khyung chen ldings pa
Mvy	Mahâvyutpatti, ed. R. Sakaki, repr. 1962
NGB	rNying ma'i rgyud 'bum
SMG	bSam gtan mig gron
VGB	Bair ro'i (Vairocana) rgyud 'bum

ACKNOWLEDGMENTS

The present work was made possible through a Leave Fellowship granted by the Social Sciences and Humanities Research Council of Canada which provided me with the funds to carry out the necessary research during a sabbatical leave granted by The University of Calgary. To both institutions I am much indebted for their support and encouragement. The Central Institute for Higher Tibetan Studies in Sarnath/Benares, India, offered excellent research facilities. My sincere thanks go to Professor Samdhong Rinpoche, Principal, who extended such warm hospitality. Professor mKhan-po Rig-'dzin tutored me with endless patience in my attempt to understand the essence of the text I am presenting here in translation. His instructions proved an invaluable help which I am acknowledging with great gratitude. But I am sure there are still things I have misunderstood or not at all understood. These failures are my sole responsibility. Dr. Bettina Bäumer, Alice Boner Stiftung, Benares, helped me with her expertise in Kashmîri Shaivism in particular and in Hindu spirituality in general. With joy and gratitude I will always remember the hours she spent with me sharing her knowledge. But I am also indebted to my colleagues and friends, particularly to Dr. Phyllis Granoff, who through critical questioning brought me to a fuller appreciation of the present text and its philosophical implications and who was so kind as to read the manuscript of the introduction. Dr. Harold Coward gave me much-appreciated advice with regard to the final manuscript. Geshey Lobsang Dargyay contributed much to the success of my work through his intellectual support but also through making daily life in a difficult environment easier.

INTRODUCTION

"The All-Creating Sovereign, the Mind of Perfect Purity" (henceforth KBG) is a Buddhist scripture. What distinguishes it from so many other Buddhist texts is the timeliness of its ideas. It constitutes a radical attempt towards deconstructing Buddhist philosophy and presents a rather unusual feminist perspective of Buddhist spirituality. Regardless of the origin of the text (which is still largely veiled in mystery) the text in itself speaks loud and clear and delivers a message germane to the present. The text is adamant in saying that "being" is the centre and depth of existence, thus accessible in everyday experience. More than any other Buddhist scripture the KBG states: the fleeting existence (samsara) is in its depth "being," i.e. a dynamic process of complete integration (nirvana). This consummation may well be described as divine reality of a feminine dimension. This divine reality, the text argues, must never be appropriated through our conceptual thinking or through the process of defining and naming it. Thus the doctrinal structure of Buddhism is not only questioned but deconstructed, and eventually rejected. The natural corollary is then that there is no spiritual goal to achieve (i.e. nirvana), no religious practice to perform (i.e. path to enlightenment), and neither disciple nor Buddha. In other words the entirety of the Buddhist doctrinal and practical system is brushed aside by a Buddhist text! These seemingly extreme positions are maintained on the ground that all that exists does so due to "pristine awareness" as the dynamic of being. Thus, one has to conclude, all that exists is already in the process of consummation. Being as such (understood as a dynamic "spinning," and not as an essence) is buddhahood. The world in its manifold variety is the manifestation of the pristine awareness which endows all that exists with order and intelligibility. Consequently the world is beautiful, and the KBG admonishes its reader to rejoice in this beauty. Even what appears to the ignorant eye as ugly and painful reveals its intrinsic beauty to the sage. With this message the KBG certainly opens a new dimension of Buddhist thought.

This is the first time that this text has been translated into a modern language. The text itself consists of several components: the "root tantra," and two additions called "later tantras." The additions are in general recapitulations of topics covered in the root text. For this reason only the latter is given in translation here. As is the case with many Buddhist texts, The All-Creating Sovereign is repetitive because the text is a meditation orbiting around one theme: the "mind"[1] as intelligent, all-pervasive ground of the universe, and as an autonomous cognitiveness or *gnosis*. This theme is contemplated in all its facets, mirrored in a hundred ways, by illuminating it in the light of leading Buddhist concepts. Therefore the text gives us the impression of moving along loops rather than along a straight line. Subtle nuances distinguish seemingly similar, if not identical statements. But in this repetitiveness the richness of the basic theme also reveals itself to the contemplative mind.

First we shall talk in a cursory way about the position mind holds in Indian thought. Because of our scant knowledge and the complexity of this topic, only those Indian texts which may have provided a philosophical background for our text will be briefly mentioned. Then we shall examine the Buddhist views of the mind as stepping stones leading us to a fuller comprehension of the KBG. Secondly we shall survey the historical context from which the text emerged, and ask in particular, what kind of text is the KBG? The text has the appearance of a sutra, which commonly means that Buddha is talking to a person who poses certain questions to him. However, the text is preserved in the tantra section of the Buddhist canon and therefore called a tantra (an esoteric Buddhist text). This incongruity will be discussed together with the authenticity of the text and its transmittance through the tradition. Thirdly, I shall summarize the basic ideas of the text to enable the reader to follow the translation with more ease. A topical analysis of the chapters (given at the end of the book) will make the structure of the text more transparent. Finally the language of the text and its inherent meaningfulness will be examined, together with a discussion of the way the Tibetan text has been translated.

1. THE CONCEPTUAL CONTEXT

The attempt to provide a background for the broader understanding of the themes covered in the KBG by illuminating areas of similar Indian and Buddhist thought is questionable, regardless of how desirable it is. From its beginnings, Indian thought orbited around a non-physical power which comes close to what we mean by "mind." A plethora of religious and philosophical texts, the majority of them neither translated nor properly studied by modern scholars, exists within the many strands of Hindu and Buddhist traditions, whereby each text and each tradition redefined the inherited assumptions and incorporated new ideas. The complexity of such endeavour and our still fragmented knowledge of the voluminous literature pertinent to the topic "mind" precludes the possibility of covering it within an introduction. The desire to discuss this topic in a scholarly and responsible way would not only require a lifelong commitment to researching it, but would also necessitate a series of monographs. It is one of the deplorable but unavoidable facts of oriental studies that compact and yet accurate information, for instance in the form of an encyclopedia, is virtually non-existent.

Having said all this, I want nevertheless to give the reader some help in exploring this vast field for him- or herself. Thus I shall mention certain literatures and traditions which contributed more than others to the Indian idea of "mind." The underlying assumption is that these works of similar ideas constitute, to some extent, the intellectual and literary environment in which the KBG arose. A study of these works of related thought may provide an opportunity to appreciate the idiosyncrasy of the KBG within its philosophical and religious context.

A. The Mind—Pivot of the Universe in Non-Buddhist Indian Literture

For centuries the West has preferred to see the universe as a gigantic machine which is either in perpetual motion (Laplace) or which converts heat into motion with a final state of thermal equilibrium, "heat death."[2] Despite of the enormous diversity of opinions about what constitutes the nature of the universe, all, except for the most recent hypotheses, perceive it from a mechanical point of view—as a matter of physics. In contrast to this modern view, India, for more than three millenia, has embraced the idea that a non-physical potency is the origin of the universe. In recent years western scientists seem to revert to some of these ancient ideas. Fritjof Capra with *The Tao of Physics* is perhaps the most widely read author and the first to draw public attention to this issue.[3] Others followed in his footsteps.[4]

(1) The Mind as Creative Potency in Vedic and Hindu Literature

The Buddhist text presented here deals with timeless questions: what is the ontological reason for the existence of the universe? what is being? what is the position of humanity within this framework? what is the nature of interaction between the different components of the universe? how does the universe come into existence? if everything is saturated with the divine, what is the role of ethics? But the text presents these questions and their answers in the trappings of its own historical and cultural environment. One has to break through this cultural shell to reach the kernel, i.e. the meaning of the text which is not confind to one era or one culture.

At present the history of the KBG cannot be traced back beyond the 8th century at the earliest, as will be shown in a subsequent chapter of the introduction. Nevertheless, the text was most likely part of a stream of Indian Buddhist texts that reached Tibet during the 8th and 9th centuries. Thus we may assume that the ideological and literary background of the KBG has to be sought in India.

However, before we embark on a journey to trace possible connections with ancient Indian ideas, we have to consider another possible root of the KBG, and that is its link with Chinese Ch'an Buddhism (in the West better known under its Japanese name "Zen"). First, M. Lalou described Tibetan texts documenting the existence of Ch'an Buddhism in early Tibet (8/9th century).[5] Later, the Italian pioneer of Tibetan studies, Giuseppe Tucci, established a connection between early Tibetan Buddhism and Ch'an Buddhism. In his influential work *Minor Buddhist Texts*[6] he expressed the opinion that the Tibetan form of Ch'an survived in camouflage as a strand known as the Great Perfection (*rdzogs chen*) to which our text belongs.[7] A further connection with China is provided by the Tibetan tradition which links some early masters of the Great Perfection school with China.[8] A problem which plagues this issue is that many of the Buddhist masters who lived and worked in China were raised and educated in places located in Central Asia along the Silk Road where Indian cultural influence was predominant. Consequently many of the "Chinese" masters were actually Sogdian or Khotanese.[9] It would be premature at this moment to venture a position as to whether the leading ideas of the Great Perfection school as expressed in the KBG came directly from India to Tibet, or *via* Khotan, Sogdia, and/or China to Tibet. Regardless what future research will discover, it is a fact that Buddhism originated and had thrived in India for more than 1500 years, and that from there it had reached Inner Asia and China. Thus the entire field of Indian thought must be considered as a primary reservoir for any development of Buddhist thought. This of course does not preclude indigenous developments which opened new frontiers in Buddhist thinking.

If, for the time being, we accept the statement of the Tibetan tradition that the KBG was translated from an Indian language into Tibetan by the end of the 8th century, then we have to infer that the text, not necessarily in the present form but perhaps as a set of oral instructions, existed in India prior to that time.

In what follows I shall refer to schools of thought and literatures which consitute the intellectual and literary context for ideas of the "mind" as the creative force of the universe, that is, ideas which show a variant degree of similarity with what we find in the KBG. These sparse references should however by no means be understood as a survey of the Indian literature about mind.

Jan Gonda has in a recent article compiled numerous evidences as to *manas* (inadequately translated as "mind") found in the Rig-Vedic and later Vedic literature.[10] Gonda comes to the conclusion that "mind" in modern usage is an abstract and erudite construct, while to the ancient sages it was a potency full of life and fire.

In the post-Rig-Vedic literature it is maintained that before non-being and being came into existence there was only *manas*.[11] In the KBG 3.6–16 we read that the "mind of perfect purity" predates everything else:

> I am the mind of perfect purity, the maker of all. If I were not existent in the past, no vigour were there for all things to originate. If I were not existent in the past, no Sovereign were there who made all things. If I were not existent in the past, none were there to be a teacher from the primordial. If I were not existent in the past, none were there to teach from the primordial. If I were not existent in the past, that which is known as retinues would not be there from the primordial.

In the Brahmanas and Aranyakas this *manas* is further qualified as "lord" and "ruler" over a number of "vital principles" (*prâna*). Vishvakarma, the Vedic "All-Maker" is endowed with *manas*, and from this statement the development leads to the saying that *manas* becomes the principle potency responsible for creation.[12] Thus the images we find in the KBG, i.e. the primary, non-appropriated mind, ruling like a sovereign over all that exists and creating everything, were available in certain strands of Indian thought at a fairly early time, perhaps even prior to Buddhism.

Well-educated Buddhist thinkers of India certainly lived in a situation of "intertextuality," that is "texts"—whether in oral or written form—constituted part of the general environment in which literary people conversed.[13] Phrases, metaphors, stereotypes, and symbolic expressions were "public domain" to be borrowed by everyone who liked these expressions. This textual and literary environment influenced, most likely unintentionally and unconcsiously, the literary style of compilers and authors of texts like the KBG. Regardless of the philosophical disagreements between Vedic/Upanishadic and Buddhist thought, Buddhist writers and thinkers still lived within the environment of Indian literature; they were exposed to its style and influenced by its predilection for metaphoric expressions. When it came to the point to verbalize mystical experiences, like those underlying the KBG, the "author" (unknown to us) could regress to earlier stylistic and symbolic expressions and still maintain a rejection of the major conceptual framework in which these stylistic elements were originally embedded.

A major stepping-stone in the development of a philosophy of mind in India are the works of Gaudapâda and Shankara, which declared the mind as the source of the ephemeral world. Occasionally the mind is said to be like *akâsa*, sky or space. In the KBG the most used metaphor of the sovereign mind is *nam mkha'*, the Tibetan equivalent to Skt. *akâsa*.

The *Yogavâsistha*, a voluminous work whose literary and ideological context is still debated, contains long passages dealing with the mind as the base of the universe. The text projects a non-dualistic world-view whose focus is the mind, perfectly pure, the ground of all being, and which is like ether. Some of the images and metaphors of the *Yogavâsistha* seem to be echoed in the KBG, or *vice versa*: for instance in 2.55–56 of the *Yogavâsistha*, the absolute is compared with an actor impersonating different characters by putting on different costumes; while KBG 73.34 talks about a dance of stillness by the sovereign mind thereby letting unfold the manifest world. Despite the extensive scholarship on the *Yogavâsistha* the text has retained much of its mystery. Thus speculations about possible connections between the KBG and the *Yogavâsistha* are premature at present.[14]

In recent years, Kashmirian Shaivism has attracted scholarly attention, although a comprehensive understanding of this system is still unachievable.[15] The system developed in Kashmir, a place with strong ancient ties to Tibet, at a time when the contacts between these two countries were particulary vibrant, from the 8th to the 11th centuries. Thus the geographical and historical context could be seen as providing a forum for contacts between the circles promoting ideas of Kashmirian Shaivism and those associated with the thinking we find in the KBG. Whether this was truly the case, however, can at the present not be decided. Furthermore, Kashmirian Shaivism seems to have certain aspects in common with the KBG: Shiva is seen as the inner self of all sentient beings and of the inanimate nature,[16] very much like the All-Creating Sovereign who as autonomous, or self-originated pristine awareness (*rang byung ye shes*) is present in all that exists. The awareness of Shiva as the inner self can not be generated because from the beginning of existence this inner self breathes life into all that exists. Thus this primordial awareness is not a new state of knowing but rather a recollection of something that has been there all the time, although unknown to the individual. A major point of dissent is that the KBG appears to be more inclined towards feminine symbols and metaphors, while Kashmirian Shaivism remains firmly entrenched in its phallocentric symbolism. The KBG further disagrees with Kashmirian Shaivism when it comes to define a method to achieve this sublime state of recollection. In Shaivism there are four stages of "means" (*upâya*) facilitating the purifying of the mind so that the individual becomes aware of its primordial divine nature. In contrast, the KBG rejects any attempt to structure such a path by firmly insisting on the full presence of the divine in the given situation. Consequently, Kashmirian Shaivism knows about a yoga leading to the realization of the divine, while the KBG rejects such an idea as a fatal error. These few remarks about possible affinities between the KBG and Kashmirian Shaivism should not cloud the fact that a detailed comparison of the two systems is beyond the scope of an introduction; the complexity of the respective thoughts warrants a monographic study.

To discuss Indian religious works as hypothetically providing a milieu from which some of the thoughts found in the KBG could arise is further justified when we consider the following information: Pho-brang Zhi-ba-'od, an 11th century prince of the Himalayan kingdom of Guge (today known as Spiti), alleged that the KBG was a text forged by Drang-nga Shag-tshul (Shâkya tshul-khrims) of Khro-gangs in Upper Nyang. This accusation is included in a letter addressed to the Buddhists of Tibet in which the prince warns them of certain texts which he deems detrimental to the pursuit of liberation and enlightenment. The alleged author he classifies as a follower of "eternalism," that is, of a view that embraces ontologically real entities; such a view is in Buddhism always branded as an extreme, in other words, a deviation from the middle path of the true Buddhist teaching.[17] In general Tibetan Buddhist writers identified Hindu philosphers as "eternalists;" thus one may speculate that our prince of Guge opined that the KBG along with a number of similar works are the result of a forgery committed by some Hindu thinker(s), and given the close association of certain ideas with Kashmirian Shaiva notions, we might even assume that he had in mind a Kashmirian Shaivite. At the same time, however, it should be mentioned that the validity of this letter is open to questioning as several of the works on this "black list" were accepted as authentic Buddhist works by masters whose integrity was beyond question. In any case, given the close ties of Kashmir to Tibet, we might be justified in assuming that Kashmirian Shaivism forms part of that environment of "intertextuality" we have referred to before.

B. *The Mind in Buddhist Thought*

The following inquiry is not intended as a comprehensive discussion of this more than complex topic, but to provide stepping-stones for readers not well-acquainted with Buddhist thought to follow the translation with greater ease. Thus the theme will be treated in a subjective and selective way.

In Buddhist texts the term *citta* (which is commonly considered to be synomymous with *manas*, the term preferred in the Vedic and post-Vedic literature) is used as a generic term to cover the non-physical components of humans and other living creatures as well as the intelligent element integral to absolute Reality. Thus the term occurs in the context of Buddhist psychology, ethics, epistemology, and metaphysics. The concept of "mind" (in the sense of *citta*) is more central to Buddhist thinking than to any other system of Indian thought. In fact, there is a common impression that much of Buddhism consists of nothing else but in gazing at one's own mind. This view is not unjustified if we look at the opening verse of one of the most ancient and most popular Buddhist texts, the *Dhammapâda*:

> The mind (*manaso*) precedes the given phenomena which are dominated by the mind, conditioned by the mind. If one speaks or acts with a distorted mind then suffering will follow this person as the wheel follows the draught animal. (Dhp.I.1)[18]

In this programmatic statement "mind" may refer to the individual mind or to Mind as a transpersonal potency inherent to being. If we embrace the first option, then the second line has to be taken as an elaboration of the first by saying that through the mind one acts and speaks. But if we take the second option, then the second line would be in contrast to what is said in the first line. That is to say, only after the transpersonal Mind has become manifest as an individual mind, does a person speak, i.e. conceptualize and communicate, and act in accord with and in dependence on that Mind. In other words, the dual character of "mind" would then be addressed in these two lines: the first speaking of the transpersonal ("absolute") Mind, while the second referring to the personal mind through which the individual conceptualizes and interacts. Some of the difficulties in translating and understanding this verse are discussed in Max Müller's translation.[19]

The Theravâda commentators embraced the first option of understanding this verse by interpreting it within the context of the twelve limbs of dependent co-arising (*pratîtyasamutpâda*). This chain of twelve causal limbs starts out with "ignorance," i.e. an obscured mind, and covers the circle of death, rebirth, and old age.[20] The problem created thereby is that the term *manas*, as a generic term, comprises the four non-physical aggregates (*skandha*), i.e. feelings, perceptions, impulses, and consciousness, which form part of the twelve limbs of dependent co-arising. This implies that the generic term, i.e. *manas*, is said to precede its specific forms, and that mind antedates or presupposes ignorance.[21] Such thinking is only possible if an independent transpersonal entity is supposed as lying behind the specific, but that would be unacceptable to the Buddhist teaching. Another possible scenario could be constructed by arguing that the word "preceding" is used in a non-temporal and non-causal sense, that is, that without mind no given phenomena could exist. But why, then, would one say that without the generic no specific could exist? And after all, this would bring us back to the previous dilemma. We will take up this problem again when discussing the view of the Sarvâstivâda school.

At the moment we shall continue our search for Mind/mind in the Pâli Canon. In the Pâli Abhidharma it is said that when the practitioner has entered the transcendental path (*lokuttara magga*) the mind will be of a transcendental nature (*lokuttaram cittam bhâveti*).[22] The *Abhidhammattha Sangaha* distinguishes four kinds of transcendental mind: the mind associated with the path of having entered the stream of Buddhist teaching (*sotâpatti magga cittam*), the mind associated with the path of returning only one more time to samsaric existence (*sakadâgâmi magga cittam*), the mind associated with the path of no returning (*anâgâmi magga cittam*), and the mind associated with the path of the arhat, the person who realizes nirvana (*arahatta magga cittam*). These four types of transcendental mind are then subdivided into many more categories as the transcendental mind of each path relates to other soteriologic aspects.[23] It seems that the term *lokuttara*, which I rendered as "transcendental," refers to the mind as being part of the advancement towards nirvana. Thus the more concrete notion of the term would be "other-worldly," with the implication that it does not refer to the this-worldy mind, but to that which strives for nirvana. This transcendental mind is characterized by "knowing the unknown," that is, a new frontier which opened itself to the mind, or, in more conservative Buddhist terms, the mind passes through the door of liberation. The transcendental mind cognizes what is essentially unknowable to the ordinary mind. If that transcendental mind is capable of doing that, one may argue, then not only is its object of transcedental nature but so is the Mind itself. In this context mind is not the individual's response to the sensory stimuli provided by the outside world but is fundamental to being.

Buddhaghosa, in his commentary on the *Dhammasanganî*, explained that passage by telling the parable of a man and four baskets:[24] A man has four baskets in a treasure-chamber. At night he has to do some business there. He lights a candle, whereby only one basket, being in the light, becomes visible to him. He carries out the business he had come for, and when he leaves the chamber darkness covers all baskets. Three times he repeats this act, but when he enters the chamber for the fourth time the sun is about to rise and all four baskets become visible. This is the moment of enlightenment. The gist of the parable seems to be that whatever insight is acquired prior to enlightenment, it is of a fragmentary character while the liberating insight gained at the moment of arhatship (entering nirvana according to the Theravâda school) is all-encompassing; it is whole and total. Thus this insight is of transcendental character. Buddhaghosa makes reference only to a mind perceived as a flux of momentary phenomena whereby the nature of the flux changes due to the changing character of the individual phenomena of which it is comprised.

A crucial problem of Buddhism has been how there can be continuity in one's striving towards nirvana and spiritual progress if all mental phenomena are conceived as momentary entities which come and go like a flash. This dilemma was continuously reformulated, and the various traditions responded to it in different ways. The predicament was not only of a conceptual nature, but at its heart lay a meditational experience. The experience the Buddhist recluse had when his or her mind was in a state of stillness, beyond all conceptual thinking, seemed to contradict the assumption of the universal momentariness of all mental phenomena. The *Short Sermon on Voidness*

(*Cullasuññatta sutta*) talks about this experience in an explicit manner.[25] In this *sutta* the Buddha says that the Buddhist mendicant (*bhiksu*) ought to empty his mind of sensory objects. The training takes the practitioner through a regimen to empty the mind from the perception of relatively coarse objects (like elephants, villages, and forests) up to more subtle ones, like thoughts and imaginations, till one reaches a state of no-thought. This is expressed in a statement indicating a dialectic jump; it says that the mendicant realizes the emptiness of his or her mind and dwells in its fullness which is experienced as bliss. How can bliss be sensed if the mind rests without the awareness of any object? What senses this bliss? What is this bliss? Something else but mind? These questions arising from meditational experience had to be reconciled with the premises of Buddhist philosophical thinking.

Western thinking originated, according to Northrop Frye, as a reconciliation of metaphorical thinking with metonymic.[26] In Buddhism the issue was to reconcile the conceptual casting of the Buddhist doctrine with how these same theorems were intuitively sensed during objectless mental absorption. Buddhist schools that considered meditational experience superior to reasoning would then argue for a non-physical, non-substantial groundedness carrying the stream of momentary mental entities. The followers of the school "All Exists" (Sarvâstivadins) called this groundedness *paramârtha citta*, the absolute Mind whose nature is ceaseless and immutable. This Mind constituted in their system the base of everything. Other Buddhist schools, like the Sautrântika, rejected this proposition.[27]

In the Mahâyâna literature this idea gained momentum and branched into several strands: the *âlayavijñâna* (frequently translated as "storehouse consciousness" but perhaps more adequatly as "foundation-consciousness"), the concept of the innate "Buddhagerm" (*tathâgatagarbha*), and voidness (*sunyatâ*) as understood by the Tibetan thinker Dol-po-pa. Although Dol-po-pa's understanding of voidness is a fascinating deviation from the mainstream Madhyamaka understanding, his thought will remain beyond our consideration because he formulated his ideas after the KBG was established as a text.

Canonical statements, supporting or believed to support such concepts, are found in the *Suvikrântavikrâmi pariprchhâ prajñâpâramitâ sûtra*,[28] the *Siksasamuccaya*,[29] the *Lankâvatâra sûtra*,[30] and the *Ratnagotravibhâga*, to name the most important.

The *âlayavijñâna* is sometimes understood as a flux of mental phenomena that constitutes a continuum existing beyond the individidual's life.[31] But, as L. Schmithausen showed in his thorough study of the *âlayavijñâna*, such an assumption is reading into the text the exegis it received in later tractates.[32] Originally the term seems to identify a reservoir for all karmic "seeds," or a continuum to which these seeds could "cling" (which is one of the many connotations of the word *âlaya*).

The text which comes closest to the KBG in all of this is the *Ratnagotravibhâga*.[33] This canonical text tells us that "This" (i.e. being as such) cannot be polluted or mutilated by anything, and that in this respect it is similar to all-pervading space (or sky) that cannot be polluted due to its subtle nature.[34] This statement is reminiscent of KBG chapter 5 (Tib. p. 15) where it is said:

> Like the sky so is Reality; by means of the sky as simile [Reality] is pointed out. The imperceptible Reality is taught by pointing at [something else which is] imperceptible.

Verses 59–63 of the *Ratnagotravibhâga* talk about the "Innate Mind" being like space, but a reversive trend of the mind generates defilements and the multiplicity of phenomena which constitute an ephemeral reality. The "Innate Mind" knows of no beginning or end, not even a stability. In its true nature this Mind is brilliant and immutable like space. A cursory reading of the *Ratnagotravibhâga* suggests that the KBG has adopted several of its terms and main ideas. Takasaki assumes that the *Ratnagotravibhâga* was compiled after Nâgârjuna and Aryadeva (commonly dated into the 2nd century C.E.) but before the *Lankâvatâra sûtra* was translated for the first time into Chinese by 433 C.E. Thus it would be possible for the compilers of the KBG (said to have been translated into Tibetan by the late 8th century) to have been fully acquainted with the ideas and the terminology of the *Ratnagotravibhâga*.

If, for the moment, we accept as true the premise that the KBG was translated into Tibetan during the later part of the 8th century, then we have to limit a possible influence of the *Ratnagotravibhâga* upon the KBG to the time when the KBG was still circulating in India. The *Ratnagotravibhâga* was translated into Tibetan during the 11th century by Blo-ldan shes-rab at Srinagar in Kashmir and consequently was not known at the time the KBG is claimed to have been translated into Tibetan. However, if we doubt the claim made in the colophon of the KBG regarding the date of its translation into Tibetan, then we may opine that the KBG is perhaps the literary result of an encounter with the *Ratnagotravibhâga*. Such a hypothesis would find support in the accusation made by a prince of Guge during the 11th century that the KBG is a forged text (see the section above on a possible influence of Kashmirian Shaivism).

In Chinese Ch'an Buddhism the development took a distinctive turn in so far as the concept of "no-mind" (Chin. *wu shin* or *wu nien*) was to displace Mind as proclaimed in the *Ratnagotravibhâga*. This concept of *wu shin* was developed by Hui-neng who adhered to the southern school of Ch'an. It was felt that when self-nature, the autonomous being innate to all that exists, is intuited, the mind as one of the five aggregates can no longer be its reference. Thus the reference for intuiting self-nature is "no-mind" or, as the KBG would say, pristine awareness (*rang byung ye shes*). Suzuki elaborates on this issue as follows:

> When thus the seeing of self-nature has no reference to a specific state of consciousness, which can be logically or relatively defined as something, the Zen masters designate it in negative terms and call it 'no-thought' or 'no-mind', *wu nien* or *wu hsin*.[35]

The obvious similarity shared by some ideas developed within Chinese Ch'an traditions and the Tibetan Great Perfection tradition was mentioned before. At present our knowledge is still scanty and does not allow a comprehensive understanding of how this similarity came about. By now however we are certain, unlike earlier scholars of Tibetan Buddhism, that the Great Perfection is not the Tibetan form of Ch'an. The present hypothesis is that the Great Perfection School preserved material that was seminal to the development of Chinese Ch'an, but which was lost later on. Further studies of the literature of the Great Perfection School are necessary to gain a better understanding of its own evolution before we may venture upon a comparative study.

Looking back at our survey of how "mind" was understood within the Indian and Buddhist traditions, we witnessed a development from an archaic concept of mind as a creative potency to a mystical awareness of "no-mind." All these various facets, created in the attempt to grasp the nature of the elusive mind, have bearings on the KBG. If we adopt for the moment Northrop Frye's theory about the phases in the development of language we may apply it to the KBG in the following manner:[36] It employs metaphoric language, typical of the Vedic literature, when it refers to the ground of being as "all-creating sovereign;" it uses metonymic language (signifying something other than the word alleges) by interpreting the term *rang byung ye shes*, self-originated or autonomous pristine awareness, as being void of any object to become aware of; in its discussion of doctrinal matters of Buddhism the texts applies a descriptive language. These three phases, metaphoric, metonymic, and descriptive, are indicative of three phases in human history: the archaic, the scholastic, and the modern. Thus the KBG is a text which aspires to include the entire literary tradition of India and Buddhism by transforming each of its distinctive traits into a cipher meaningful only within a web of paradoxes. This fabric of signs, each eluding rational conceptualization, is designed to lead the reader to experiencing the overpowering message of silence or the muteness of language. Language itself becomes a web of illusion veiling the depth of being. The text will take us from the surface of Buddhist doctrinal elements (such as the three forms of Buddha's existence) to the depth of final integration where all distinctions coincide in oneness.

2. THE HISTORICAL CONTEXT

The historical context within which the KBG became crystalized as a coherent religious text is the history of Buddhist literature in general and of that of the canon in particular. First we shall survey the formation of the Buddhist canon before we discuss the transmittance and authenticity of the KBG itself.

A. Formation of the Buddhist Canon in India

Buddhist scripture is the word of the Buddha; this is the basic definition given by the tradition. A close examination shows however that this stern sentence asks for modifications and that Buddhist scriptures are only an approximation of this maxim. The very fact that Buddhist scriptures were not put into writing before the 1st century B.C.E., that is 400 years after Buddha's death, makes the statement that they record Buddha's word questionable. At an early time the problem of what exactly constitutes the word of the Buddha arose for the tradition. Buddhists more than anybody else were aware of the fleeting character of the spoken word, so what was commended to writing? The word spoken by the Buddha, or the word heard by the disciples, or the word most suitable for demonstrating the way to enlightenment; what hermeneutical devices were suitable to decode the not always apparent meaning of a sacred text?

In the course of history each Buddhist community created its own collection of sacred texts. Thus there are several Buddhist canons which comprise different collections of sacred texts: the Pâli canon, or *tripitaka*, of the Theravâda tradition; the Chinese canon, mostly referred to as *san ts'ang*, recognised by the Buddhists of the Far East; and the Tibetan *bka' 'gyur* (Kanjur) accepted as "Buddha Word" by the Buddhists of Central Asia. There were also further collections which are extant in fragments or which have vanished altogether.

(1) The Pâli Canon

In the Theravâda tradition, custodian of the Pâli canon, it was assumed that the word spoken by the Buddha was faithfully imprinted in the disciple's mind. Ananda, Buddha's attendant for decades, was equipped with an extraordinary memory, and so it became his task to rehearse the sermons after Buddha's entry into nirvana. These sermons reproduced from Ananda's memory became the cornerstone of the Pâli canon. This collection of texts was first put into writing in the Aluvihâra of Ceylon, or Sri Lanka as this island is known today, under the reign of King Vattagâmanî Abhaya (r. 89–77 B.C.E.) after 400 years of oral transmittance. The text's authenticity rested at that time upon the credibility of the rehearser.

When Buddha's sermons started to proliferate in a number of Middle-Indian vernaculars the problem of authenticity and faithfulness became more acute.[37] The Indian civilization of that era had already developed sophisticated methods to ensure an accurate transmitting of oral texts as substantiated by the transmission of the Rig-Veda. But the historical Buddha rejected this approach with its emphasis on memorization, dissecting the text into its linguistic elements and so on. As the prime focus of Buddha's instructions was the realization of liberating insight or nirvana, the form of these instructions became irrelevant. Thus monks from different regions of India and other countries used their own languages and dialects to repeat Buddha's words. This was the source for the enormous diversification of the Buddhist canon.[38] But the Theravâda tradition rejected this view by upholding the opinion that Pâli was the Buddha's own language and that his disciples should use it as the sole medium in transmitting the Buddha word. The result was the codification of what is known as the Pâli canon, a well-defined body of scriptures, organized in three collections: the collection of regulations pertinent to the monks and nuns; the collection of Buddha's sermons (*sutta*); and the collection of theoretical abstracts (*abhidharma*) which was added later on. In our effort to trace the development of "mind" and its understanding in the early Buddhist literture we came accross some of the texts incorporated in this canon.

(2) The Canons of the Mahâyâna Tradition

When a segment of the Buddhist community distanced itself from the Pâli tradition and its canon, it gradually developed ideas from which a movement originated known as Mahâyâna. The concept of scripture asked for redefinition in the light of these new ideas.[39] By that time, the presence of the historical Buddha, whose paramount figure had dominated the early disciples' minds, had faded away in favor of a symbolic understanding of Buddha's nature. In the words of the Buddhist doctrine we may say that the *dharmakâya*, Buddha's intrinsic awareness of reality, displaced the *rûpakâya*, Buddha's visible presence or his historical existence. The word of the Buddha was not anymore grounded in the earthly, historical Buddha's uttering but in its conformity with the spirit of what the historical Buddha had experienced: enlightenment. Consequently those who had achieved enlightenment could speak "in the spirit" of the Buddha. On this basis the Mahâyâna sutras claimed to be authentic scriptures, regardless of whether the words of the text had ever been voiced by the historical Buddha. But also the concept of what constitutes the content of the sacred text changed during this process of actualization. In the attempt to capture "things as they are" (*yathâbhûtâ*) the Buddhists found themselves in the predicament to have to express the inexplicable. Thus Buddhist scripture changed from being a pragmatic instruction of how to achieve enlightenment (as expressed in the parable of the man hit by an arrow) to being an expression of encountering a reality that was by its very nature beyond the reach of words (resulting in a language full of paradoxes and negations).

In the course of time, the Mahâyâna took over the various previous schools with the sole exception of the Theravâda. Ideas which were generated amidst the older schools became seminal for the development of Mahâyâna thought.[40] With the begining of the Common Era, the Mahâyâna canon began to grow. It started with individual sutras, sermons considered as Buddha word, and ended with a canon comprising a much larger quantity of texts than the older Pâli canon. Only a few of the Pâli texts were included in it. The details of how the Mahâyâna canon developed are still unknown. The general assumption is that the Mahâyâna texts were originally conceived in an Indian language, in most cases in Sanskrit, before they were translated into Chinese, Khotanese, and then into Tibetan, and other Asian languages. But the Indian originals were largely lost, and only a few fragments have been discovered in the arid soil of Central Asia.

This makes the translations into Chinese, Khotanese, and Tibetan all the more valuable. In general the Mahâyâna canon comprises the collection of the monastic regulations (*vinaya*); the collection of Buddha's sermons, or sutras; and the tantras, esoteric teachings of the Buddha which incorporate elements not usually found among the sutras. But each redaction of the canon resulted in new changes and revisions of the previous version. Some texts were newly incorporated, while others were dismissed as inauthentic; the individual sections of the canon were rearranged all the time. There were no two redactions of the canon which were identical.

The first edition of the Chinese canon was produced under Emperor Wu-ti of the Liang dynasty in 518 C.E. Most of the 2,213 works included in that edition are considered to be lost. During the next two centuries a number of canons were compiled in China. Gradually more works of Chinese Buddhist thinkers found entrance into the collection. During the Sung dynasty (960–1126) the canon was printed for the first time. Copies of the Chinese canon reached Korea, Japan, and Vietnam.

B. *The Reception of the Buddhist Canon in Tibet*

(1) General Developments

The inception of Buddhism in Tibet may have started with casual contacts between Tibetan tribes and the surrounding Buddhist nations. But the existence of Buddhism in Tibet is not significant before the mid 8th century, which Tibetan sources identify as part of the period of the early dissemination of Buddhism. King Khri-srong lde-btsan (r. 755–797) became the main figure in transplanting Buddhism to Tibet, but during the time of his reign only the royal family and some of the court nobles were affected by this new religion. When Khri-srong lde-btsan's father was still in his boyhood he came across a prophecy by one of his royal forefathers. In this statement the ancient ruler foresaw the advent of Buddhism and its growth in Tibet; the young prince felt that it was his duty to carry out his forefather's predictions. Thus the prince sent envoys to India to bring the Buddhist tradition to Tibet. This account is given in the *sBa bzhed,* one of the oldest texts recording the introduction of Buddhism in Tibet.[41] Initially the reception of Buddhist scriptures in Tibet was connected with a belief in their power to give presence to the divine which reportedly should result in establishing the subjects in happiness. Thus the sacred texts were in high regard not because of their message (which is the reason usually given in Buddhist tradition) but because of their assumed supernatural power to evoke and embody the divine presence.[42] Later the same king sent two court officials to China to collect more Buddhist texts. It was the time when early Ch'an Buddhism took most of the Far East by storm. The two Tibetans came into contact with a Korean Ch'an monk, Chin Ho-shang, who had taken up residence in Szechuan, a country wedged between the mainland of China and Tibet. Chin Ho-shang gave valid advice to the Tibetan delegates for handling the precarious situation in their homeland where anti-Buddhist forces had become active.[43] If we are inclined to see a Ch'an influence upon the Great Perfection School and its KBG, then this encounter with Chin Ho-shang could be a possible link between the two traditions.

During the reign of Khri-srong lde-btsan, Tibet's contacts with the two Buddhist nations, India and China, intensified. They resulted in Indian and Chinese masters coming to Tibet, bringing along with them those texts they thought to be most beneficial for the newly converted Tibetan Buddhists. After the inauguration of the first Tibetan monastery at bSam-yas (approximately 775 C.E.) and the ordination of seven Tibetan young men as monks, the translation activity gained prominence over other religious interests. Sacred texts imported from China as well as from India were translated into the native idiom under the assistance of Chinese and Indian scholars. This ambitious undertaking was financed by the Crown. The result of this translation activity was the production of a library of independent Buddhist texts housed in the royal palace. Later they became known as the Old Translations (the KBG is counted among them). The selection of Buddhist texts available in Tibetan by the late 8th century reflected the doctrinal predilections of the Tibetans' Buddhist preceptors.[44] As far as we know, there was no attempt to translate a complete set of the *tripitaka*. This did not happen before the period of the Later Translations (beginning with the late 10th century).

By the end of the 8th century, tensions between the masters of Chinese Buddhism and their followers, and the Indian masters of Buddhism became tangible in a debate held at bSam-yas, the first Tibetan monastery. The accounts of the debate are conflicting, nevertheless, later historiographic writings tell us that the Indian party won the debate. The Chinese representative Ho-shang Ma-ho-yen (in Tibetan texts known as Mahâyâna), a Buddhist from Tun-huang who was trained in the system of Northern Ch'an,[45] was expelled from Tibet. But, so we are told, he had left behind his "shoes" as a symbol of the lasting impact of his teachings. Since then any Buddhist theory loosely connected with the Ch'an teachings of Ma-ho-yen was considered heresy by the mainstream Buddhists of Tibet. As we shall see, the teachings of the Great Perfection School were the preferred target for this allegation. Thus during the period of the later dissemination (from the late 10th century onwards) the Old School tried to clear itself of any such accusation, which lead to profound changes in their teachings.

The Later Translations were produced during the "later period" of Buddhist propagation in Tibet. After the earlier translation work had come to a standstill by the mid-9th century, the Later Translations started due to the efforts of Rin-chen bzang-po (958–1055), a native of Guge, a petty kingdom nestled in the western Himalayas. He, together with a number of equally motivated Tibetans, started to translate Indian Buddhist texts which were not yet available in Tibetan. Under the guidance of Rin-chen bzang-po this editorial team also revised some of the Earlier Translations. At the same time the works of the Earlier Translations were scrutinized as to whether they should be considered genuine Buddhist works. Members of the royal family of Guge were particularly critical about some of the Great Perfection texts which claimed to have been translated during the 8th century. Among many other texts, the KBG was rejected as a work of forgery.

The Tibetans who came to India during and after the 11th century tried to save whatever they could of Buddhism as they saw Muslims of Afghanistan destroying Buddhist libraries in India. The Buddhist community of India, the prime target of the Muslims' attacks, saw the dusk of Buddhism coming.[46] The attempt to compile a complete set of Buddhist scriptures in Tibetan was a natural response to that situation. The compilation of the Tibetan canon was a direct result of the political changes in India and the beginning demise of Buddhism there. For the first few centuries the Tibetan canon was transmitted in the form of manuscripts, but from the beginning of the 15th century the canon was reproduced as woodcut prints. At present seven different recensions of the printed canon are known.

(2) The Scriptures of the Old School (*rNying ma*)

While the Tibetans came into formal contact with the Buddhist civilizations of India and China from the 7th century C.E. onwards, they started to translate Mahâyâna texts in the 8th century. This translation activity climaxed towards the end of this period, resulting in a literature known as "the old translations" of which the KBG forms a part. When the promulgation of Buddhism came to a halt during the middle of the 9th century, later generations questioned whether the "old translations" were faithfully preserved or whether they had been tampered with.[47]

The followers of the Old School of Tibetan Buddhism assert that the old translations are genuine Buddhist texts and scriptures, while those schools which originated after the 11th century, i.e. during the period of the "later translations" (e.g. the bKa' gdams pa, dGe lugs pa, Sa skya pa, etc.) deny this. Most of the old translations themselves claim to be translations of Indian, and in a few cases of Chinese Buddhist texts. As the KBG is part of the old translations and incorporated in the body of scriptures of the Old School we shall examine this body of scriptures more closely.

There are two main collections recognized as authentic Buddha word by the Old School in addition to the Tibetan canon which is accepted by all Schools; they are: The Hundred Thousand Old Tantras (*rNying ma'i rgyud 'bum*), and The Hundred Thousand Tantras of Vairocana (*Bairo rgyud 'bum*). Besides these two collections there are many other collections, but none of them enjoys the same authority as these two do. Each collection consists of many tantric texts (but none comprises one hundred thousand texts) whereby several occur with some variations in both collections. Some texts were at a certain time incorporated in the Kanjur, while other old translations remained excluded. The question arose whether all the texts which claim to have been translated from a Sanskrit original were indeed based upon lost Indian Buddhist scriptures. And we shall see that this applies particularly to the KBG and its related literature.

At present we know little about how the old translations were organized during the period of the early dissemination. During the later dissemination writers of the Old School linked the organization of their scriptures with the structure of the Buddhist teaching as they saw it. The Old School organizes the Buddhist teaching into nine stages (*theg pa rim pa dgu*). The first three of them comprise mainstream Buddhism, i.e. the vehicles of the hearers (*shrâvaka*), of the solitary Buddhas (*pratyekabuddha*), both known as Hînayâna, and of the bodhisattvas which constitutes the Mahâyâna. The next three stages comprise the "external tantras" which are characterized by ritualism and purifications: Kriyâyoga, Caryayoga, and Yoga. The last three stages are known as the "internal tantras" and consist of Mahâyoga, Anuyoga, and Atiyoga. Mahâyoga and Anuyoga represent advanced stages of what constitutes the "external tantras," while the Atiyoga is free of any attempt to reify reality or to conceptualize the world as we perceive it. The Atiyoga stage is divided into three segments: "mind class" (*sems sde*), to which the KBG belongs, "expanse class" (*klong sde*), and "sacred instruction class" (*man ngag sde*). The Tibetan tradition knows of eighteen texts of the "mind class" but there is widespread disagreement as to which texts belong to this group.

The Atiyoga is also known as *rdzogs chen* or Great Perfection. There is Atiyoga teaching, practice, and literature. The Atiyoga literature is mainly contained in the first two volumes of the Hundred Thousand Old Tantras, but some of the texts are also found in the Hundred Thousand Tantras of Vairocana. The history of the Hundred Thousand Old Tantras is not known in full. The collection's core texts of Atiyoga are mentioned in the historical accounts of the Old School when they talk about the Indian roots of their own tradition,[48] but most of these accounts cannot be substantiated through independent evidence. Ratna-gling-pa (1403–1479) gives the following account in his The Lion's Roar, an apologia of the Old School's teachings (*Chos 'byung bstan pa'i sgron me rtsod zlog seng ge'i nga ro*):[49]

> Further, there were many tantras of the Great Perfection [tradition] [buried] underneath a vase-shaped pillar at Vajrâsana. Previously Srîsimha and 'Jam-dpal bshes-gnyen had entrusted them to guru [Padmasambhava] and Vimala[mitra].[50] Now [we shall talk] about the remaining [tantras]: At the time when the three [Tibetan] translators, bKa'-[ba dPal-brtsegs], Cog [Klu'i rgyal-mtshan], and rMa [Rinchen-grags], were about to invite Vimala[mitra], the scholar, [to Tibet] the Indian pandits planned a plot. Through [their] slander Vairocana, who was a sickness to their heart, was banned to Tshaba-rong, and [they advised] King Milakutra to ban Vimala[mitra] to Tibet[51] because he had become too famous as a scholar. But it was announced that [King Milakutra] could not refuse the request made by the King of bSam-yas. In their sick mind, the pandits pretended to be pleased if [Vimalamitra] went to Tibet. Vimala[mitra] as master and [the three translators] as his attendants approached the king and his pandits by saying "Now that I am going to Tibet I need a religious stronghold never heard of before." The pandits replied "Underneath [the vase-shaped pillar at] Vajrâsana are countless sacred [texts] of the Great Perfection [tradition] but we Indian pandits have no authority to explain them as this is not the right time [for such a doctrine]. Furthermore as your journey to Tibet is so important take out whatever [you deem suitable] and bring [these texts] with you [to Tibet]. As Vimala[mitra], the master, together with [the three translators as his] attendants were so ambitious and because Vimala[mitra] thought that he would never return to India at a later

> time, they took out all the sacred [texts] of the Great Perfection [tradition]. Thereby the root of all Indian books [of the Great Perfection] was severed.

Two things in this account are particularly relevant to the present discussion: the fact that Indian pandits felt the time was not right for promoting any one of the Great Perfection texts, and that Vimalamitra together with the Tibetan translators had removed all the remaining texts from Vajrâsana (i.e Bodhgaya in Bihar). For the Old School there is no doubt that the Great Perfection texts originated as authentic Buddhist teachings in India. Other Buddhist schools of Tibet debated, and sometimes rejected this claim. From a critical viewpoint one may argue that the entire story smacks of a cover-up, that it wants to explain why there are no Indian traces of Great Perfection texts.

That the Great Perfection literature, at least in some specimens, had come to Tibet as early as the 8th or 9th centuries can be inferred from the fact that some of these texts are found among the Tun huang documents. As the caves containing these documents were closed by the mid 11th century, and because Tibetan domination over this area ceased by the mid-9th century, the general assumption is that the Tibetan texts were put there prior to 850 C.E. This would mean that a segment of the Great Perfection literature was known to the Tibetans at the time when they started to convert to Buddhism.

Ratna gling-pa (1403–1479) was the first Tibetan known to make an effort towards collecting the various texts belonging to the Great Perfection. In his biography it is said that Ratna gling-pa compiled these manuscripts, which filled twenty volumes. Later he had them copied with silver and gold ink.[52] Unfortunately nothing is said about where Ratna gling-pa had found these manuscripts. Dudjom Rinpoche, the late hierarch of the Old School, reported in his account of this school that Ratna gling-pa found most of these manuscript in the district of Zur 'ug-pa-lung in central Tibet, but supplemented them with mansucripts found at various other places.[53] For the next three hundred years we do not know what happened to the Hundred Thousand Old Tantras. In the 18th century another master of the Old School, 'Jigs-med gling-pa (1729–1798), re-edited the Ratna gling-pa edition and composed the first catalogue of the Hundred Thousand Old Tantras. Under the editorship of 'Jigs-med gling-pa the number of volumes increased from twenty to twenty-five.[54]

Most texts of Atiyoga promote ideas with a certain degree of affinity to early Ch'an thought, such as sudden enlightenment, no-interference, no-deed, etc., while most other texts of the Old School are in accord with mainstream Vajrayâna conventions.

The Old School underwent major changes after the inauguration of the "new translations" from the late 11th century onwards. Along with the "new translations" a new form of Buddhism was introduced to the Tibetans: the gradual path towards enlightenment (known as *lam rim* in Tibetan) which was promoted by the Indian scholar Atisha (who entered Tibet in 1042) and his subsequent disciples.[55] Atisha's gradual path was in direct contrast with some of the "older translations," which asserted that enlightenment will be spontaneously realized. When Atisha's system became dominant among the Tibetan Buddhists, the Old School had to incorporate at least some of the newer concepts into its own system. Klong-chen-pa Dri-med 'od-zer (1308–63) was the genius who achieved this amalgamation. Because we know so little about the teachings and the literature of the Old School prior to the beginning of the later dissemination, we are ill-advised to use writings of the later dissemination to elucidate problems we encounter in the writings of the earlier period. The first step is to conserve what we know about the literature of the early dissemination; in a second step we may ask how these texts were interpreted by later thinkers of the same tradition.

3. THE ALL-CREATING SOVEREIGN—MIND OF PERFECT PURITY AS A LITERARY WORK

After an examination of the conceptual and historic contexts in which the KBG is embedded we shall turn to study this text as a work of literature. First we shall examine how the KBG was transmitted, and whether it may be considered as an authentic Buddhist text. Secondly, we shall examine some of the leading ideas encapsulated in it. A topical analysis of the chapters is incorporated at the end of the book. Thirdly some thoughts about the language of the text and the manner of its translation will be shared.

A. Transmittance and Authenticity of the KBG

The KBG is a tantra found in the Kanjur section of the Buddhist canon in Tibetan and in two collections of tantras which were not universally accepted as authentic Buddhist scriptures, i.e. the Hundred Thousand Tantras of the Old Translations (*rNying ma'i rgyud 'bum*) and the Hundred Thousand Tantras of Vairocana (*Bairo rgyud 'bum)*.[56] The Tibetan title of the text identifies it as a sutra, a categorization supported by the evidence of the text's appearance. But the fact that the text was incorporated in several collections of tantras suggests that, at least at the time when these collections were compiled, the KBG was no longer considered a sutra. Although the KBG is a canonical and not an apocryphal text, it attracted the attention of only a few Tibetan masters, most of them just paying lip service to the importance of the text without exploring its spirit, and the text has been neglected by Western scholars altogether.

Despite these facts, the KBG constitutes the main scriptural source of the "mind class" (*sems sde*) of the Great Perfection (*rDzogs chen*), a mystical strand of Tibetan Buddhism. Many parts of the KBG are included in other *sems sde* texts, or make up independent texts. At present it would totally premature to guess which text(s) constituted the source for the other(s).

The authenticity of the KBG cannot be discussed except within the broader context of the authenticity of the old translations in general. The core of the old translations are the Hundred Thousand Old Tantras. At present several of these Old Tantras are incorporated in the Kanjur of the Tibetan Buddhist canon, where they form a separate section.[57] This fact indicates that the compilers of the canon who did incorporate these Old Tantras accepted them as authentic scriptures. Thus questions arise as to when the Old Tantras were for the first time included in the canon, who was responsible for this compilation, and what were the reasons for doing so.

When by the 14th century the Tibetan Buddhists started to compile numerous pieces of scriptures to form an authoritative collection, the textual transmission was mainly based on manuscripts. By the beginning of the 15th century the Tibetan canon was printed for the first time, not in Tibet, but in China. The printed version proliferated and branched into various "trees" or *stemma*.[58] The oldest extant manuscript version of the canon is known as the *Them spangs ma*. Its earliest copy is known to exist in Gyantse (Tibet), while copies of this copy exist in Tokyo and in Ulan Bator.[59] This *Them spangs ma* manuscript canon is based upon the original compilation of the canon arranged at sNar-thang from which all other canons derived. Another version of the canon which stems directly from the sNar-thang canon is the *Tshal pa* canon.

Now, the KBG is present in volume 94 of the Ulan Bator copy of the *Them spangs ma*. At present it is assumed that the *Them spangs ma* was compiled during the 15th century, and that an exact copy of it was presented to the Mongol dignitaries towards the end of the 17th century.[60] But the KBG is absent, along with all other Old Tantras, in the *'Jang sa tham* canon which is a copy of the old *Tshal pa* canon.[61] But above all, the KBG was excluded by Bu-ston, the chief editor of the sNar-thang canon, from being incorporated into the oldest Tibetan canon. He did so despite the fact that he had studied the KBG along with other key scriptures of the Old School under his grandfather Tshul-khrims dpal-bzang-po.[62] This exclusion was interpreted by the opponents of the old translations to imply that the Old Tantras were later fabrications and not authentic scriptures. But Bu-ston in his catalogue of the canon which was appended to his Great History of Buddhism (*chos 'byung chen mo*) admitted that although some Buddhist scholars of the 11th century rejected the Old Tantras as inauthentic, his own teachers, Rig-ral and sMra-ba Nyi-ma'i mtshan-can, had seen their Sanskrit originals housed at bSam-yas.[63] The question, why he did not then include them in his edition of the sNar-thang canon when he considered the Old Tantras to be genuine translations from Indian sources, remains unanswered. Scholars of the Old School speculated that the political bias of his patrons forced Bu-ston to disregard the Old Tantras when he prepared the authoritative edition of the canon. This surmise has some substance if we consider more closely the political affiliations of Bu-ston's patrons, the princes of Zha-lu. They were feudatories of the Sa-skya hierarch, who ruled as viceroy over Tibet, and of the Mongol emperor, lord over most of Asia. Consequently the Zha-lu princes had to show a certain amount of loyalty and veneration for the Sa-skya hierarchs and their doctrinal dispositions. One of their most esteemed members was Sa-skya Pandita, who wrote a scathing tractate on the old translations, i.e. the "Treatise on the Distinction of the Three Vows" (*sDom pa gsum gyi rab tu dbye ba'i bstan bcos*).[64] Consequently it is reasonable to assume that the Zha-lu princes adopted Sa-skya Pandita's verdict on the authenticity of the old translations, and therefore refused to sponsor the publication of such questionable texts. Bu-ston was apparently obliged to follow suit.

Whatever the case may have been, it is a fact that the KBG, together with other texts dating from the era of the old translations, was considered authentic by the Old School and a large number of followers of other schools. However, a few individuals, among them Pho-brang Zhi-ba-'od, a member of the royal house of Guge, and Sa-skya Pandita, voiced their concerns about the authenticity of these texts. The general argument brought forth against the Great Perfection is that its teachings are identical with or similar to Ho-shang Ma-ho-yen's (Hva-shang Mahâyâna) ideas. In the eyes of the Tibetan Buddhists, this statement means that the accused is guilty of heresy. If one compares the KBG or other Great Perfection texts with the whole range of Mahâyâna thought then we have to come to the conclusion that it is not more heretical than the *Ratnagotravibhâga*, or some other texts. The doubts about the authenticity of the KBG seem to be more a response to an inner-Tibetan dispute about which strand of Mahâyâna and Vajrayâna is the most preferable, than an unbiased assessment. In fact, many a text discredited by Pho-brang Zhi-ba-'od in the same manner as the KBG was later without hesitation incorporated into the authoritative body of scriptures. In other words, the voices of criticism have to be evaluated within their contextual situation, and should not be taken as definitive statements.

From the vantage point of a modern scholar it seems that the Old Tantras of the Great Perfection preserved a form of Buddhist mysticism that was later on displaced by a more scholastic form of thinking that produced the astonishing quantity of Tibetan philosophical and epistemological works. The antiquity of the Great Perfection literature is, as we have mentioned earlier, to some degree substantiated through the fact that several of its tractates were discovered among the Tun huang documents.

Reading the KBG and other texts of the Great Perfection will instill the impression that they convey a message similar to the texts of Ch'an Buddhism. However, the 9th century Tibetan Buddhist master gNubs-chen Sangs-rgyas ye-shes tells us in his work *bSam gtan mig sgron* that the two schools are different. One of the most significant differences is that Ch'an promotes meditation as *the* means to realize enlightenment while the KBG emphatically denies the validity of meditating. Furthermore Ch'an considers the teaching of the Perfection of Wisdom sutras (*Prajñâpâramitâ*) to be a valid method for spiritual progress while the KBG rejects every teaching that affirms causality, the acquisition of certain phenomena or the abandoning of others. A detailed consideration of these points is beyond the scope of this introduction; suffice it to say that to see the KBG as a Ch'an text or Ch'an-related text would be inadequate despite the fact that both have certain characteristics in common.

B. *The Message of the Text*

A text is as much a part of the historical and philosophical context from which it originated as it is part of the reader's world. When we read a text as distant in time and place as the KBG then we generate a process of appropriation, to make the text ours, to gain access to its meaningfulness. This process may go on undetected by the reader; or it may be intentionally started. Regardless of what our methodological positions are, as readers we are part of our own contextual situation and the text we read originated from another contextual situation. Thus a far more fundamental "translation" than the one from Tibetan into English has to happen. Unlike the translation from one language into another, which is done by someone for the reader, the contextual translation has to be performed by the reader him- or herself. While reading, the reader will inevitably translate the text into his or her own contextual situation. Therefore every reader sees the text in a different light. Thus no matter how remote a text may be from the reader's own situation, it will become part of it as soon as the reader starts to read the text.

The process of the reader's appropriation may be affected by the mass of historical and philological information with which tradition and scholarship encumbers a text. A text like the KBG was never truly appropriated by the Tibetan tradition. For this reason there is no well-defined exegetical context within which we could interpret the text. A scholar of Buddhist thought may regret this, but this lack turns into a challenge and opportunity for the reader. The text invites the reader of the late 20th century as much as it invited the reader of 8th century Tibet to interpret the text within the given situation of our own time. A text as unorthodox as the KBG particularly lends itself to this appropriation by the reader. Despite the historical and circumstantial information I am providing here, I do not want to discourage this process from happening. A comprehensive interpretation of the system of thought presented in the KBG would harness the reader's creative appropriation and dialogue with the text. As the Tibetan tradition has not created a context within which a "secured" interpretation of the text could occur, I do not want to impose my own appropriation of the text upon the reader. In the following chapter, I am merely trying to provide some help for understanding and appropriating the text by referring to the text itself. But some topics and issues are not clearly defined in the text and, therefore, must remain somewhat unclear. Hopefully, further studies of this so-little-known literature will provide us with the answers.

In order to make the cultural shell of the KBG more transparent, I shall focus on metaphoric expressions, like "All-Creating Sovereign," "three-fold nature," "ten characteristics," the concept of "entourage" and "manifestation." A topical analysis by chapters will provide further help in understanding the text (see end of book).

(1) The All-Creating Sovereign

The expression "All-Creating Sovereign" is a metaphor to elucidate the very nature of what is the ground of the universe. This ground is thought of as an intelligent and intelligible potency. The Buddhist text equates the "All-Creating Sovereign" with the phrase "the mind of perfect purity" (Tib. *byang chub sems*).

For this reason we shall first examine the term "mind of perfect purity" before we go on to study the phrase "All-Creating Sovereign". In general the Tibetan term *byang chub sems* corresponds to Skr. *bodhicitta* which is customarily translated as "mind of enlightenment" or "enlightened or awakened mind." For instance, in the Perfection of Wisdom Sutras we find this term as the main characteristic of the bodhisattva. There it means the firm intention to achieve enlightenment for the sake of all other sentient beings and to realize enlightenment in its fullest form as omniscience. Thus the practice of universal compassion and the understanding of emptiness are the two main components of the "mind of enlightenment" as understood in general Mahâyâna Buddhism.[65]

In Vajrayâna the term "mind of enlightenment" has a new connotation in so far as its main components, compassion and emptiness, are associated with masculinity and femininity. Consequently the union of the two components was symbolicly expressed through terms denoting the sexual union of man and woman. Within this context, the "mind of enlightenment" was seen as the most crucial element in the process of realizing enlightenment. It became the very essence of one's spiritual life and the sole force which inspired the practitioner to continue his or her pursuit of enlightenment. Thus the "mind of enlightenment" was frequently glossed as the "life force" symbolicly present in semen and blood.[66] This meaning of "mind of enlightenment" is found in the works of the three external tantras (i.e. Kriyâyoga, Caryayoga, and Yoga) and of the first two stages of the internal tantras (Mahâyoga and Anuyoga). But the two meanings which we have discussed so far are absent in the Atiyoga tantras to which the KBG belongs.

The KBG as well as other Atiyoga texts reject the ideas expressed in the eight other levels of the Buddhist path (see *theg pa dgu*). Thus the understanding of the term "mind of enlightenment" as given in these texts is quite different from its more common meanings. The KBG defines the term in chapter two in the following way:

> My own being is the mind of perfect purity. 'Pure' is taught to be the nature of the limpid (*dag pa*) in its three aspects of totality. 'Perfect' is taught as the nature of the limpid as encompassing the three reasons.[67] [The limpid] is all-encompassing like the sky. The nature of what is called "mind" is taught as the ceaseless, all-encompassing All-Creating Sovereign. Everything is made, all is generated in the mind of perfect purity.

This passage defines the "mind of enlightenment" in a way which renders the common translation of the term meaningless. Consequently I have chosen a translation which is based on the interpretation of the term in the text itself: "mind of perfect purity."

The mind of perfect purity is in an allegoric manner addressed as the "sovereign" who governs the universe. This is well expressed in a passage of chapter forty-one of the KBG:

> I am the core of all the Buddhas of the three times. I am father and mother to all sentient beings of the three-fold world. Also, I am the cause for all that exists as animated and inanimated. Not one thing is that does not emanate from Me.

The All Creating-Sovereign is not a male god presiding as judge over the world but its governing life force which is beyond any gender-related distinction. The Sovereign is the intelligent ground of the universe. Only in an allegoric fashion can this ground talk like a person. This "person" is male as well as female. In the root-text the Sovereign Mind is seen as "father" and "mother" of all that exists. In the second appendix the issue of gender equality is taken one step further. In a chapter dealing with the different names given to the Sovereign Mind it is said:[68]

> Because all the Buddhas of the three times (past, present and future) merge from Me, I am called the Buddha-Mother.

Other Atiyoga texts support this position. The *rDo la gser zhun* states that if the nature of All Good as a female (Samantabhadrâ) is not grasped the bliss of truth cannot be appreciated.[69] Another Atiyoga text, the Instruction on The Chain of [Doctrinal] Views (*Man ngag lta ba'i phreng ba*) ascribed to Padmasambhava, represents the five great elements as five "mothers" of "own being." It further says that the totality of what exists as compound and non-compound phenomena (this includes nirvana) is the feminine creative force (*chos bya ba mo*), "All Good," that is "own being" which exists from the primordial.[70]

Thus within the context of the Atiyoga literature it is accurate to render the ultimate as of feminine gender. This is an essential point which should be kept in mind when reading the translation. I shall address the issue of gender-specific language versus an inclusive language when I talk about the nature of Buddhist language (see chapter four of the Introduction).

The term "All-Creating Sovereign" is always paraphrased as "mind of perfect purity." In this context "mind" is an inadequate reference to the non-physical, order- and meaning-giving force which is the base of all that exists. Because this force arrays the things of this world in order, it makes them intelligible. On numerous occasions the text talks about the fact that the universe is accessible to the intellect, not in a way of counting, measuring, or reckoning, but in an intuitive, yet intelligent way. Thus the force is an intelligent one. This force is said to be in balance, as it is free of any partiality, particularity, or peculiarity. It rests squarely in itself. Thus the text calls it "self-originated;" it knows neither cause nor conditions nor results. It is not tainted by subject-object dichotomy, thus its nature is "pure" and "limpid." It transcends the parameters of time and place; it *is* from the primordial. The most common simile given in the text to say something about this force, which otherwise is called inexplicable, is *nam mkha'* which means the expanse of the sky, the heavens in their limitless space, that which cannot be tainted, which is intangible, and limitless. The term has a clear spiritual connotation which uses the visible sky only as a metaphor. The metaphor points to the fact that this non-physical and intelligent force is all pervasive and all encompassing at the same time, very much as the dome of the sky encompasses all and like space permeates everything. The word "sky" is among the most frequently used words in the entire text.

This intelligent ground is called the one. It is one, yet manifest in all. This, however, does not mean that its nature is divided into many individual entities. Wherever it is (and there is nowhere it is not) it is there in its totality. Like the sky in its endless reach it encompasses all and permeates everything but remains the immutable one. The intelligent ground is self-originated pristine awareness (*rang byung ye shes*) which abides in its own lucid nature. It is not dependent on anything. The ground's oneness is its decisive characteristic but it presents itself in a threefold way. These two statements are not mutually exclusive but complementary. The intelligent ground is one, immutable and timeless, but it is present in all that exists in a such way that we as human beings can speak of its three aspects or three natures. Both statements are equally true and valid.

(2) The Threefold Nature of the Intelligent Ground

From the perspective of the ground it is one and nothing but one, but from the perspective of the world and its creatures it is sensed in a threefold manner. In other words, the indescribable intelligent ground is described in details and particularity for us humans who depend so much on conceptualizing things. This description, which is suitable for us, is not relevant for *It*. The three natures or aspects are:

1. The own being (*rang bzhin*) of the intelligent ground as pristine awareness;

2. the actuating force or essence (*ngo bo*) inherent in the intelligent ground and which is the factor responsible for the existence of the universe;

3. compassion (*snying rje*) which is the sole force determining the interaction among the different components of the world.

This scheme is not unanimously accepted in all Atiyoga texts. In many of them *ngo bo* is considered to be primary being, and *rang bzhin* its actuating force, while the third facet of the consummate Mind, i.e. compassion, remains unaffected. This inversion of terms is possible because in common usage the two Tibetan terms *ngo bo* and *rang bzhin* are considered to be synonymous. At the present stage of our knowledge it would be premature to speculate whether or not this change in terminology has more far-reaching implications. The translation of these terms suggested here reflects the way these terms are used and defined within the KBG. In other contexts they need to be translated in a different way.

Each of these three aspects warrants further examination. The pristine awareness which is all-pervasive consists in the oneness of the universe and constitutes the own being of the All-Creating Sovereign. Its nature constitutes the laws of the universe. In its pristine and consummate being it is the one. It is the ground from which the universe in its multiplicity and particularity arises: the All-Creating Sovereign, mind of perfect purity. In chapter forty-seven we read:

> This incomparable pristine awareness which does not stem from any cause, i.e. the self-originated pristine awareness which is ceaseless and all-permeating, generates everything; from nothing else the phenomena (*dharma*) arise.

The pristine awareness imprints its own luminous nature upon the universe which becomes thereby intelligible. This point is repeated throughout the text. But this intelligibility of the universe is not of the same order as the factual knowledge we accumulate during our life. It should not be mistaken for the scientific attempts to measure, analyze, or reckon the universe. To the contrary, the intelligibility of the universe rests in itself, in its own luminosity and equipoise without any object-oriented mental activity. It can be intuited through unmediated experience where there is no attempt to reify this pure experience. The orderly structure of this experience mirrors the meaningful organization of the universe. Our text talks about the universe being arrayed like a precious set of jewels, where aesthetics, balance, and harmony are integral elements. Thus the pristine awareness permeates existence and becomes apparent in its meaningful and orderly structure which is sensed as beauty.

The reason why people in general fail to perceive the universe in this way is that they are searching the surface for something which is integral to the depth of their own being from beginningless time. As the text points out in the last chapter, we cannot become Buddhas because we are already Buddhas. One might say that in the view of this text we are like people totally engulfed by the hustle of everyday trivia, overlooking the fact that the enormous silence of the universe comforts us as a mother comforts her child. Another way to make clear what the text conveys is to use David Bohm's concept of implicate order in modern physics as a metaphor for the fact that the pristine awareness is veiled from the eye of the ordinary person yet permeates all.[71] The order-giving, lucid nature of being is its governing force yet is hidden in invisibility from the eyes of those who want to distinguish the "governor" from the "governed." Therefore, the text says, there is no path to buddhahood on which we could progress, there is no goal which we could reach, and there is nothing of which we should rid ourselves. This statement however is not a permit to follow one's vices; this point will become clear in the discussion of compassion as the third aspect of the intelligent ground.

With regard to its all-pervasiveness the pristine awareness is the true being (*rang bzhin*) of the All-Creating Sovereign, as his and her mind, pure and consummate, consists in nothing else but this pristine awareness. But because every thing, every creature, in its true being, also rests in this limpid awareness it governs all things. For this reason it is called "Sovereign". The concept of sovereignty in this text is that the sovereign "sees everything," that his and her presence is felt in every aspect of his and her domain. This concept is very close to the Taoist concept of the ruler who should remain as invisible and as the Tao itself. Chuang Tzu says about the ruler and the way of conducting good government the following:[72]

> Resolve your mental energy into abstraction, your physical energy into inaction. Allow yourself to fall in with the natural order of phenomena, without admitting the element of self,—and the empire will be governed.

But the image of sovereignty offered by the KBG is remote from the Indian concept of the ruler who is defined by his exercise of punishment (*danda*). As a good (Taoist) ruler implementing harmony and happiness, is apparent in every part of the empire, so is the pristine awareness present in every aspect of existence.

The pristine awareness is the ground of the universe, but it would be incorrect to say that this awareness came into existence at a certain time. Such a statement implies that before this act it was non-existent. To describe the trans-temporal character of the pristine awareness the Tibetan uses the term *ye nas* which literally means "since the beginning;" but in this context it is quite obvious that there is no beginning in a temporal sense. Thus this phrase has to be understood in an ontological sense.

The pristine awareness rests in the depth of itself, fully integrated. Its second facet, i.e. "actuating potency" (*ngo bo*) is the force which arouses the pristine awareness to become manifest, tangible, perceptible, thinkable. The "actuating potency" makes the transition from a state of undifferentiated cognitiveness to the world of multiple phenomena possible. The "actuating potency" propels the pristine awareness from its stillness to manifestation. In a metaphoric context, pristine awareness is seen as the ultimate "ur-Buddha" thus the manifestations produced through "actuating potency" are metaphorically speaking the hosts of his attendants and disciples, or entourages, as Buddhist texts like to call them. Thus the metaphoric image is as follows: the ur-Buddha rests in the centre, unreified, beyond conceptualization; he and she is surrounded by the different forms of the manifest world. The opening chapter of the KBG depicts this vision by identifying individual "entourages" with certain components of the manifest world, such as the elements. The text looks at the common Buddhist teaching with its numerous paradise-like Buddha worlds, where the teacher is surrounded by hosts of listening disciples, and interprets this image as a meaningful diagram for laying out its own propositions: the world of phenomena is nothing but the manifest form of awakened awareness. To make this process of emanation plausible to its Buddhist audience the text engages common Buddhist terminology, like *dharmakâya*.

The true nature of the All-Creating Sovereign as part of the three aspects of its true being is already the first stage of emanation. As such it is identified with what, in traditional Buddhism, is known as the *dharmakâya*, i.e. the manifestation of ultimate truth which is the true being of a Buddha. The Sovereign's own being as part of these three aspects is therefore somewhat different from the true being as pristine awareness. Therefore the manifestation of truth as the Sovereign's own being is labeled "retinue," while this term would be inadequate for the intrinsic awareness in its primary state of undifferentiatedness. The term entourage implies that it is oriented towards some thing else, i.e. the centre. Consequently the centre can never be called an entourage, which would amount to labelling it as something on the perimeter.

The second phase in the ontological but not temporal or causal emanation of the universe is the Sovereign's actuating potency (*ngo bo*) which evokes a response from the depth of its own being. Many times this creating force is glossed with the expression "central vigour" (*snying po*). This response is known as the retinue of *sambhogakâya*, i.e. the manifestation of consummate joy, the second of the retinues. It is the phase where the ultimate in its oneness rejoices in a situation characterized by the experience of "you." In the metaphors of Buddhist thought it is described as the manifestations of joy rejoicing in sharing the truth with other living beings. In Buddhist art this event is portrayed as a paradise where a princely Buddha or bodhisattva teaches similarly advanced persons the truth of the doctrine. Our text makes it abundantly clear that this phase is not to be understood as a form of heaven but as a phase where the one intelligent ground of the universe begins to unfold into the multiplicity of the existing world, and this event is one of joy and exuberance. In more concrete terms this second phase is characterized by the emergence of the primary elements of the physical world: earth, water, fire, wind, and sky. These five primary elements are called the adornment of the world. This statement is in contrast to the common Buddhist world-view which sees the world in rather negative terms, while this text praises the wonder of creation. In chapter fifty-two we are encouraged to rejoice in the wonder of being manifest in the variety of living beings.

This joy reveals the third aspect of the Sovereign's being: compassion (*snying rje*). It is the force which provides the mode of interaction between the one and the emanated multiplicity, and it is the sole base for all such interactions.

For this reason, the KBG stipulates natural ethics and not a set of prescribed morals. Common Buddhism knows of five basic rules to be embraced by the laity: to abstain from taking life; to abstain from taking what is not given; to abstain from sexual misconduct; to abstain from false speech; and to abstain from intoxicants as tending to cloud the mind.[73] In the later tradition these five precepts become expanded and form a group of ten precepts. Monks and nuns observe many more rules enforcing strict abstention from all sexual activities, renunciation of property, limitation of their needs, etc. (several hundred more rules regulate their lives in every detail). The KBG criticizes the ten moral precepts, i.e. the moral guidelines of ordinary Buddhism. The point of its criticism is the fact that by following a set of morals certain activities or attitudes are rejected while others are sought. Such an attitude is seen as improper, as all activities and attitudes are saturated with pristine awareness. Consequently, to reject certain activities implies a rejection of their innate divine nature. Such partial denial of the divine reality jeopardizes the realization of totality. The person who is rooted in the intelligent ground will act in accordance with compassion not because it is said to be moral or because it will produce advantageous results (i.e. "merit"), but because such a mode of acting is integral to the person's nature. Our text strongly rejects all attempts to use the Vajrayâna for condoning licentious behaviour such as drinking, sexual misconduct, black magic, etc. even if these activities are carried out within a ritual context. The Atiyoga's rejection of prescribed morals is not a free ticket for the pursuit of one's passions but is motivated by a deep concern for regaining natural ethics.

Compassion becomes visible as the earthly manifestations of the Buddha, for instance as Buddha Shakyamuni, whom the Western world calls the historical Buddha; but compassion also generates all other sentient beings who populate the universe. They all constitute the third retinue. The corporeal manifestations of the Buddhas preach what is suitable for the different disciples. Not all their teachings reflect the sublime and subtle truth of the Atiyoga, as many people are not capable of understanding it. Therefore the earthly Buddhas replace the definitive lore with a teaching which is in need of commentaries and interpretation.

The ideas described above are given in the text in the following passage:

> In the untainted mansion of pristine awareness [the All-Creating Sovereign's] own being (*rang bzhin*), Her actuating essence (*ngo bo*),

> Her compassion and pristine awareness became manifest as [various] retinues in the following way: The retinue [emerging] from Her own being is known as the retinue of truth manifestation (*dharmakâya*); the retinue [emerging] from Her actuating essence is known as the retinue of joy manifestation (*sambhogakâya*). The retinue of Her actuating essence, the manifestation of consummate joy is called the retinue [of the element] water;[74] . . . retinue [of the element] fire; . . . retinue [of the element] wind; . . . retinue [of the element] sky. Furthermore, the manifesting of [Her] compassion and pristine awareness as retinues [in the form] of corporeal manifestations (*nirmâna*) happened in this way: the retinue known as sentient beings of the realm of desire (*kâmaloka*), the retinue known as the sentient beings of the realm of form (*rûpaloka*), and the retinue known as the sentient beings of the realm of formlessness (*ârûpaloka*). Furthermore, the retinues equal to Her own being correspond to the four yoga: the retinue of Atiyoga (*shin tu rnal 'byor*), the retinue of Anuyoga (*yongs su rnal 'yor*), the retinue of Mahâyoga (*rnal 'byor chen po*), and the retinue of the Bodhisattvayoga (*sems dpa' rnal 'byor*). As Her own being, Her actuating essence, and Her compassion are inseparable from Her nature, there is only one method.[75] (chapter 1)

This passage makes it abundantly clear that the entire universe constitutes a "retinue" of the All-Creating Sovereign. In other words, all that exists does so in dependence on the intelligent ground. As there is no Buddha without disciples to teach, so there are no disciples without being taught by a Buddha. In the same way, the intelligent ground and the existent universe are mutually dependent and mutually integrated. Neither one is without the other. This makes every attempt to purge, cleanse, or abandon the one for obtaining the other obsolete. The divine reality is not located in another world but is present in every moment and every aspect of this existence.

(3) The Ten Characteristics of the Nature of the Consummate Mind (*rang bzhin bcu*)

Chapter nine of the KBG mentions these ten traits for the first time, but there are many references to them throughout the text. The Tibetan term would warrant a literal translation of "ten natures" which however would lead to a misunderstanding. The fact, as substantiated by this passage, is that these are ten characteristics of the All-Creating Sovereign's own being, and they typify the Atiyoga teaching. Thus the ten characteristics highlight Atiyoga's otherness by setting it apart from all other Buddhist teachings. In other words, by means of the ten characteristics the idiosyncrasy of this teaching can be appreciated. The importance of this topic asks for a more detailed discussion of each of the ten characteristics.

Klong-chen-pa talks about these ten characteristics in his *Don khrid*, but his list is different from the one given in the KBG.[76] Therefore we shall concentrate on the KBG list. The pertinent passage in chapter nine first lists these ten characteristics, which mainly consist of rejecting common Buddhist ideas and practices, before it gives a more detailed description of what will happen if such precautions are not heeded. We shall try to juxtapose these opposing statements to achieve a clearer understanding of this concept.

(1) The first characteristic is the absence of *lta ba* (Skr. *darsana*), doctrinal "view," which deserves to be contemplated. Such contemplation of the doctrinal view may be carried out in six ways: two appreciative judgements are made with regard to the three facets of the primary being. One may embrace or pursue (*blang*), or reject (*dor*) each of the ten characteristics in its correlation with the three facets, which are essential vigour, suchness, and the true nature of things or Reality.[77] If one would contemplate a doctrinal view from these six perspectives, the One, i.e. the pristine awareness, would be clouded with error. This amounts to nothing less than a rejection of the entire abhidharmic (or scholastic) tradition of Buddhism. The underlying assumption is that all abhidharmic categories result in distinction, and distinction is according to the KBG discrimination against the primary Mind. Therefore the entire scholastic system of Buddhism is rejected in this statement.

(2) The second characteristic deals with the irrelevance of vows whose observance is recommended by Buddhism in general. The taking of vows is intended to stimulate the individual to modify his or her behaviour in order to achieve a certain ideal form of life. Such discrimination is in opposition to the Oneness of the primary Mind.

(3) Consequently the third characteristic states that all the salutary acts (*phrin las*) are achieved without the slightest effort. This is so because the primary Mind does not know of any striving or achieving.

(4) The fourth characteristic sets the one and primary pristine awareness apart from other forms of awareness, such as the six sensory awarenesses. Those who are inclined to assume that the primary awareness is subject to the same restrictions applicable to the six sensory awarenesses, are in error.

(5) The practice for achieving the ten bodhisattva stages (*bhûmi*) is

declared as being not in accord with the primary Mind which is not in need of any practice.

(6) Thus there exists no soterilogical path with a promise to let the individual reach a spiritual goal. The assumption of "progress" in itself is rejected as erroneous.

(7) The seventh and eighth characteristics deal with the nature of things as seen by the abhidharmic tradition. The KBG rejects any definition of the nature of things, be it "subtle," "dualistic," or "dependent." Therefore it is said things are neither subtle (*phra ba chos med*),

(8) nor dual, nor dependent.

(9) The ninth characteristic says that there is no accurate sacred instruction firmly established except for that which reveals the Mind as *the* primary potency.

(10) The last of the characteristics warns against any attempt to define the instructions except that they are beyond praise and blame. This is considered to be "the [right] view of the great perfected mind of perfect purity."

In summary, the ten characteristics make and articulate a plea for not appropriating the Atiyoga lore in such a way as to destroy its spiritual meaning in the hair-splitting of scholastic reasoning. Through deconstructing Buddhist abhidharmic thinking an attempt is made to regain the original vitality and freshness of liberating insight (*samyaksambodhi*).

C. *The Climax of Atiyoga*

If every existent creature and thing is fully integrated in the intelligent ground and its divine nature, what then, we may ask, has the text to teach? It certainly rejects the concept of a goal which has to be reached by proceeding on a strenuous path leading from an undesirable situation, i.e. samsara, to another thought to be desirable, i.e. nirvana or buddhahood. Thus it would not be right to talk about a goal of Atiyoga. Yet without any doubt, the text wants to convey a message. But what is it? The answer the text wants to instill in us is an awareness that existence in total integration (i.e. being) is the consummation.

The notion of individual existence ceases in the unmediated experience of totality which is translated as "oneness." The statement that being is one does not imply a negation of the diversity of existence; on the contrary it means that in its diversity the experience of totality rests. In this totality the usual dichotomy of subject/object is subsumed into a sense of being one with everything else. Oneness and diversity are not mutually exclusive concepts, as they are under ordinary circumstances, but complementary aspects of the same reality.

Those who are grounded in this unreified experience of totality differ in an essential way from all other people. They will not indulge in activities designed for obtaining results but will abide in deedlessness. Deedlessness does not mean that the adepts of Atiyoga remain in complacent quiescence but that they engage in the only meaningful activity, integration in the totality of being. Every moment presents itself anew in its total integration. The adepts of Atiyoga are in harmony with this. Their acts come forth spontaneously and not as a reaction to something else, nor are their acts destined to change or produce anything. Thus their acts fulfill the most sublime purpose but are in an ordinary sense purposeless.

The idea of deedlessness (*bya bral*) is well known from the writings of philosophical Taoism where the term is known as *wu wei*. In Taoism it means to act in accordance with the tao and the "nature" of the affected thing. The Taoist sages "act without action."[78]

The state of mind typifying the Atiyoga is beyond the scope of conceptual thinking as all distinctions become irrelevant. The adepts of Atiyoga refrain from doctrinal debates as well as from ritualism as both are based on a distinction-making attitude. The adepts will accept every event in its own right without imposing definitions or judgments on it. In a figurative way they become speechless in a nameless world of blissful silence in integrated being. For this reason the Atiyoga rejects the entirety of Buddhist philosophy, scholasticism, and all formal meditation techniques. All the scriptures of Buddhism are said to be of a meaning that requires interpretation. They are of an ephemeral nature and their content does not reveal the truth in its finality. In contrast to the scriptures, Atiyoga is not a teaching taught by the Buddha, it is the matrix of buddhahood.

No method is revealed as to how to realize this sublime state of Atiyoga, no path is described to pursue this elusive goal, and rightly so. If there were such instructions we would have reason to doubt the authenticity of this teaching.[79]

4. TRANSLATION CONSIDERATIONS: TOWARDS A PHILOSOPHY OF BUDDHIST LANGUAGE

The bulk of Buddhist texts were originally composed in four Indic languages: Pâli and Prakrit, both Middle Indic , Sanskrit and, in the terminology of Franklin Edgerton, Hybrid Buddhist Sanskrit.

These four languages belong to the Indo-Germanic family of languages; they share similar grammatical structures and many of their words are derived from the same stem or root. The Indo-Germanic family of languages is widespread, as it comprises languages as different as Latin and Sanskrit, and English and Russian. What they all have in common is a certain grammatical structure characterized by distinguishing between different categories of words, such as nouns, verbs, and adjectives; and by making the verb dependent upon the agent which functions as the grammatical subject in a sentence.

If we assume that language is a system of symbols permitting us to express our experiences and our thoughts, then we have to view the structure of language as a reflection of the structure of our minds. Philosophers of phenomenology have argued for some time that sensual perception and the expression it finds in our thoughts, in our speech, and finally in our writings are mutually interdependent.[80] If this assumption is correct then we have to expect that the speech of Buddhist writers reflects a Buddhist view of the world. In other words we have to be prepared to find in Buddhist speech less or no emphasis on the "I" or a similarly dominant agent. Such grammatical and syntactical preferences result in a sentence structure not quite in accord with what is deemed good English. A Buddhist writer who sees the world as a web of interrelated and interdependent fleeting phenomena will express his or her perception of the world accordingly. The sentence structure will emulate this Buddhist view by preferring a syntax that is flexible and often ambiguous and where the individual phrases and clauses reach out to all other components of the sentence to create this web of interrelatedness. Meaning in such speech is not confined to one single possibility, but meaning is revealed in various ways because the correlations of the individual components of the sentence are not fixed. Buddhist speech invites the reader's mind to become engaged in multi-directional associations to let his or her mind float in an ocean of meaning.

This brief characterization of Buddhist speech versus speech based upon occidental ideology makes it clear that translating a Buddhist text requires a certain sensitivity towards this issue. It is neither sufficient to translate word-for-word, which would result in a senseless hodgepodge of words and sentences, nor is it sufficient to paraphrase the original in such a way that the product reads as plain English or whatever modern language of the Indo-Germanic family we may use. On the one hand the meaningful idiosyncrasy of Buddhist speech should be preserved because it bespeaks an authentic

Buddhist perception of reality. On the other hand the English translation should follow its own grammatical and syntactical conventions. Thus a translation is a compromise, a middle road between extremes of "purism."

One issue which comes to mind here is the gender of the term *kun byed rgyal po*, translated here as "all-creating sovereign." The text itself makes it abundantly clear that the *kun byed rgyal po* is beyond any distinction of sexual orientation. In chapter twenty-one of the KBG the following statement is made:

> By being the Sovereign who has made all things, I am father and mother of the teacher in his three manifestations, and the progenitor of all the Buddhas of the three times.

Consequently the neutral pronoun "it" would seem to be the right choice. But the *kun byed rgyal po* acts and speaks in the text like a person and interacts as such with other persons. Many sentences start with "My nature . . . " Can such be said of an "it?" The Tibetan, the language in which the text is preserved, knows of reflexive pronouns which do not specify the gender of the pertinent noun (e.g. *rang*). Consequently the issue of gender does not arise in the original text. The pronoun *rang* is equally used for things as well as persons of both genders. When such sentences are translated into a modern Indo-Germanic language the possessive and reflexive pronouns create a dilemma, forcing the translator to change the text from an inclusive to a gender-biased speech. This is a regrettable situation, particularly at a time when we in the West struggle to integrate the two sexes and the grammatical genders in a more holistic view of the world. Initially I was inclined to give in to the pressure of conventional Buddhist translations, that is to render the All-Creating Sovereign as male. But after reading through most of the works belonging to the "mind section"(*sems sde*), and after considering the impact patriarchy had upon how Buddhist thought was presented throughout time, I decided to follow the intent of the Atiyoga texts and render the All-Creating Sovereign as feminine. Thus the reader will find "her" where the Tibetan text reads "his/her/its." To provide a more balanced view of the text, I chose to speak of the Buddha, at least in the Introduction, as "he and she" whenever the term Buddha referred to the depth of being and not to the historical teacher. Until the present the rendering of Buddhist thought, in the West as well as in the East, was mainly done by men who were sometimes forgetful of the fact that, at least in some branches of the Mahâyâna, every male Buddha has a female equivalent "Buddhâ," that buddhahood is neither male nor female, and that the perfection of wisdom is seen within feminine symbolism. The social structure of the past has prevented women from developing their own perception of Buddhist thought. Thus a religion which had the potential of not being gender-oriented became encapsuled in a patriarchal crust. It is time to understand this fact and to challenge Buddhist thought from a more inclusive perspective.

Some may say that in the Tibetan term *kun byed rgyal po* a male connotation is included as *rgyal po* means "king." However in this text, the term "king" is used as a metaphor. The question is, what does the text want to say by applying this metaphor. The text speaks about the intelligent ground being omnipresent, and thus it is called "king."[81] This statement helps us to develop the right understanding of what is intended when the text uses the metaphor "king." Just as a good but energetic ruler can be felt in every corner of the country governed by his or her laws, so the divine ground of existence is present and can be sensed everywhere. In order to diminish the male connotation of "king," and be more in tune with the spirit of the text, I chose "sovereign" over "king" to render the Tibetan *rgyal po*.

In many cases the Tibetan does not specify the subject of a sentence or the indirect object of an action expressed in the verb. In such cases I have supplied them from the context. To distinguish my insertions from the translation of the text proper, I put my additions between square brackets. The text prefers a non-active mode, as most Buddhist texts do, and indeed as many non-Buddhist texts in Sanskrit and Sanskrit-based languages also do. For this reason the reader will find more passive sentences in my translation that one may normally expect in English. But in the light of the above-mentioned considerations I felt that replacing the non-active style of the original with an active mode would distort the text and the meaning it wants to convey.

On occasion the text fails to specify the intelligent ground in any form, referring to it by using demonstrative pronouns (*de* in Tibetan) without a noun as a reference in its vicinity. As I have pointed out in the notes added to the translation, such usage is well established in the spiritual writings of India. One may also point to Merleau-Ponty who sees in the demonstrative pronoun the least "interpreted" expression.[82] To distinguish this use of the demonstrative pronoun from its more ordinary usage I have capitalized it.

Buddhist philosophy rejects one basic assumption made by all Indo-Germanic languages, that is, the assumption of the I as centre and origin of all activities and events. To put it bluntly, a sentence like "I read a book" is wrong from a Buddhist viewpoint: It is not that I do something to the book; rather, a Buddhist would argue, something happens in a field consisting of a book, a person ("me"), and an event, i.e. "reading." Consequently a Buddhist way of saying it would be "there is the reading of a book with regard to me." Indo-Germanic languages do not allow for such flexibility in their grammatical structures. The example sentence is bad English just as it would be bad Sanskrit, if I had bothered to translate it literally. Because of the Buddhists' unhappiness with the active mode, the prominent position of the agent, etc., they preferred in their Sanskrit writings nominal constructions.[83] That is, they transformed a structure essentially governed by the subject and its dependent verb into one that is governed by verbal nouns. Our example from above would then read "book-read-by-me." In the course of time Buddhists developed this form of language into a true art, so that they were able to produce long and complex sentences consisting of nothing but verbal nouns and their attributes. Under the influence of such thinking the activity becomes an event that happens in a field of interdependent factors with none superior to the others. By the late 8th century C.E. the Buddhists had largely transformed the Sanskrit language into a tool suitable to express a Buddhist world-view.

When the Indian Buddhist texts were brought to Tibet during the late 7th and 8th centuries to be translated into her native idiom the difficulties dwindled away. Tibetan was still a very young language at that time, and flexible enough to accept readily Buddhist philosophy as a basis for developing a more formalized grammatical structure. A factor which encouraged this trend was that Tibetan did not belong to the Indo-Germanic languages but to the Tibeto-Burmese family of languages. These languages do have quite different grammatical premises. For instance, they do not distinguish different categories of words (a word may function as a noun one time and as a verb at another time); active and passive modes are rather the exception than the rule; and expressions which can be understood in only one way are considered a sign of mental immaturity. All these characteristics influenced the way the text is translated here. After all, the reader of the translation should be able to catch a glimpse of the aesthetics of this Buddhist text.

NOTES

1. The term mind is considered by many modern thinkers to be too vague to be used in a scientific context (see the comprehensive discussion in *Historisches Wörterbuch der Philosophie,* ed. by Joachim Ritter. Darmstadt:

Wissenschaftliche Buchgesellschaft, 1974, vol. 3, p. 154ff). I use the term here as an empty "sign" that receives its meaning from the context provided by the KBG. The vagueness of the term "mind" suits this purpose better than a premature identification of the Tibetan term *sems* (rendering the Sanskrit terms *manas* and *citta*) with any of its modern definitions.

2. Prigogine, Ilya/Stengers, Isabelle. *Order out of Chaos, Man's Dialogue with Nature.* New York: Bantam Books, 1984, 115f.

3. Capra, Fritjof. Boston: New Science Library, 1975. *Wendezeit* Bern: Scherz Verlag, 1987.

4. Among other publications see Dürr, Hans Peter (ed.). *Physik und Transzendenz.* Bern/Munich/Vienna: Scherz Verlag, 1986; Wilber, Ken (ed.). *The Holographic Paradigm and Other Paradoxes.* Boston: Shambhala, 1982.

5. Lalou, Marcelle. "Documents Tibétain sur l'expansion du dhyâna Chinois" *Journal Asiatique* 1939, 505.

6. vol. 2. (Serie Orientale Roma IX). Rome: Istituto Italiano per il Medio ed Estremo Oriente, 1956; s. also his *Tibetan Painted Scrolls.* Rome: La Libreria dello Stato, 1949, vol. 2p. 615, n. 252.

7. Op. cit. pp. 21 and 44.

8. See for instance Klong-chen rab-'byams-pa Dri-med 'od-zer. *Lo rgyus chen mo* (in *sNying thig ya bzhi* vol. 9) p. 110. This material is discussed in Dargyay, E. *The Rise of Esoteric Buddhism.* Delhi: Motilal Banarsidass, 2nd ed. 1979, 22 ff.

9. Yampolsky, Philip. "New Japanese Studies in Early Ch'an History" in *Early Ch'an in China and Tibet,* ed. by Whalen Lai and Lewis R. Lancaster (Berkeley Buddhist Studies Series). Berkeley: Asian Humanities Press, 1983, p. 3.

10. Gonda, Jan. "The Creator and his Spirit (*Manas* and *Prajâpati*)" in *Wiener Zeitschrift für die Kunde Südasiens* vol. 27, 1983, pp. 5–42.

11. Shatapatha Brahmana 10,5,3,1 ff; Aitareya Brahmana 2,40,2, and many others, s. Gonda op.cit. p. 16.

12. For further references s. Gonda "The Creator and His Spirit" p. 18 f.

13. See Kristeva, J. *Le texte du roman. Approche sémiologique d'une structure discursive transformationelle.* The Hague: Mouton, 1970.

14. Some of the more recent works on this text may provide further information: Thomi, Peter (tr.). *Cûdâlâ. Eine Episode aus dem Yogavâsistha.* Wichtrach: Institut für Indologie, 1980; Thomi, Peter (tr.). *Yogavâsistha. Die Lehren des Weisen Vasistha.* Interlaken: Ansata Verlag, 1988; Mainkar, T.G. *The Yogâvasistha Râmâyana: A Study.* Sangli: Prabha Press, 1955; Granoff, Phyllis. "The Yogavâsistha: the Continuing Search for a Context."

15. Some scholars prefer the more accurate name Pratyabhijñâ over Kashmirian Shivaism because more than one form of Shaivism had flourished in Kashmir (Chatterji, J.C. *Kashmirian Shaivism*. 1914, rpt. Albany, NY: SUNY Press, 1986, p. xviii) Dyczkowski, Mark S.G. *The Doctrine of Vibration. An Analysis of the Doctrines and Practices of Kashmirian Shaivism*. Albany, NY: State University of New York Press, 1987; Muller-Ortega, Paul Eduardo. *The Triadic Heart of Shiva. Kaula Tantricism of Abhinavagupta in the Non-dual Shaivism of Kashmir*. Albany, NY: State University of New York Press, 1989.

16. Chatterji 1986, xviii.

17. S. Karmay. "An Open Letter . . . ," *The Tibet Journal* 1980, 3, p. 4.

18. Manopubbangamâ dhammâ, manosetthâ manomayâ / manasâ ce padutthena, bhâsati vâ karoti vâ / tato nam dukkham anveti cakkam va vahato padam / (Kashyap, Bhikshu J. *Kuddakapâtha—Dhammapda—Udâna—Itivuttaka—Suttanipâta (Khuddakanikâya I)* (Nâlanda Devanâgari Pâli Series). N.p.: Pâli Publication Board (Bihar Government), 1959, p. 17).

19. Müller, F. Max. *The Dhammapada—a collection of Verses* (Sacred Books of the East X). Rpt. Delhi: Motilal Banarsidass 1968, p. 3 n1.

20. See Conze, E. *Buddhist Thought in India* (Ann Arbor Paperbacks). Ann Arbor: The University of Michigan Press, 1967, p. 156 ff.

21. This kind of argument may be brought forward against Kalupahana, David J. *A Path of Righteousness—Dhammapada*. Lanham/New York/London: University Press of America, 1986, p. 63, where he understands the *manaso* of verse 1a as "empirical mind."

22. Kashyap, Bhikshu J. (ed.). *Dhammasanganî* (Abhidhamma Pitaka vol. 1). N.p.: Pâli Publication Board (Bihar Government), 1960, p.89.

23. *Abhidammattha Sangaha* chap. 1.9–10.

24. Buddhaghosa. *Atthasâlinî* VIII, iii, tr. by Pe Maung Tin. *The Expositor (Atthasâlinî). Buddhaghosa's Commentary on the Dhammasanganî, the First Book of the Abhidhamma Pitaka*. Ed. and rev. by Rhys Davids. London: Pali Text Society, 1921, p. 323 ff.

25. Tr. in *Collection of the Middle Length Sayings,* vol. III, by I.B. Horner; text edition *Majjhimanikâya*, ed. by Bhikkhu J. Kashyap. Bihar: Pâli Publication Board, 1958, vol. 3, p. 168–73.

26. *The Great Code*. San Diego: Harcourt Brace Jovanovich, 1982, p. 15 .

27. According to *Vibhâsâprabhâ vrtti* 262 f., quoted in the article on *citta* in *Encyclopaedia of Buddhism* vol. 4.

28. For full bibliographical information see Conze, E. *The Prajñâpâramitâ Literature,* 2nd rev. and enlarged ed. (Bibliographia Philologica Buddhica, Series Maior 1). Tokyo: The Reiyukai, 1978, p. 56.

29. p. 86.

30. Verses 100–101.

31. Osaki, Akiko. "What is meant by destroying the âlayavijñâna?" *Indogaku Bukkyôgaku Kenkyû* (Journal of Indian and Buddhist Studies: Univ. of Tokyo) XXVI.2.

32. Schmithausen, Lambert. *Alayavijñâna. On the Origin and the Early Development of a Central Concept of Yogâcâra Philosophy* (Studia Philologica Buddhica, Monograph Series IV). Tokyo: The International Institute for Buddhist Studies, 1987, p. 197 ff.

33. Takasaki, Jikido. *A Study on the Ratnagotravibhâga (Uttaratantra) Being a Treatise on the Tathâgatagarbha Theory of Mahâyâna Buddhism* (Serie Orientale Roma 33). Rome: Istituto Italiano per il Medio ed Estremo Oriente, 1966.

34. Op. cit., p. 235.

35. Suzuki, Daisetz Teitaro. *The Zen Doctrine of No-Mind,* ed. by Chr. Humphreys. New York: Samuel Weiser, 1973, 29.

36. Frye, Northrop. *The Great Code,* chap. 3, p. 53ff.

37. These events are fully treated in the pertinent literature. More information on this subject is given in Lancaster, Lewis. "Buddhist Literature: Its Canons, Scribes, and Editors" in *The Critical Study of Sacred Texts,* ed. by Wendy D. O'Flaherty. Berkeley: Graduate Theological Union, 1979, pp. 215–229; Coward, Harold. *Sacred Word—Sacred Text.* Maryknoll, NY: Orbis Books, 1988, p. 138ff.

38. Bechert, Heinz (ed.) *Zur Schulzugehörigkeit von Werken der Hînayâna-Literatur* (Abhandlungen der Akademie der Wissenschaften in Göttingen). Göttingen: Vandenhoeck & Ruprecht, 1985, vol. 1, p.21 f.

39. Greg Schopen discusses the religious situation prevalent at the begining of the Common Era in his article "The Inscription on the Kusân Image of Amitâbha and the Character of the Early Mahayana in India", in *Journal of the International Association of Buddhist Studies* vol. 10,2, 1987, pp.99–137.

40. S. H. Bechert, op. cit. p. 51.

41. Stein, R.A. (ed.). *Une chronique ancienne de bSam-yas: sBa-bzed* (Publications de l'Insitut des Hautes Etudes Chinoises, textes et documents I). Paris: Adrien Maisonneuve, 1961, p. 1.

42. S. Detweiler, Robert. "What is a Sacred Text?" in *Reader Response Approaches to Biblical and Secular Texts* (Semeia 31), ed. by Robert Detweiler. Decatur, GA: Society of Biblical Literature, 1985, p. 222 f.

43. These events are described in the afore-mentioned *sBa bzhed* but also by Seizan, Yanagida in "The *Li-tai Fa-pao Chi* and the Ch'an Doctrine of Sudden Awakening" in *Early ch'an in China and Tibet* (Berkeley Buddhist Studies

Series 5). Ed. by Lai, Whalen and L. Lancaster. Berkeley: Asian Humanities Press, 1983, pp. 13–49.

44. A title list of this royal library is preserved under the name the *lDan dkar ma Catalogue*. Further evidence about which books did exist by the 8/9th centuries in Tibetan is provided by the Tun Huang manuscripts.

45. S. Yampolski, Ph. "New Japanese Studies . . . " p. 10.

46. A vivid descriptions of these events is given by a 13th century Tibetan pilgrim who visited most of the sacred sites of Buddhism in India (Roerich, George, ed. and tr.). *Biography of Dharmasvâmin (Chag lo-tsa-ba Chos-rje-dpal) a Tibetan Monk Pilgrim*. Patna: K.P. Jayaswal Research Insitute, 1959.

47. This subject has received tremendous coverage in the writings of the Tibetan scholars. For more information on this topic see: Karmay, Samten G. "An Open Letter by Pho-brang Zhi-ba-'od to the Buddhists in Tibet" *The Tibet Journal* vol. 5, no. 3, 1980, pp.3–28; Dargyay, Eva K. "A Rnying-ma Text: The *Kun byed rgyal po'i mdo*," *Soundings in Tibetan Civilization*, ed. by Aziz, Barbara N. and M. Kapstein. New Delhi: Manohar Publications, 1985, pp.283–293; Broido, Michael. "Sa-skya Pandita, the White Panacea and the Hva-Shang Doctrine" *The Journal of the International Association of Buddhist Studies* vol. 10, no.2, 1987, pp.27–68.

48. A detailed coverage of the various strands of this transmission is given in my early work *The Rise of Esoteric Buddhism*. 2nd rev. ed. Delhi: Motilal Banarsidass, 1979.

49. Ratna-gling-pa. *The Nyingmapa Apology of Rin-chen dpal-bzang-po, Chos 'byung bstan pa'i sgron me rtsod zlog seng ge'i nga ro*. Repr. by Kham-sprul Don-brgyud nyi-ma. Tashijong, Palampur (India): n.p. 1972, pp. 89.3–91.2.

50. Here the question arises as to whether the text should not better read Vairocana instead of Vimalamitra, as the subsequent story tells how the latter has received his share of Great Perfection texts. Furthermore, the first part of the quote deals with Vairocana and not with Vimalamitra. Most *chos 'byung* accounts of the Old School credited Vimalamitra with the transmission of the Atiyoga texts in general and of those of the *man ngag* section, while Vairocana is said to have transmitted those of the *sems sde* and *klong sde* sections (Dargyay, 1979, p. 26, 50f).

51. Read *bod du spyug byas te* for *bar du spyug bas te*.

52. Don-grub rgyal-po of Nyang. *Rig 'dzin chen po Ratna gling-pa'i rnam thar skyes rabs 'bring po tshigs su bcad pa*, in *Selected Works of Ratna gling-pa*, reproduced from a manuscript from the library of Ri-bo-che Rje-drung of Padma-bkod by Tseten Dorji. Tezu, Dist. Lohit (India): n.p., 1973, vol. 1, p. 365, cp. p. 411.5.

53. Dudjom Rinpoche. *Gangs ljongs rgyal bstan yongs rdzogs kyi phyi mo snga 'gyur rdo rje theg pa'i bstan pa rin po che ji ltar byung ba'i tshul dag cing gsal bar*

brjod pa lha dbang g-yul las rgyal ba'i rnga bo che'i sgra dbangs. Kalimpong: n. p., 1967, p. 570.

54. Ibid., p.625f.

55. Later Tibetan tradition considers the Indian scholar Kamalasîla to be the first one to promulgate the gradual path among the Tibetans. For this reason he is pictured as the antagonist of Hva-shang Mahâyâna (the correct form of his name is Ho-shang Ma-ho-yen), the Chinese monk, who reportedly was defeated in the debate of bSam-yas. Recent research, however, does not corroborate this traditional view but suggests that the so-called bSam-yas debate was a more complex issue resulting from different interpretations of certain Buddhist concepts. Therefore I do not count Kamalasîla as the protagonist of the gradual path teaching.

56. The Tibetan text is contained in Cone vol. Dza 1b.1–92a.1; sNar-thang vol. Dza, 1b.1–120b.1; Lhasa vol. Dza 1b–123a; Peking vol. Dza (9), p. 93, 1.1–126.5.2; and Derge vol. 97, 1b–86a (information as to where the individual xylographs or modern reprints are to be found is given by G. Grönbold, *Der buddhistische Kanon;* NGB vol. 1, pp. 1–220, ed. by Jamyang Khyentse; VGB vol. 1, no. 4, chapters 58–84, p. 384.1.1–435.5. .

57. The canon of Buddhist scriptures in Tibetan is divided into two large sections: (a) The Kanjur with over 1,000 individual texts arranged in more than 100 volumes. They contain those texts which in view of the Buddhist tradition were proclaimed by the historical Buddha Shâkyamuni himself or under his inspiration by one of his disciples; some of the texts are ascribed to other Buddhas. The Kanjur constitutes the core of Buddhist scriptures. (b) The second section is known as Tanjur which contains almost 3,500 individual works which were composed by the Buddhist scholar-saints of India. This section constitutes the commentaries on which the exegesis of the Kanjur rests. This gigantic collection of texts exists in several printed edition (carved from blocks of wood), and in an unknown number of manuscript editions. One or the other printed edition may be found in most research libraries of the West.

58. This complex subject is discussed by Eimer, Helmut. "Some Results of Recent Kanjur Research" *Archiv für zentralasiatische Geschichtsforschung*, ed. by Schuh, Dieter and M. Weiers. Sankt Augustin, West Germany: VGH Wissenschaftsverlag, 1983, fasc. 1; Grönbold, Günter. *Der buddhistische Kanon, eine Bibliographies*. Wiesbaden: Otto Harrassowitz, 1984, p. 15 ff.

59. S. Eimer, Helmut. "Some Results . . . " p. 13 f.

60. Bethlenfalvy, Géza. *A Hand-list of the Ulan Bator Manuscript of the Kanjur Rgyal-rtse Them spangs ma*. Budapest: Akadémiai Kiado, 1982, p.7.

61. Imaeda, Yoshiro. *Catalogue du Kanjur Tibetain de l'edition de 'Jang Satham* (Bibliographica Philologica Buddhica Series Major IIa) Tokyo: The International Institute for Buddhist Studies, 1982.

62. Ruegg, D.S. *The life of Bu ston Rin po che* (*Serie Orientale Roma* 34). Rome: Istituto Italiano per il Medio ed Estremo Oriente, 1966, p. 68f.

63. See Dargyay, Eva K. "A Rnying-ma Text: . . . " p. 285.

64. Published in vol. 4, no. 132, of the *Sa-skya bka' 'bum*, Tokyo 1968.

65. For further information see Conze, Edward. *The Large Sutra on Perfect Wisdom*. Berkeley, Los Angeles, London: University of California Press, 1975, pp.2–3, 45ff.

66. See Guenther, Herbert V. *The Tantric View of Life*. Berkeley, London: Shambala Publications 1972, 15.

67. These three reasons are: 1. the self-arising pristine awareness, 2. the five awarenesses, and 3. the five elements.

68. KBG 218.6.

69. NGB vol. 1, p. 499: *kun tu bzang mo'i spyod pas ma zin dge ba'i chos ni gang yang rung*. For a further discussion of a feminist reading of certain Buddhist texts and ideas see the publications by Anne Klein (s. Bibliography).

70. The short tractate is preserved in a number of collections, among them: *Selected Writings of Padmasambhava*, ed. 'Chi-med Rig-'dzin bla-ma. Leh: n.p., 1974, pp.1–18; Kong-sprul Blo-gros mtha'-yas (ed.). *gDams ngag mdzod*. Delhi: n.p., 1971, vol. 1, pp. 16–26; cf. Loseries, Ulrich. *Guru Padmasambhavas "Instruktion 'Die Kette der Anschauungen'"* (Inaugural-Dissertation Friedrich-Wilhelm Universität, Bonn). Bonn: n.p., 1989.

71. Bohm, David and Weber, Rene. "Implizite und explizite Ordnung: zwei Aspekte des Universums" in *Das holographische Weltbild*, ed. by Ken Wilber. Munich/Bern: Scherz Verlag, 1986, pp.48–114.

72. Giles, Herbert A. (tr.) *Chuang Tzu, Taoist Philosopher and Chinese Mystic*. 1889, rpt. London: Allen and Unwin, 1980, p.87.

73. Conze, Eward. *Buddhist Scriptures* (Penguin Classics). Harmondsworth, UK: Penguin Books, 1984, p.70.

74. The Tib. text repeats the first part of this sentence every time. I have replaced this sentence with an ellipsis to avoid cumbersome repetition.

75. The term "method" (Skr. *upâya*, Tib. *thabs*) refers to the Buddha's method of rescuing the sentient beings from the endless abyss of samsara. Its most crucial component is the "great compassion" which enables the Buddha to see all things as essentially one. Sometimes the term is also translated as "skill-in-means." In this text, the term "method" is—as most other terms of sutra literature—loaded with a different meaning. As shall become clear later on, method in this text means "no-method" as reality is since beginningless time in the state of consummation.

76. *Byang chub kyi sems kun byed rgyal po'i don khrid rin chen gru bo* p. 169, l. 4, in *gDams ngag mdzod* by 'Jam-mgon Kong-sprul. Delhi: n.p., 1971, vol. 1, pp. 159–184.

77. see KBG p. 31.

78. *Tao te ching* 2, tr. in *A Source Book in Chinese Philosophy*, tr. and ed. by Wing-tsit Chan. Princeton: Princeton University Press, 140; Visvader, John and William C. Doub. "The Problem of Desire and Emotions in Taoism and Ch'an," in *Early Ch'an in China and Tibet*, ed. by Lai, Whalen and L.R. Lancaster. Berkeley: Asian Humanities Press, 1983, 285.

79. The fact that in Atiyoga texts which were composed during the later period of dissemination (*phyi dar*), that is from the mid-10th century onwards, such methods are given is not a contradiction. In my opinion these texts demonstrate that the followers of the Old School felt enormous pressure to give in to the gradual method promoted by Atisha, who came to Tibet in 1042, and his disciples. This pressure led them to design "methods" to achieve a goalless goal.

80. For more information see Lanigan, Richard L. *Speaking and Semiology. Maurice Merleau-Ponty's Phenomenological Theory of Existential Communication*. The Hague: Mouton, 1972, where the issue receives extensive coverage.

81. KBG chapter 4.

82. Lanigan 1972, p.158.

83. I like to point to a theory of literary criticism formulated by feminist scholars that says that the occidental obsession with the "I" as a monolithic entity is an extension of the phallus as symbol of male dominance. This is obviously not the right place to elaborate on this issue but more information on this subject may be obtained from Moi, Toril. *Sexual/Textual Politics: Feminist Literary Theory*. London and New York: Methuen, 1985, p. 8 f.

THE ALL-CREATING SOVEREIGN, MIND OF PERFECT PURITY, THE CONSUMMATION OF ALL

Translated from the Tibetan

*

From the Ocean "The Tantras of the Old Translations," [part of the] Vajrayâna of Secret Spells, such [texts] as The Great Consummate All-Creating Sovereign [which belong to] the section on the mind (*sems sde*) will follow here.

{p.2} In Indian language: *sarva dharma mahasanti bodhicitta kulaya râjâ* In Tibetan: *chos thams cad rdzogs pa chen po byang chub kyi sems kun byed rgyal po* (The All-Creating Sovereign, Mind of Perfect Purity,[1] the Consummation of All)

1

Homage to the All-Creating Sovereign, the mind of complete purity, the victorious one!

At a time this sermon was taught in the realm No-Below (Akanishtha) [where] Reality is [like] the sky, and the dimension of Reality itself (*dharmadhâtu*) [like] the vastness [of the sky]. There is the place where the Mind itself (*sems nyid*) exists.[2]

In the untainted mansion of pristine awareness [the All-Creating Sovereign's] own being (*rang bzhin*), Her actuating essence (*ngo bo*), Her compassion and pristine awareness became manifest as [various] retinues in the following way: The retinue [emerging] from Her own being is known as the retinue of truth manifestation (*dharmakâya*). The retinue of Her actuating essence, the manifestation of consummate joy (*sambhogakâya*) is called the retinue [of the element] earth;[3] {p.3} . . . retinue [of the element] water; . . . retinue [of the element] fire; . . . retinue [of the element] wind; . . . retinue [of the element] sky. Furthermore, the manifesting of [her] compassion and pristine awareness as retinues [in form] of corporeal manifestations (*nirmâna*) happened in this way: the retinue known as sentient beings of the realm of desire (*kâmaloka*), the retinue known as the sentient beings of the realm of form (*rûpaloka*), and the retinue known as the sentient beings of the realm of formlessness (*arûpaloka*). {p.4} Furthermore, the retinues equal to Her own being correspond to the four yogas: the retinue of Atiyoga (*shin tu rnal 'byor*), the retinue of Anuyoga (*yongs su rnal 'byor*), the retinue of Mahâyoga (*rnal 'byor chen po*), and the retinue of the bodhisattva yoga (*sems dpa' rnal 'byor*). As Her own being, Her actuating essence, and Her compassion are inseparable from Her nature, there is only one method.[4]

Furthermore, the retinues cognizing Her own being are such: the retinue resting in Her, i.e. the Buddhas of the past; the retinue realizing Her objective, i.e. the present Buddhas; the retinue that brings forth Her deeds, i.e. the Buddhas to come later. Because they are inseparable from Her own being there is only one method.

After that, the All-Creating Sovereign, the mind of perfect purity, absorbed into Her mind and heart all the retinues so that they were blessed with Her own being. {p.5} She then let the self-originated pristine awareness become lucid. To endow all things with Reality, She then dwelt as one in the void focus (*bindu*) after She had united all things.

After that, Sems-dpa' rdo-rje, who abided through Her in the great void focus of [Her] own being, emerged from this [state] and sat down with a mind of joy and a pure and bright appearance in front of the All-Creating Sovereign, the mind of perfect purity. The All-Creating Sovereign, the mind of perfect purity, spoke to Sems-dpa' rdo-rje:

"Sems-dpa' rdo-rje, *emaho*, generate a mind of joy, *emaho;* produce a pure and bright countenance, *emaho:* You have come forth from Me, *emaho!*"

Thus She spoke.

Then Sems-dpa' rdo-rje addressed Her:

"Oh teacher of the teachers, All-Creating Sovereign! Is the void focus of the non-conceptual (*spros med*) also the teacher Herself, or is the void focus of the non-conceptual also the entirety of retinues, or is the void focus of the non-conceptual also the entirety of teachings, {p.6} or is the void focus also time and place,[5] or how does the teacher of the teachers teach if everything abides in the nature of this void focus? For what purpose do the retinues circulate as Her retinues? Why is a teaching taught to the retinues? How can it be that time and place are one?"

Thus he asked. After that the All-Creating Sovereign, the mind of perfect purity, gave Sems-dpa' rdo-rje the following instruction:

"Oh great bodhisattva, direct your mind towards this instruction! Let me explain the meaning. Oh Sems-dpa' rdo-rje, Mind-as-such, i.e. I, the All-Creating Sovereign, am the central vigor (*snying po*) of all things. This central vigor, which is non-conceptual, is the primordial void focus. The void focus in its final value (*don*) is without conceptualization from the primordial. The teacher, the teachings, the retinues, time and place, they emerged from Me as the primordial void focus. My own being is known as the void focus."

Such the All-Creating Sovereign, the mind of perfect purity, spoke.

This is the first chapter, the introduction.

2

{cont'd p.6} After that the All-Creating Sovereign, the mind of complete purity, dwelt in what is called a contemplation (*samâdhi*) of 'all things emerge from Her.' Then Sems-dpa' rdo-rje arose from the own being of the retinues and, approaching with a smiling face the teacher, the All-Creating Sovereign, the mind of perfect purity, asked Her and sat down:

"Oh teacher of the teachers, All-Creating Sovereign! As I am in an integrated way present in Your retinues, what is then the objective of my existence (*'tshal*)?[6] Please teach me about the objective of my existence!"

Such he spoke.

{p.7} Then the All-Creating Sovereign, the mind of perfect purity, laid out all things on the basis of Her own being, Her actuating essence, and Her compassion. That from the one great self-originated awareness the five great self-originated awarenesses come, is as follows: the great self-originated awareness as hatred, as attachment, ignorance, jealousy, and pride—these five self-originated awarenesses bring forth the five great [elements] as cause of adornment.[7] She set up the three great realms (*'khams*) as a receptacle of what is perishable. That the cause of adornment obtained its five forms[8] as one is as follows: There is the form of earth as the cause of adornment; there is the form of water, fire, wind, and sky as causes of adornment. All these forms were obtained as one.

The five awarenesses were organized according to the five 'families': the family of the self-originated awareness of hatred, that of the awareness of attachment, of ignorance, of jealousy, and of pride. The beautiful appearance of the forms of the "families" associated with the five self-originated awarenesses was set up as the Reality of those endowed with a body (i.e. sentient beings). As Reality was set up in accord with Her own being, even the All-Creating Sovereign, the mind of perfect purity, dwelt in this manner.

{p.8} Then Sems-dpa' rdo-rje again abode in front of the All-Creating Sovereign, the mind of perfect purity:

"Oh teacher, All-Creating Sovereign! From the self-originated awareness, one with Your[9] mind, the five forms of self-originated awareness come, and from that the five causes of adornment come. Oh All-Creating Sovereign, what is the reason for this [fact that] the five self-originated awarenesses adopt five [different] forms?"

Such he asked.

The All-Creating Sovereign, the mind of perfect purity, explained further:

"Oh great bodhisattva, this you must know: Besides Me, the All-Creating Sovereign, the maker, there is no other maker. None besides Me creates Reality. None besides Me establishes the teacher's three forms of manifestation (*sku gsum*). None besides Me establishes the hosts of retinues. None besides Me establishes [the things] as they are (*tathatâ*) in their Reality. Sems-dpa' rdo-rje, by Me you are! I shall show you My own being. My own being has three aspects (*rnam pa*). My own being is the mind of perfect purity. 'Pure' is taught to be the nature of the limpid (*dag pa*) in its three aspects of totality. 'Perfect' is taught as the nature of the limpid as encompassing the three reasons.[10] [The limpid] is all-encompassing like the sky. The nature of what is called 'mind' is taught as the ceaseless, all-encompassing All-Creating Sovereign. Everything is made, all is generated in the mind of perfect purity."

Such She spoke.

This is the second chapter of the *All-Creating Sovereign, the Mind of Perfect Purity,* in which is explained how Reality has become apparent.

3

{p. 9} Then the All-Creating Sovereign, mind of perfect purity, spoke about "How I[11] have become in the past the maker of all things:"

"Oh great bodhisattva, lend your mind to the ear! Understand [My] words by virtue of listening. Oh, I am the All-Creating Sovereign. I am the mind of perfect purity, the maker of all. If I were not existent in the past, no vigor were there for all things to originate. If I were not existent in the past, no Sovereign were there who made all things. If I were not existent in the past, none were there to be a teacher from the primordial.[12] If I were not existent in the past, none were there to teach from the primordial. If I were not existent in the past, that which is known as retinues would not be there from the primordial. Sems-dpa' rdo-rje, do not have doubts. Also you, oh great bodhisattva, are an emanation of Me."

Such She spoke.

Then Sems-dpa' rdo-rje addressed the All-Creating Sovereign, mind of perfect purity:

"Oh All-Creating Sovereign, mind of perfect purity, You are from the primordial the great one. Because you, the creator of teacher, teaching, and retinue as well as of all things, have made them, how then do all things come into existence? It seems that you, the creator, have made them. Has then one teacher appeared or many? Is there one teaching or many? Are the retinues one or many?"

Such he asked.

Then the All-Creating Sovereign, mind of perfect purity, spoke again:

"Oh the self-originated pristine awareness, sole teacher of all, appears as the three aspects of My own being, and with regard to the number of teachers {p. 10}, they come into existence as three. Because I am one with suchness (*de bzhin nyid*) the Reality of all things is this suchness. Nothing is except My self, i.e. the mind of perfect purity. From Me emanated the teacher's three forms of manifestation that teach the retinues the three forms of teachings. My actuating essence has been manifest as one and because My own being is declared to be one, all is one as My, i.e. the All-Creating [Sovereign], retinue. But the retinues of the teachers, though emanating from Me, are of three divisions."

Such She spoke.

Sems-dpa' rdo-rje asked:

"Oh teacher of the teachers, All-Creating Sovereign! From You, the teacher's three forms of manifestation emanated, but is there a path for the sentient beings to Your stage (*sa*) or not? If not, can one reach Your stage or not? If so, does one reach it by means of progressing [on a spiritual path] or by not progressing?

[The All-Creating Sovereign:]

"Listen great bodhisattva! The teacher's three forms of manifestation emanate from Me, but there is no path on which you could proceed towards My stage. I have shown[13] the self-originated pristine awareness. But all the Buddhas of the three times have taught the retinues, associated with the teacher's three forms of manifestation, a universal path (*kun gyi lam*), i.e. the path to liberation in five stages.

The five paths of the five self-originated pristine awarenesses are attachment, hatred, ignorance, pride, and jealousy. This is [the true] universal path, i.e. the five aspects of self-originated pristine awareness."

Such She said.

[Sems-dpa' rdo-rje:]

"Oh teacher of the teachers, All-Creating Sovereign, expound the five paths in accordance with the self-originated pristine awareness. How has come to be what is known as 'self-originated'; what are the synonyms for the term 'awareness'; what is given as meaning of 'path'. I beg You to expound {p.11} the meaning of the five paths as to the five aspects, i.e. attachment, hatred, ignorance, pride, and jealousy!"

Such he asked.

[The All-Creating Sovereign:]

"Great bodhisattva! With regard to the path of the five aspects of the self-originated pristine awareness [it is as follows:] 'self-originated' [is said because it is] without cause and condition; 'pristine awareness' [is said because it is] lucid in its ceaselessness. There is no reason to proceed on this path, as it is without cause or conditions. The five self-originated [pristine awarenesses] are known as the five paths on which one can not progress. 'Desire' is to want the things for oneself; 'attachment' is to covet that which one desires for oneself; 'mind (*zhe*)' is the nature of the unborn, and 'wrath' is to hate its miraculous variety; 'ignorance' is not to achieve clarity about the divisions of sameness and Reality through meditating on the non-conceptual. I am the unerring mind of perfect purity. In this suchness I am Sovereign from the primordial. Because everything is one in suchness, to appreciate and depreciate [the notion of] existence and non-existence will create a jealous feeling. This is the explanation about the five paths on which there is no progress.

Oh great bodhisattva listen! All things, in the way they appear, come forth from these five paths of the self-originated pristine awareness. The realm of desire is the self-originated pristine awareness, so is the realm of form, and so is the realm of formlessness. Because I, the All-Creating Sovereign, have created them, all things made by Me are known as the actuation (*ngo bo*) of the pristine awareness. That all the beings of the six [different] categories [living] in the threefold world are not the self-originated pristine awareness, such I have never proclaimed. Furthermore, {p.12} I do not say that the mind of perfect purity is not the progenitor of all Buddhas. My, the All-Creating Sovereign's nature, is declared as the three aspects of Reality. The unborn Reality does not truly appear, [but] is explained as the realm of formlessness. With regard to the wonders of existence as form, it is taught as the realm of form. [Given the fact that] compassion comes forth as an actuation of pristine awareness, compassion becomes manifest as the realm of desire in order to exhaust the karma of good luck and ill by compassion."

Such She spoke.

This is the third chapter of *The All-Creating Sovereign, Mind of Perfect Purity,* in which is explained how all things originated as deeds done by the All-Creating Sovereign.

4

{cont'd p. 12} Then the All-Creating Sovereign, mind of perfect purity, gave the following talk about the Reality of the names [given] to Her own being.

"Oh great bodhisattva, listen! From the primordial I am the self-originated pristine awareness. From the primordial I am the central vigor (*snying po*) of all things. I am the All-Creating Sovereign, mind of perfect purity. A bodhisattva ought to understand My name. If a bodhisattva recognizes My name, he or she will understand all things without exception. I am called the central vigor as I am the central vigor of all things. I am called self-originated because I am totally beyond [the scope of] striving and achieving and as central vigor I am free of causes and conditions. I am called pristine awareness because by virtue of this ceaseless and stainless [awareness] I am the teacher of all things. I am known as mind of perfect purity. {p. 13} The meaning of 'from the primordial' is that I exist right from the beginning. 'All things' is said because all the teachers are [present] in Reality, and so are all the teachings, and the retinues [manifest in] place [and time] are [present in] Reality. Not a single thing is that is not [present] in Reality. This Reality which is called inner vigor is the inner vigor which gives rise to everything.

In the own being of the mind of perfect purity, the three teachers are also coming from [this Reality], the three teachings are also coming from it, and the retinues [appearing] in place and time are also coming from [that source]. As everything comes from it, it is called central vigor.

About Me [you should know] that as central vigor of the mind itself I have created all things without any exception. 'All' is said with regard to all things [or] everything. 'All things'—whatever can be cognized as teachers, teachings, retinues, place and time. 'Creating'—I am called master of creation (*bya ba mkhan*). As I have created the teachers, teachings, retinues, place and time, I am the master of the self-originated pristine awareness. I am called Sovereign as I am superior to everything as the creator of all things and as the inner vigor of the self-originated pristine awareness.

The meaning of purity is that it is the central vigor of the mind of perfect purity. By means of the self-originated which is pure from the primordial, the All-Creating Sovereign makes everything. Because I am pure in total immaculateness I am known as the pure one. 'Perfect' is said in this [sense]: due to the central vigor of the self-originated pristine awareness [all things] which appear or exist, in short the animated and inanimated, as all the Buddhas of the three times {p.14}, and the six categories of sentient beings in the three realms are vastly established and totally perfected in suchness. Therefore 'perfect' I am called.

The meaning of 'mind' is as follows: The central vigor of self-originated pristine awareness discerns with strength the perishable in all that exists as animated and inanimated. Therefore it is known as mind. The causeless and condition-less central vigor exercises power over everything, and creates all. Oh great bodhisattva, if you understand My own being you will also understand all the teachers, and all the teachings; you will understand the thoughts of the attendants, and that the entirety of place and time has become one. Because I am all and everything you will understand all things if you understand My own being. Therefore by non-striving you will be spontaneously self-perfected in what is totally beyond doing deeds, and beyond striving and achieving."

Thus She spoke.

This is the fourth chapter of *The All-Creating Sovereign, Mind of Perfect Purity,* in which Her name is explained.

5

After that the All-Creating Sovereign, mind of perfect purity, instructed Sems-dpa' rdo-rje in the concise meaning of the teachings about Her own being:

"Oh great bodhisattva, listen! My own being is like this: Its intrinsic being (*yod*) is nothing but one. Its teaching (*bstan*) is taught in two aspects. Its origin (*byung*) is revealed in the nine vehicles. Its integration (*'dus*) is integral to the Great Perfection. Its explicit being (*yin*) is the mind of perfect purity. Its existence (*gnas*) abides in the dimension of Reality (*chos nyid dbyings*). Its luminosity illuminates the space of intuitive wisdom (*rig pa'i mkha*). {p. 15} Its pervasiveness (*khyab*) covers the entire animated and inanimated world. Its manifestation (*byung*)[14] manifests as the entirety of what appears and exists. Teaching [on it, means] things do not have [fixed] characteristics. Seeing it [means] one will be free of objects of perception. Knowing it [means] one will not attempt to express it through words.

This essential vigor, which does not come from any cause, is free of all fetters [created] by the methods [of explanation]. If one wishes for a thorough understanding of this matter one has to take the sky as a simile: the point is that Reality is unborn, and that as the main characteristic the mind is ceaseless. Like the sky so is Reality; by means of the sky as simile [Reality] is pointed out. The imperceptible Reality is taught by pointing at [something else which is] imperceptible. [The Reality] which cannot be expressed through words is explained [through something] which is inexplicable. The quintessence of the imperceptible is taught as the main point of a teaching that is joined [with similes]. The essence of this meaning is given in comments. Thereby you ought to understand the meaning of Me. Thereby you will be led to understand the meaning of Me. If you don't understand thereby the meaning of Me you will never meet Me, [regardless of] how many words you have learned. If you deviate (*gol*) from Me I shall be veiled, and for this reason, you will not obtain the pith of Reality (*chos kyi snying po*)."

Thus She spoke.

This is the fifth chapter of *The All-Creating Sovereign, Mind of Perfect Purity,* in which "meaning" is commented upon.

6

Then the All-Creating Sovereign, mind of perfect purity, gave this sermon [in which She declared] that the perfection of all things rests in Her own being:

"Oh great bodhisattva, listen to these words! I am the All-Creating Sovereign, and I have arranged all things from the primordial. I made the things apparent. I will show you My actuating essence. After I show you My own being I shall point out its meaning in words, and sounds, and you will be able to envisage [My] actuating essence [as] taught [to you]. [My] own being, when explained, you will understand it as [the letter] A.[15] By means of speaking these words you will perceive the meaning."

Such She said, and did not say anything more. She abided in the actuating essence of all things. Because of that Sems-dpa' rdo-rje arose from amidst the attendants and sat with a sombre face in front of the All-Creating Sovereign, mind of perfect purity.

The All-Creating Sovereign:

"Oh great bodhisattva, you are sitting here before Me in a sombre [mood]. Ask what you wish to know!"

Then Sems-dpa' rdo-rje asked:

"Oh teacher of the teachers, All-Creating Sovereign! If all things are Your own being, what then did You[16] establish as teachers, teaching, and retinues? What are the perfect entities?"

This question he asked.

Then the All-Creating Sovereign, mind of perfect purity, spoke these words:

"Oh great bodhisattva, listen! Things are made in a perfect manner. This is so because I am the nature of perfection. I shall show you My own being. Because My own being is non-conceptual and uncreated, I have made [things] as to exist in the realm of Reality (*chos dbyings*). They do not rest on anything else but the mind of perfect purity. As My own being is immaculate and all-pervasive [the things] do not rest upon anything else but on the self-originated awareness itself in the mansion of awareness, i.e the lucid sky. {p.17} As I am the central vigor[17] of all things which come into existence, i.e. the five great [elements], the threefold world, the six categories [of sentient beings]: they are nothing else but My form, utterance and spirit. I have established [the things] as My own being. I am revealing to you the Buddhas of the three times and the sentient beings of the threefold world as My own being. Because My actuating essence is unborn, and non-conceptual, it does not exist (*mi gnas*), but transcends all areas of perception. It even transcends the objects of meditation and does not become apparent in mental absorption. Although My own being is imperceptible, I reveal My actuation to you as the threefold world, [consisting of] the five great [elements], and the six categories [of sentient beings]. From the five [elements] which are the apparent [form of My] own being, i.e. the perfect and pure mind, come the five self-originated and vigorous awarenesses. The five awarenesses bring forth the five sensual objects; after the five desires have come forth the five passions come forth. The five passions bring their individual results which individually appear as the six categories of the sentient beings. I am teaching you the appearance [of the universe] to be like that.

Even if I taught you the three forms of manifestation, and the six vehicles, you would not understand them. Each of them (i.e. the teacher's three forms of manifestation and the six vehicles) is endowed with My true being in an individual fashion, and each of them is My actuation in individual fashion as form, utterance, and spirit. The individual actuation lets you see the whole. In such way My own being is also taught. I, as [the mind of] perfect purity, the actuating essence of all that is pure, let emerge from Me the play (*rol pa*) of the threefold world, and the six categories of sentient beings, because I am actuating the dimension of the non-conceptual, and I am the existential ground (*gnas chen*) of all Buddhas. Particularly I teach that, if you are not mistaken about the pure, all acts of happiness and misery are My compassion. {p.18} I, the All-Creating, will not teach such lore to those who adhere to the vehicle of cause and result. If I taught them My lore as definitive, they would cast praise and slander on Me, the All-Pure, as they assert that cause and result do exist because of good and bad acts. For this reason they will not meet Me, the All-Pure One, for a long time. I am the teacher, the All-Creating One, the mind of perfect purity. The mind of perfect purity is the All-Creating Sovereign. The mind of perfect purity creates the Buddhas of the three times; the mind of perfect purity creates the sentient beings [living] in this threefold world; the mind of perfect purity creates what appears and exists as the animated and inanimated world.[18]

To bring [the concepts of] cause, result, simile, objective, and definition into agreement [with this teaching, you ought to know:] at the time of cause, the five great elements are created; at the time of result the sentient beings in this threefold world are created; at the time of simile the sky as a simile of everything is created; at the time of the meaning the unborn is made by Me as the meaning of everything; at the time of sign the All-Creating Mind of Perfect Purity [is revealed]; at the time of definition the self-originated awareness is taught. This is how cause, result, simile, meaning and definition are brought into agreement with [this teaching].

By means of the mind of perfect purity all is made; not one thing is not made by it. [The All-Creating's] own being, the mind of perfect purity has made all, and not one is that is not made by it; there is no reason for itself to be created. My own being, the All-Creating One's, is beyond cognition (*ma brtags par*), but I am perceived with certainty in the things I have created. By means of a longing desire the appearance [of these things] is achieved, but they will perish because of their impermanent and illusory nature, a nature which is impartial and like a man born blind. Although the All-Creating Sovereign is impartial in Her creating, {p. 19} the senses get obstructed when they experience suffering when the six sensory objects are perceived by the six sense faculties. For this reason, the All-Creating Sovereign is impartial in Her creation. Thus, no result does exist which could annihilate cessation and origination.[19] Certainly, the two truths arise from this One (i.e. the mind of perfect purity). The ultimate and the conventional arise as two, existent and non-existent, despite [the fact that] Reality is created by Me, the All-Creating One. Therefore the two truths[20] do not lead to the overcoming of cause and result. Within [the concept of two truths] no result [is achieved which] leads to the overcoming of cause and result. By engaging in a contemplation which [attempts to] purify and search what does not exist and in a meditation of wonderful steps, which will never arise, you will not achieve a result which is free of pursuing and rejecting.[21] Who contemplates the three aspects of a single-purpose meditation, and who performs a step-by-step meditation in accord with the four practices of religious services and evoking the gods, will not achieve a result which overcomes striving and achieving, i.e. that which is totally free of activity and which acts because it is spontaneously self-perfected. Because I teach the unborn, signless, self-less you should understand the inexplicable as being free of praise and dispraise.

A simile for all things being the mind of perfect purity is that all [things] created are in their own being like the sky; this is the main point of the mind of perfect purity. Sky, wind, water, earth, and fire, these five elements come miraculously forth from the mind of perfect purity as Buddhas, the three-fold world, the five paths, and the six [categories of] sentient beings. The apparent yet immutable (Akshobhya) Buddha whose deeds are well-ripened is from the primordial the perfect purity of the threefold world [as expressed] in form, utterance, and spirit. Therefore whatever appears as animated and inanimated has consequently no place to exist [except in the mind of perfect purity] like the centre of the sky [which exists only in itself]. Because of the vast scope of the mind of perfect purity as the actual object (*yul chen*), all that appears and exists as animated and inanimated, i.e. Buddhas and sentient beings, {p.20} is free of praise and dispraise, is non-dual in so far as all is the entirely pure Reality. Who does not see the mind as the vigor of non-being will not achieve the goal for many eons. The root of all things is alone the mind of perfect purity. The vigor of perfect purity from which all and everything comes forth, i.e. Buddhas, sentient beings, all that appears and exists as animated and inanimated, cannot be expressed through counting what is not even one. Also the Buddha's form and utterance, and the sentient beings' body and speech are the mind of perfect purity, and therefore they are free of [such concepts as] subject and object (*gzung 'dzin*). Who accomplishes freedom from [such concepts as] subject and object will master the root of all things, and [will be known] as all-accomplished. With joy one will recognize an understanding of [what constitutes] thinking—the uniqueness of the mind of perfect purity. I teach what is beyond reckoning and duality.

How is it that the own nature of Reality is this sole mind, and that the three aspects of this own nature make the mind manifest? The three [aspects] of this own nature are the three best arrangements (*bkod pa*), and this is the Reality of perfection. This one nature, although non-dual, is connected with everything. If it is put in relationship with balance (*rnal ma*) it [unfolds] into four aspects: "the four yogas" as the objects of [My] teaching. I teach the one mind [permeating] the five great [elements]. Because the mind's own being is endowed with five faculties (*yon tan*) they are called the five great [elements].[22] If judgments regarding the existence or non-existence of the one, that is definitive, would arise, then these many errors, obscurations, doubts and judgmental thoughts are removed by the All-Creating One who transcends striving, achieving, and judgmental thought. To purge these judgments regarding existence and non-existence and [the resulting] doubts {p. 21} I establish this unerring and definitive lore because [those other people] cannot understand the perfect purity through suchness. In order to show you that this [lore] clearly deserves your faith I teach the ultimate which is free of striving, achieving, and deeds by means of the ten instructions[23] which deserve your faith and which let you avoid deviations (*la dor*).[24] So trust them!

The proclamation of the nine words of truth which are non-existent: as to the one vigor, nine visible objects emerge. If they are individually recognized one speaks of the nine words of truth.

Because in Me, the All-Creating One, all is consummate you should foster [your understanding of] the meaning of the perfect and pure mind. The root of all things is the All-Creating One, the mind of perfect purity. Whatever appears is My actuation. Whatever comes into existence is My wonder. Whatever sounds and words arise, all arise as sounds and words of My intrinsic meaning. The Buddhas' form, wisdom and qualities, and the sentient beings' body, karmic inheritance (*bag chags*) etc., what appears and exists as animated and inanimated, this all together is from the primordial the actuation of the mind of perfect purity. With the exception of the mind, from Me all things have come forth. The previous Buddhas did not teach these sacred instructions now given by Me, the All-Creating Sovereign, and the presently residing and the future Buddhas will not teach these sacred instructions of the perfect purity, the All-Creating Sovereign."

Such She spoke.

This is the sixth chapter of *The All-Creating Sovereign, Mind of Perfect Purity,* [in which] the sole root [of the universe is discussed].

7

{cont'd p. 21} After that the All-Creating Sovereign, mind of perfect purity, taught how the things which emerged from the creation [done] by Her [became] the things in their particularity (*dbye ba'i chos*).

{p. 22} "Oh great bodhisattva, how is the mind the actuation [of Reality]? How is it that all particularity is totally absent in the non-dual great bliss? What is known as the fathomless one transcends all perceptible objects and dwells from the primordial in a non-conceptual [state] (*spros bral*)—just like the sky. No simile [permits one] to fathom (*bgrang*) the mind of perfect purity. The things created by the mind are purified of particularities. It is said that whatever is created by the mind, i.e. what appears and exists as the animated and inanimated world, the Buddhas and sentient beings, is produced from the mind's own being as its actuation.

I shall now teach you how [the universe] manifests after it was produced. The five great [elements] and the appearing of the six categories of sentient beings realize their purpose through form and body. They become measurable after they emerge from the pure own being of the mind."

Such She spoke.

Then Sems-dpa' rdo-rje asked:

"Oh All-Creating Sovereign, *emaho!* All Good (Kun-tu bzang-po) *emaho!* Oh You mind of perfect purity, *emaho!* When first the mind of perfect purity arises, unaware of itself and the things, these are united as the retinues of You, the omniscient one. You, the omniscient one, may explain this to me as I am unfamiliar with the object of my question. Briefly explain how all things are united as one, the mind of perfect purity; teach me, how two are in one; how can the purpose [of existence] be fathomed?"

This he asked.

Then the All-Creating Sovereign, mind of perfect purity, proclaimed:

"Ho, I am spontaneously self-perfected (*lhun gyis grub*) from the primordial. I am the vigor of spontaneous self-perfection of all Buddhas. {p.23} I am the actuating essence of compassion. I shall teach the purpose of what I have created for the good of those who take joy [in My deeds] at a time appropriate for such joy.

Listen, oh Sems-dpa' rdo-rje! The one [thing] you ought to take joy in, is that I am teaching that the actuating essence of the mind of perfect purity, i.e. the essence of the mind, creates all because all things are encompassed in this one. For those who like to enumerate characteristics, I teach that it is insufficient to specify the variety of what is created by the All-Creating Sovereign. But I also teach My own being: the one is my vigor; what emerges as two is created by Me. You may count the created things, whereby the counting is one, two, [etc.], but in the end, this counting is inexplicable. The inexplicable is the vigor of all things. I teach the inexplicable, the vigor [of all things] to be one. This one is the all-creating mind of perfect purity, while the created things are in a state of duality. Cause and result are of two kinds, therefore ultimate and conventional are of two kinds, and therefore there are definitions of these three, i.e. example, meaning, and characteristic.

Sacred instructions of definitive meaning and those of a debatable meaning are classified as two [types]. On the basis of the five great [elements] as cause, the result [in form] of the three realms and the sentient beings becomes apparent. When the three realms and the sentient beings function as cause, the Buddhas are called the result. If cause and result are taught in terms of simile and meaning, then the cause is given in the sentient beings of the three realms, while the result is called the Buddha's teachings. This is known as a debatable teaching. You ought to distinguish between these two: the cause is the five great [elements], yet all the created things become apparent because of the mind. {p.24}

If one does not understand suchness, one surely considers such things as the six sensory objects in terms of object and subject by [applying these] wrong and erroneous concepts. For this reason the six perishable (i.e. sensory perceptions) and the six receptacles (i.e. sensory objects) are known as the "perishable receptacle" (i.e. the world). The six objects are the support of the six desires, thus the six desires [lead to] suffering, and therefore they are called misery.

What is called the overcoming of misery is: one does not consider the things as the six objects, and no birth happens in the place of the six forms of existence. Because of the overcoming of misery, it is called the transcendence of suffering.

How is it that from the perfect purity, the vigor, the true being effortlessly arises, that also the five great elements are understood as its own characteristics, that perfect purity is the vigor of all, that one is able to grasp the actuating essence which is [otherwise] imperceptible? This is explained as the characteristic of the characteristics. Because of the five great [elements'] arising from [the purity's] own being, a vigor generating all things [becomes apparent, and] which in turn generates all sentient beings. Not to understand that [these emanations] are self-originated [will result in the following assumptions:] After considering this path of practice (*spyod lam*) as the cause [for spiritual progress] one will desire to obtain the result of that cause. Therefore what is called cause is declared to be the vehicle to obtain whatever result [is desired]. This is taught as abandoning, obstructing, and practising.

What is called result is known as the result (or fruit) which [is produced] by the essential cause (*snying po rgyu*). Its essential own being is an own being free of birth and decay, and is called 'diamond' (vajra) [nature]. There are two ways of achieving this diamond [nature]: (a) The outer one is the desire to achieve results by means of performing [certain acts] and abandoning [others]—[acts based on] form, utterance, spirit and wisdom; it is like [reaching for] the moon [reflected] on the water; {p. 25} (b) While the inner [achievement of the diamond nature] which is free of performing and abandoning [certain activities] is to see the scope of one's own self (which is identical with the dimension of own being) by means of the essence and the three stages.[25] You will overcome any salutary acts which [essentially] are no-acts when you become [one with] the essence of all, i.e. this deedlessness which has no support whatsoever. I am establishing the sacred lore of the bliss of non-striving by giving up the bliss of the deedless. If the followers of the vehicle of striving, who [may have practised their system] for three eons, or seven life spans, or one year and six months, or a mere sixteen months, are instructed in the intrinsic nature of the deedless they will dwell in the bliss of effortless spontaneous self-perfection. It is impossible not to be perfected therein.

The one is consummate, and thus are the two consummate, and all is consummate, thereby the creation is in [a state of] consummate bliss. "The one is consummate" means the mind of perfect purity is consummate; "the two is consummate" means the creation by the mind is consummate; "all is consummate" means that absolutely everything is consummate. Through this sacred instruction that the one is consummate, which is the Buddha's intention, you shall dwell in the Buddha's intention. The meaning of "all is consummate" is that everything is made in its utmost perfection. Who dwells in the deedless is Buddha in the Reality of Her intention, although that person's body may be that of a human being or of a god. By this means you will reach the bliss free of striving and achieving and fulfill the purpose of a sentient being."

This She spoke.

This is the seventh chapter of *The All-Creating Sovereign, Mind of Perfect Purity,* in which the fathoming [of Reality] was summarized.

8

{cont'd p. 25} Then the All-Creating Sovereign, mind of perfect purity, declared that all created things are one in their suchness, that from this suchness the three aspects of [the All-Creating Sovereign's] own being appear, {p. 26} and [She explained] how each individual appearance will occur.

"Oh great bodhisattva, My suchness, the one, appears in its fullness in three aspects (i.e. own being, actuating essence, and compassion). Likewise [My] unborn own being is suchness which appears in the objects. Each object contains the entirety of suchness. Further, after one has investigated this all, one will gaze at suchness. The stainless, self-originated pristine awareness appears as the teacher's three forms of manifestation (*sku gsum*) [teaching] causation. Some [manifestations] appear as teachers of causation; some as teachers of interdependence (*'brel pa*); some as teachers of result. From the five [forms of] self-originated pristine awareness, that emanate from compassion, the Buddhas and sentient beings [come forth], and they appear as objects of [My] teaching and as retinues.

In a similar way the three manifestations of the teachers of cause and result teach the retinues different views, although there is only one object—suchness. They teach some to give up and obstruct [certain] objects, some to purify and progress [on the spiritual path], some to purify through blessings, some to achieve [nirvana] through acquiring and rejecting, some are taught to realize the pure mind through striving and achieving. In this way the teacher's three manifestations taught [the retinues] the concepts of cause and result. Although [the manifestations teach that] cause and result are two [different entities] I, the All-Creating, teach only the lore of stillness and of suchness.

Suchness [has to be understood] as follows: I, the All-Creating, am suchness, but also what I created is suchness. The six sensory objects, I made them; the six sensory faculties are My intelligence; all the sense awarenesses are My self-originated pristine awareness. {p.27} The five great [elements] also are the five causes, and the entirety of the five causes is suchness. That compassion is [nothing but] the five [forms of] self-originated pristine awareness, that the six categories [of sentient beings] in this threefold world are the actuation of suchness—such I declare.

The suchness of [My] own being is in its actuation non-dual. Yet the four stages of resting in tranquility (i.e. the four yogas) come forth from their being one with [My] own being. The following constitutes the four yogas:

Listen great bodhisattva, the central vigor of everything, the Mind of perfect purity is the actuation of the stillness of all things. From the primordial it dwells just like this in suchness. By means of the four yogas, i.e. Atiyoga, Anuyoga, Mahâyoga, and [Bodhi]sattva-yoga one will see the deedless stillness of the true central vigor. The object of this cognition is these four aspects.

At [the stage of] [Bodhi]sattva-yoga they will see the objects and [enjoy the] sensory faculties, the five [forms] of enlightening insight (*byang chub lnga*) and the four miracles, and the two deities of the [Bodhi]sattva-yoga after the blessings [are performed]. But they will not see the stillness and true central vigor. They still ought to meditate on non-conceptual suchness.

Those who [mastered] the Mahâyoga will see the deedless stillness of the true vigor (*don gyi snying po*). They will see themselves perfectly accomplished [through] expansion and contraction [of the visualized deities] after they have perfected the limbs [of the *pûja*] through the four services: the mandala of the gods of cause and result in their own mandala from the primordial pure mind. But still, they will not see the stillness of the true vigor. They should thoroughly meditate on uncontrived suchness.

Who mastered the Anuyoga (*yongs su rnal 'byor*) will see the dimension [of Reality], the stillness of the true vigor as cause {p. 28} and they will view the great pristine awareness as the result of that stillness. They will understand the oneness of the the central vigor in its dual aspects of cause and result, yet they will not see the stillness as beyond cause and result. They should meditate on the non-contrived Anuyoga just as it is.

Who will be able to understand the great perfection of the Atiyoga as the deedless stillness of the true vigor, will recognize the mind of perfect purity as the vigor of all. This they will see as the stillness of the non-contrived essence (*don*). They ought to contemplate this view which is unfathomed from the primordial. They ought to contemplate the vows which from the primordial are not to be observed. They ought to contemplate salutary acts which from the primordial are not to be sought. Through these contemplations, they will harness suchness.

The four yogas should be known in their peculiarities: each subject (i.e. each of the four yogas) is to be divided into four aspects.

(1) There are four peculiarities regarding the [Bodhi]sattva-yoga:

(a) [At this stage] the mind does not reflect upon objects or the sensory faculties, therefore it is called [Bodhi]sattva-yoga (*sems dpa'i rnal 'byor*).

(b) When the wondrous blessing of perfect purity is released then it is called Mahâyoga.

(c) When it is associated with the four great seals (*mudrâ*) it is called Anuyoga.

(d) Those who see that the vows of awareness lack own being, will aspire to the mind [of perfect purity] and understand it as Atiyoga.[26] They do not see the yoga free of acquiring and rejecting.

(2) The four peculiarities of Mahâyoga:

(a) First, a person [who has acquired] the three *samâdhi* is known as [being at the level of] [Bodhi]sattva-yoga.[27]

(b) Those who are able to see the pristine awareness by means of their own pure mind are known as [being at the level of] Mahâyoga.

(c) Those who have perfected the four services (*bsnyen sgrub*) are known as [being at the level of] Anuyoga. {p. 29}

(d) When they see everything as the great self (*bdag nyid chen po*), they will be known as [being at the level of] Atiyoga. They do not see the stillness beyond striving and achieving.

(3) The understanding of the four peculiarities of Anuyoga:

(a) at this stage of *samâdhi* they do not generate the deity as their own individuality, but because the people are dwelling in the pure nature of Reality; [this stage] is known as [Bodhi]sattva-yoga.

(b) Because they do not depend on "father" and "mother" as method and wisdom, but have perfected the mandala in its essential parts only, they are known as [being at the level of] Mahâyoga.

(c) Those who dwell in [the contemplation of] Reality, which is without own being, yet apparent, are known [as being at the level of] true Anuyoga because of their general bearing.

(d) When all things in the entirety appear, just as they are, and when the [practitioners] see the dimension [of Reality] as cause and pristine awareness as result—they are known to be at [the level of] true Atiyoga. But they do not yet see the stillness beyond cause and result.

(4) The four peculiarities of Atiyoga:

(a) The mind of perfect purity, free of acquiring and rejecting, this is called [Bodhi]sattva-yoga.

(b) The mind of perfect purity beyond striving and achieving is called Mahâyoga.

(c) The mind of perfect purity beyond cause and result is called Anuyoga.

(d) [The mind seeing] the things as being beyond praise and dispraise, beyond existing and non-existing, this is called Atiyoga by Me.

As the three [lower stages], such as Anuyoga, and so on, are not associated with the great self-originated pristine awareness, those [who are still in these phases] should practice the stages [of the bodhisattva path] (*bhûmi*) during their progressing on the path. Because [such practitioners] preserve their vows and contemplate the doctrinal views there is no practice or theory of a vivid or relaxed meditation.[28]

{p. 30} The practice of the lore of Atiyoga is as follows: because from the primordial the All-Creating Herself has made [everything], there is no progress on the path, and no practice of the bodhisattva stages (*bhûmi*). There is no observing of the vows nor a contemplation of doctrinal views. Because from the great path of perfect purity everything emanates, there is no proceeding of the perfect purity in the perfect purity. Because there is no other bodhisattva stage (*bhûmi*) for progress outside of perfect purity itself, perfect purity is not practised with regard to perfect purity. As the nature of the vows is the perfect purity itself, the perfect purity needs not to be preserved with regard to the perfect purity. As the nature of meditation is perfect purity in itself, the perfect purity itself does not meditate upon itself. As the goal of the doctrine is perfect purity in itself, perfect purity does not reflect upon itself. This is the deedless practice of the lore of Atiyoga.

If one's meditation of the self-originated pristine awareness is vivid, one will meditate on the All-Creating Sovereign. This is not the practice of those attached to the vehicle of cause and result."

This is the eighth chapter of *The All-Creating Sovereign, Mind of Perfect Purity,* in which is explained how all things are set up in the Reality as objects due to the own being of things.

9

{p. 30} Then the All-Creating Sovereign, mind of perfect purity, talked about what constitutes errors and obscurations with regard to the great perfection, because to proceed on the path of the vehicle of cause and result is wrong.

"Oh great bodhisattva, the very nature of the mind of perfect purity is like that: it is the central vigor of absolutely all things; it is stainless because it is pure and unborn. There is no error in it because it is without a path to proceed on. It is effortless as it is totally perfect from the primordial. The mind of perfect purity, i.e. the essential vigor of all things, is one. {p. 31} But if one would count it as one then it constitutes an error. To proceed on something which is without progress constitutes an error. Viewing the imperceptible constitutes a wrong with regard to the invisible.

Although everything is one in suchness, there are some who, by working on the causes, desire to obtain later the results and by means of the ten perfections (*pâramitâ*) they aspire to achieve the ten bodhisattva stages (*bhûmi*). These [practitioners] will be obscured with error for three eons. Even if they purify the state of their vows and pledges by [practising] the three purifications of the outer, inner, and intellectual [realms], the five [forms of] enlightening insight, and the [four] limbs of miracles,[29] they will still be obscured by error for seven lifespans. Those who hold a view that by preparing the causes [they will obtain] the results, and by considering doctrinal views and religious practice to be two different things, they will be in a state of error and obscuration as to what is non-dual for three lifespans.

If [these practitioners] observe pursuit and abandoning (*blang dor*) with regard to the one essential vigor, they will not be able to see it in its oneness but in its duality, and therefore they will be clouded by erring till they free themselves from pursuit and abandoning. Those who contemplate [the ultimate] in three [aspects], although it is the one which is self-originated, they are said to err as to the goal which is free of striving. Those who do not understand that the essential vigor of things, which appear and exist just the way they are, is suchness, they will view the dimension [of Reality] and the pristine awareness as cause and result. Because of this praising the cause and dispraising the result, they will be obscured till they are confident that there is no [reason for] praise and dispraise.

There are six desires for a result that does not exist:

(1) to achieve [a true appreciation] of the two truths as cause [for spiritual progress];

(2) to achieve the result [of spiritual progress] by performing the three purifications;

(3) the wish to achieve [results by] keeping the doctrinal views and the religious practice separately;

(4) the wish to achieve [results] by the practice of pursuit and abandoning;

(5) the wish to achieve [results] through a meditation in three stages;[30]

(6) the desire to achieve [liberation] by seeing the dimension [of Reality] and pristine awareness as cause and result.

{p.32} These are the six [wishes] for achievement (*thob rnam drug*).

There are six errors and six obscurations in turn. I say [the practitioners] should rid themselves of the faults of these six wishes for achievement because [such desire] is faulty, obscuring, and wrong with regard to the mind of perfect purity. I also declare examining and reflecting to be an error and obscuration as I do [with such concepts as] subject and object, and doctrinal views and religious practice.

Doctrine and practice, pursuit and abandonment, striving and achieving, causation, [all these concepts] are an obscuration as they are wrong with regard to the great bliss which is without effort.

The mind of perfect purity is like the sky. This mind itself, i.e. the Reality, is like the sky and therefore [it is said]:[31]

(1) No doctrine is to be contemplated,

(2) nor vows to be observed.

(3) The salutary acts (*phrin las*) are without effort and

(4) pristine awareness is without obscuration.

(5) There is no practising of the [ten] bodhisattva stages (*bhûmi*) and

(6) no path to proceed on.

(7) Things are neither subtle (*phra ba chos med*),

(8) nor dual, nor dependent.

(9) There is no accurate sacred instruction firmly established except for that about the mind.

(10) There is no definition of the instructions except that they are beyond praise and dispraise. This is the [right] view of the great perfected mind of perfect purity.

(Opposite of the first statement:) By meditating in six ways upon what is not to be meditated upon, i.e. that one beyond doctrinal view, an erroneous obscuration will come because of such a view full of error and obscuration.

(Opposite of the second statement:) By observing the six vows, with regard to that one which is beyond observance, an erroneous obscuration of these vows will occur because of such obscuring error.

(Opposite of third statement:) By pursuing the six salutary acts with regard to that one which is without effort, an erroneous obscuration of these acts will occur because of such obscuring error.

(Opposite of fourth statement:) By generating the six pristine awarenesses with regard to that one, free of obscuration, an erroneous obscuration of this pristine awareness will occur because of such obscuring error.

(Opposite of fifth statement:) By generating the six achievements of practising [the bodhisattva stages], with regard to that one which is not to be practised, an erroneous obscuration of the [ten] bodhisattva stages will occur because of such obscuring error.

(Opposite of sixth statement:) By generating six forms of progressing on the path, with regard to that one which is of no progress, an erroneous obscuration of this path will occur because of such obscuring error.

(Opposite of seventh statement:) By generating six ways of

grasping, {p. 33} with regard to that one which is not to be grasped, an erroneous obscuration of the [existing] things will occur because of such obscuring error.

(Opposite of eighth statement:) By generating six ways of linking, with regard to that one which is non-dual, an erroneous obscuration of this linking will occur because of such obscuring error.

(Opposite of ninth statement:) By producing six certainties, with regard to that one truth, an erroneous obscuration of these sacred instructions will occur because of such obscuring error.

(Opposite of tenth statement:) By producing six ways of explanation, with regard to that one which is inexplicable, an erroneous obscuration of the religious instructions will occur because of such obscuring error.

This mind of perfect purity is the essential vigor of all. There is no need for accomplishing [the goal] by seeking the [realization] of the ten characteristics of [My] true nature because My own being is consummate from the primordial. An all-[encompassing] symbol of My own being is the sky as no one made any effort [to purify] the pure sky. Even if everyone sought [to purify] the pure sky, the sky which made everything (*nam mkhas kun byas*) is beyond such seeking and achieving. Likewise, the mind of perfect purity, the essential vigor which creates all of all created, I[32] transcend the scope of all sensory perception (*spyod yul*), and therefore from the primordial, there is no point in theorizing Me or in meditating upon Me. Likewise, not even the ten [characteristics of My] true nature can affect Me who transcends [everything]. Those who follow the vehicle of causation and who try to seek Me through these ten characteristics by desiring to see Me and My own being, they will fall like somebody who attempts to walk over the sky will fall upon the earth. Who desires to proceed by means of these ten characteristics will likewise fall. My own being is firmly taught to be the origin [of the universe]. Because I am transcending the scope of sensory perception (*spyod yul*), no doctrinal view [about Me] should be contemplated upon. Likewise, [because] the ten [characteristics of] My true nature lack meaning, so do not reflect upon a possible meaning of them. {p. 34} Contemplate suchness, but don't make up doctrinal views [about Me] as I am never an object to be seen through doctrinal views.

There is no need to observe the moral [precepts] and vows as there is no reason to rid [yourself] from what is non-conceptual and unborn. Because the essential vigor is from the primordial spontaneously self-perfected, there is no need for striving and achieving. Because the self-originated pristine awareness is without obscuration, you should not generate clarity with discriminative knowledge (*rig pa'i ye shes*). There are no bodhisattva stages (*bhûmi*) which could be reached through practice because everything exists in My stage. There is no path on which to proceed towards Me because everything exists by being encompassed in Me. There are no designations like "subtle" to be attributed [to Me] because from the primordial I am neither object nor subject. Because I am encompassing all with My form, there is nothing from the primordial which could be called two. I am from the primordial the self-originated pristine awareness, and therefore others should not make firm statements about Me. I am the essential vigor of all, the [mind of] perfect purity, and thus no other secret instructions exist. Because I am beyond all praise and dispraise, I firmly declare that [neither praise nor dispraise should be applied] to all things.[33] Beside Me there are no other objects, therefore I also firmly declare that there is no doctrinal view to be contemplated. Because besides Me nothing should be guarded, I also firmly declare that the vows should not be guarded. Because there is nothing else than Me to be sought, I also firmly declare that no salutary acts should be performed. Because there is no dwelling in anything else but Me, I also firmly declare that the bodhisattva stages (*bhûmi*) should not be practised. Because there is no fault of Me from the primordial, I also firmly declare that I am the self-originated pristine awareness. {p. 35} Because I am the unborn Reality, I firmly declare that I am the subtle Reality. Because there is no progress other than in Me, I firmly declare there is no path to proceed on. Because everything which appears and exists as the inanimated and animated, i.e. the Buddhas and sentient beings, has emerged from Me, the essential vigor, i.e. the perfect purity, I firmly declare that from the primordial I am non-dual. Because the self-originated pristine awareness came down as correct revelation (*gtan la 'bebs pa*), I firmly declare that the sacred instructions of the Great Perfection (*lung chen*) came down like a flash of lightning. Because all things do not exist outside of Me, I firmly declare that I am all—the All Creating One.

Not to know Me, I declare to be the actuation of obscuration. To seek anything else than Me produces error. A teaching [claiming] action and knowledge to be two [different things] is not seeing [what is right and wrong], and this is obscuration to action; not knowing [Reality] is an obscuration to knowledge. Likewise I declare that striving and achieving is an error, and so is the claim that ignorance and not-knowing are the essence of this dual obscuration because all things which appear are the actuation of the mind of perfect purity, the essential vigor.

Oh, great bodhisattva, listen! If you recognize the things which appear just the way they are as being of no other nature than yourself, this constitutes an obscuration of yourself due to yourself. Do not understand your own nature in this manner! Enter into [a state of] bliss [consisting in a knowledge] of sameness and non-discriminative thinking because all things, which appear just the way they are, are nothing but the mind[34] and not different from itself.

With regard to that, the meaning of "bliss" is as follows: there is no need to seek the ten [characteristics pertinent to My] great nature. {p. 36} By not seeking the ten [characteristics of My] great true nature, there will be no limit to these 360 errors and obscurations, that is six times sixty errors.

Oh, great bodhisattva, that all things appear as they do, due to the manifestation of perfect purity as the essential vigour of My own being—if not this, nothing else I teach about the things. I tell you, do not try to intellectualize this! I recommend that you, oh great bodhisattva, will teach the hosts of retinues in the same way as I taught you."

Such She said.

This is the ninth chapter of the *All-Creating Sovereign, the Mind of Perfect Purity,* in which the removal of faulty errors and obscurations [is taught].

10

{cont'd p. 36} Then the All-Creating Sovereign, mind of perfect purity, talked about Her own being as consummation:

"Oh, great bodhisattva, listen! Because everything is incorporated in Me, for this reason, I am called the consummate. I am called the All-Creating One because from the three aspects of My own being, i.e. that of the All-Creating One, emanate these three things: teacher, teaching, and retinue.

First [I shall teach you] the consummation of the teacher. From the self-originated pristine awareness, i.e. Me, the All-Creating One, emerge the three aspects of My own being. They are taught to be the three teachers in their three forms of manifestation (*trikâya*). They are known as the manifestation of truth (*dharmakâya*), the manifestation of highest communal joy (*samyaksambhogakâya*), and the corporeal manifestation (*nirmânakâya*).

The nature of these three forms of manifestation is explained as follows: The nature of the truth manifestation is explained as dwelling in the own being because it is unborn and free of a subject-object [dichotomy]. The nature of the manifestation of highest communal joy is dwelling in perfect joyful fulfillment of whatever desires there are. {p. 37} The nature of the corporeal manifestation is explained as dwelling in the manifest body which is likewise disciplining.[35]

The teaching pertinent to the three forms of the teacher's manifestation is explained under three [aspects], i.e. outer, inner, and secret (*gsang ba gsum*). The teaching pertinent to the truth manifestation is explained as follows. The secret is told to be of a threefold nature. From the ground (*gzhi*),[36] i.e. the pure nature of Reality, the nature of secret generation [stems] as well as that of the secret perfection, and that of the great secret perfection. They are labeled secret because they are not within anyone's field of sensory perceptions. The secret teaching is to generate the three stages of no-Reality, thus it is labeled the secret generation (as pertinent to *bskyed rim*). The teaching about [the different forms of] manifestation (*sku*) is called secret perfection. Do not investigate the secret by means of contemplating the inner knowledge. All things which appear just as they do, are explained as the essential knowledge and this [constitutes] the inner contemplation. After you have transformed your own pure mind into an eternal deity, you will wish the inner and outer sense-fields (*âyatana*) of your own diamond body to be the embodiment (*bdag nyid*) of non-duality [free] of doctrinal views and practice, acquiring and abandoning. This is declared to be the perfection of the inner secret.

The secret of the great perfection is taught as follows. All things which appear as they do, are not produced as mind of perfect purity by means of the three *samâdhi;* they are not made perfect because of uttering the essential characters [of the mantras]. I, the All-Creating One, am the great one who perfects [all things]. Nothing exists which is not perfect in Me.

My own being is taught to be threefold, and it is taught as the three [stages of] the great perfection, i.e. the mind of perfect purity.[37] This is the explanation of the secret great perfection. This is also explained as the teaching of the teacher manifest as truth.

The teaching of the teacher manifest in the form of highest communal joy (*samyaksambhogakâya*) consists of the three outer sections of the rituals to be performed (*bya byed pa*).[38] {p. 38} The [tantra] section of rituals to be performed along with discursive thinking [consists of] mainly contemplating the three purifications of the outer, inner, and conceptual realms by means of a non-discursive *samâdhi;* and you should enter [the *samâdhi*] at a time when the planets and stars [are suitable] for such penetration.[39] [At this stage, you will strive for the *siddhi* of form, utterance, and spirit, although non-existent, by means of *bodhicitta* and the various miracles after having performed the offerings by executing the three purifications by [considering] the visualized deity and yourselves to be [like] lord and servants.

It is declared that both the ultimate and the conventional are an illusion. If doctrinal views and religious practice are divided into two [separate units] then, by relying on this dichotomy, a belief arises in the achievability of the final purpose, which is one. Those who pursue an impossible goal by practising what is there, are like a she-wolf stretching herself out on the sky which [offers] no support.

The secret of the outer [tantra sections] in terms of acquiring and rejecting, is to bless everything through unreflective *samâdhi* and blessed miracles. After that the wisdom deity (*ye shes lha*) is formed. These [practitioners] hope that they, being endowed with the four seals (*phyag rgya bzhi*) and [the deity's] form, utterance, and spirit, will obtain whatever *siddhi* they desire. But they will not realize the *samâdhi,* free of hope for desirelessness, by acquiring and rejecting certain doctrinal views and religious practices. This is the explanation of the teaching pertinent to the manifestation of highest communal joy.

The teaching of the teacher in corporeal manifestation is explained in the three *pitaka,* whereby those of the hearers, the solitary awakened ones, and the Mahâyâna sutras are declared to be external because of characteristics known as external. The five pleasurable sensory objects (*'dod yon lnga*), which are the actuation of Me, the All-Creating One, come forth as the actuation of the five awarenesses, and from them come attachment, hatred, and ignorance. The remedies for controlling these [afflictions] are taught as the 84,000 dharma-doors (i.e. teachings). {p. 39} The five pleasurable sensory objects emerge, and therefore form, sound, smell, taste, and touch come forth. They bring forth attachment, hatred, and ignorance. The remedy for their control are the three *pitaka.* As remedy for the control of attachment, the 21,000 precepts of the *vinaya* are taught. As remedy for the control of ignorance, the 21,000 sermons of the *sûtra pitaka* were taught. As remedy for the control of hatred, the 21,000 tractates of the *abhidharma pitaka* were taught. For equally controlling all three poisons the 21,000 teachings of the three *pitaka* were proclaimed as remedy. In general, the 84,000 teachings were proclaimed as an external remedy for controlling the three poisons.

The vehicle of causation and philosophy consists of three sections: the [dharma]-doors of the *sûtra-*, *vinaya-*, and *abhidharma-pitakas.*

There is a teaching that is known as being of a condensed meaning, and there is the *sûtra pitaka* explained in twelve ways. Each teaches in detail an individual meaning.

The three poisons as causes effect the three evil forms of existence. By regarding the sentient beings as cause, good and evil [deeds], doctrinal views and religious practice effect good or evil rebirths. This is well proclaimed in [the vehicle] of causation and philosophy. It was proclaimed in the past; it is presently proclaimed, and it will be proclaimed later on. Its meaning, as far as it is an inexplicable meaning, was not proclaimed at previous times, nor is it proclaimed at present, nor will it be proclaimed in the future by the [different] corporeal manifestations. Therefore this is known as the teaching of the corporeal manifestations.

Oh great bodhisattva, the first retinue of the teacher's three manifestations arises from the three aspects of My, the All-Creating's own being. {p. 40} The three retinues of the teacher's three manifestations, are now explained.

Oh great bodhisattva, listen to this explanation of the retinues of the teacher's truth manifestation! All the retinues created by Me are the retinues of [the teacher's] truth manifestation, which is My own being. All that appears and exists as inanimated and animated [world], i.e. as Buddhas and sentient beings—nothing exists which is not united in the retinues of the truth manifestation."

Such She spoke.

"Oh great bodhisattva, listen to this explanation of the retinues of the teacher's manifestation of highest communal joy! Those who surpassed the stage of the four perfections in devotion,[40] and who have mastered the first bodhisattva stage, [called] the "very joyful," up to the tenth, "dharma cloud," they are declared to be the retinues of the [teacher's] manifestation of highest communal joy.

The explanation of the retinues of the teacher's corporeal manifestation: Those who had deviated from the utmost path of enlightenment as *tîrthika, mu stugs, phyal pa,* and *lokâyata,* after being blessed by [the Buddha's] compassion, were converted and became Buddhist monks and nuns, lay men and lay women—they are known as the retinue of the teacher's corporeal manifestation."[41]

Such She spoke.

"Oh great bodhisattva, listen to this explanation of the individual realm of each of the three manifestations who are the teacher's three manifestations emanating from Me. The realm of the teacher's manifestation of truth is explained as the palace of Akanishtha, the dimension of Reality. Akanishtha is hereby explained as the ultimate purity.

The realm of the teacher's manifestation of joy is explained as a divine mansion, a towering building in the Akanishtha realm, which is above the boundaries of this world. The realm of the teacher's corporeal manifestation is explained as {p. 41} Gridhrakûta, the place where Shâkyamuni, the seventh Buddha, became manifest. The realms of the other manifestations of [Buddha's] compassion are undefined."

Such She spoke.

"Oh great bodhisattva! I shall explain in which individual realm (*zhing khams*) the teacher in three manifestations, emanating from Me, disciplines [the sentient beings]:

———the realm of disciplining [suitable] for the teacher's truth manifestation is the limitless dimension of Reality which extends as far as the sky. This is the realm suitable for the disciplining [of sentient beings by the teacher's] manifestation of truth.

———the realm of disciplining [suitable] for the teacher's joy manifestations: They discipline where there is enjoyment sought in form, sound, smell, taste, and touch—which originate from Me.

———the realm of disciplining [suitable] for the teacher's corporeal manifestations: by means of their self-originated pristine awareness and compassion they discipline the six categories of sentient beings in all 100,000 millions of worlds. In accord with this, different teachings [were proclaimed].

The teacher's three manifestations, emanating from Me, are the same with regard to cause and to result, and are of one own being. The cause, that is the mind of perfect purity, is one with everything; the result, that is the buddha[hood], is also one with everything. This is declared as the own being of Reality, the one actuating being. The [right] time for disciplining was not divided into earlier and later."

Such She spoke.

"Oh great bodhisattva, listen further! Now the ways of promulgation [as practised by] the teacher's three forms of manifestation that emanate from Me, the All-Creating One!

The teacher's truth manifestation promulgates the teaching by means of blessings; the manifestations of perfect joy promulgate the teaching by means of their own actuating being; the corporeal manifestations teach those persons who are able to hear the word and the meaning [of the dharma] by integrating the word with the meaning.

{p. 42} Now the promulgation [of the dharma] by means of blessing by the truth manifestation: all created things are taught to be My own being. Although unborn, in the wonder of genesis, all things which appear and exist as animated and inanimated come forth as a miracle of [My] compassion and actuating being. This is called the promulgation by means of blessing of My own being.

Now the promulgation by the manifestations of perfect communal joy by means of their own actuating being: all things, which appear in whatever form, are taught to be perfect, in so far as they are pleasurable sensory objects for which one may feel desire as form, sound, smell, taste, and touch. This I teach as the promulgation by means of My actuating being.

The promulgation by the corporeal manifestations by means of the integration of words and meaning: [At this stage] it is not appropriate to teach all things which appear and exist in whatever way as the teacher's actuating being because what is called 'teacher' is in a peculiar way the creation of one's own desires. [The corporeal manifestations] promulgate the meaning of the teaching through the sound of words and letters, and due to this [activity, the disciples] understand the meaning by means of words and letters. This is the meaning explained through words and letters.

Oh great bodhisattva, listen! I, the the All-Creating Sovereign, am actuating the three forms of manifestation. Without reflection (*mi rtogs*), just existing in balance, I am actuating the truth manifestation as non-conceptual (*spros bral*). The wonder of genesis which comes from My own being, this is the manifestation of perfect joy as the origin of desires which are fulfilled by disciplining in whatever way by means of compassion. This is [also] the actuation of the corporeal manifestation. The All-Creating Sovereign, through the three forms of Her nature (i.e. the three forms of manifestation) causes teachers to appear in bodily form to discipline by whatever [method is suitable]. Although the nature of the teaching is inexpressible in its meaning, the meaning is expressed in whatever way is suitable. This is called the perfect teaching.

{p. 43} The nature of the retinues is that those apt for unity will become the first-borns [in the "Buddha families"] after they have been united. This is called the perfect retinue.

I am the teacher, the All-Creating One, the mind of perfect purity. The All-Creating is one, but is known in Her three aspects (*rnam pa gsum*): I, the All-Creating, My own being, and the things created by Me—these are the three aspects. I am the teacher, the All-Creating One, the progenitor of everything. My nature is taught in terms of ten characteristics: they are declared as the essential vigour of all teaching. I, the All-Creating, have made all and everything. The Buddhas dwell in the three times as one, and without discrimination they make all the sentient beings living in the threefold world their noble retinue. Because the One, the All-Creating One, has made everything in a perfect manner, for this same reason, all the mind's needs are perfected by the All-Creating One. Whatever amount of needs and what kind of needs there are—it is said that I, the All-Creating One, perfectly fulfill them.

The teacher's own being is taught under three aspects (*ston pa'i rang bzhin rnam pa gsum*): manifestation of the truth, manifestations of pristine awareness, and manifestations of compassion. Under whatever forms the teacher in three manifestations disciplines, they perfect the retinues who abide in accord with himself.

I, the teacher of the teachers, the All-Creating Sovereign, show you My nature in its three aspects. As the first retinue, the teacher in Her three manifestations arises; this is the unborn pristine awareness which is free of subject and object. As the first retinue, the teacher in Her truth manifestation arises; it is the miracle of genesis, the all-pure play (*lîla*). The [manifestations] of perfect joy arise [next from which] the diverse desires, whatever they may be, come. {p. 44} In accordance with oneself [the teacher] satisfies every one. Then the various forms of corporeal manifestations are known [to come]. Those who have gazed into the direction of what is known as the teacher in the three forms of manifestation, the Buddhas and bodhisattvas, and those who have achieved patience (i.e. *tshogs lam* and *sbyor lam*) are united as the teacher's manifestations. In accordance with this, they dwell in their [appropriate] realms and teach the essential point.

The teaching's nature is such that it is an instruction [given] to the retinues by one of the three manifestations. As to the retinues that need to be disciplined, one way or the other, the Buddha promulgates what is known as perfect in order to discipline and teach gods and humans of good karma in this world. The Buddhas of the three times, who abide in the dimension of the truth manifestation which is non-explicitly existing, teache all sentient beings living in the threefold world the non-conceptual mind of perfect purity by means of this truth manifestation.

[The manifestations] of enjoyment [dwelling] in Akanishtha [in a state of] pristine awareness, explain to the bodhisattvas of the tenth stage the mind of perfect purity by means of their manifestation and their wisdom.

The various undefined manifestations of [the Buddha's] compassion also teach their retinues, those united in their pursuit of patience, the main points of disciplining by whatever unspecified [methods they find suitable]. For those of good karma, due to their pledges, and [if] not interfered by other circumstances, the time when My compassion becomes embodied has come. Join the retinues I am going to teach.

I teach the non-dual true meaning by three means (i.e. through the three manifestations). The accumulations [of merit and wisdom] will lead to perfecting the time, place, and nature [in which the three manifestations proclaim the dharma]. The fully perfected [teaching] in its three aspects, i.e. the three jewels, is taught as being precious. They are explained as form, utterance, and spirit of Me, the All-Creating Sovereign.

The teacher, the precious Buddha, the jewel, {p. 45} is the manifestation of truth, the manifestation of enjoyment, and the corporeal manifestation. The best and precious promulgation of the teaching, the noble dharma, is the three best promulgations [as explained in what follows] of the inexplicable All-Creating One. As to the best sangha, as part of the retinues, I shall give instructions on whatever they need.

I, the teacher, the All-Creating, the mind of perfect purity, created the teacher who generated the three manifestations. The teaching of the noble dharma is arranged in three ways. It is arranged into external, internal, and secret.[42] Each of these three divisions is divided into three sections, thus nine [divisions] are known. The corporeal manifestations make three promulgations to discipline in this way by means of their compassion. The joy manifestations make three promulgations in terms of external, internal [and secret] of the ritual acts. The truth manifestation makes three promulgations of the secret, ultimate lore. These are the three types of promulgations, i.e. the external, internal, and secret ones. From body, speech, and mind [at the human level], and from form, utterance, and spirit [at the level of the deities] emanates that from which the nine vehicles (*theg pa rim pa dgu*) come. By crossing nine mountain passes, and nine valleys on nine paths you will progress towards the one vehicle, i.e. the all-creating mind of perfect purity. Then you will have reached the stage of perfect purity (enlightenment) which is beyond progress, that is the All-Creating, free of acting and agent, and beyond striving and achieving."

Such She spoke.

This is the tenth chapter of *The All-Creating Sovereign, Mind of Perfect Purity,* in which the all-perfected structure [of the universe] is explained.

11

{cont'd p. 45} Then the All-Creating Sovereign, mind of perfect purity, explained the root in which all things are united.

"Oh great bodhisattva, listen! The root of all things in correlation with [My] own being is as follows: As I am all things' own being, there is not another thing outside of My own being. {p.46} The teachers' three forms of manifestations—they are My own being. The Buddhas of the three times—they are My own being. The bodhisattvas—they are My own being. The four yogas—they are My own being. The threefold world of the realm of desire, the realm of form, and the realm of formlessness—they are declared to be My own being, i.e. that of the All-Creating One. The five great elements are also My own being. The six categories of sentient beings are My own being. All that appears (*snang ba*) is My own being. All that exists (*srid pa*) is My own being. The entirety of the animated and inanimated world is My own being. Outside of My own being, nothing is, therefore the root of all things consists in Me. Not one thing exists that does not consist in Me.

[My] own being unfolds in three aspects (*rang bzhin rnam pa gsum*), i.e. the unborn, the miracle of genesis, and compassion. These are the own beings of the three teachers. With regard to the three times, i.e. past, present, and future, all the Buddhas exist in oneness because I Myself, i.e. My own being, exists in oneness. This is also known as My own being. I am free of subject and object [-related thinking], and therefore I am pure and like the sky all-encompassing.

Because I have created the central vigor of all things, My own being also is the mind of perfect purity. Those who combine the four yogas with My own being, which is balance in itself, they will be united in the one. In such way My own being is taught.

As to the sentient beings' body, speech, and mind[43] [it is said] that they come into existence because they come from My own being; {p. 47} that they are encompassing because they are encompassed in My own being, and that they are explicitly existent because they exist as My actuation. For this reason it is said that the threefold world is My own being.

My own being, i.e. that of the All-Creating, is of five[fold] aspect (*rang bzhin rnam lnga*): from My actuation come forth the five elements—sky, wind, water, earth, and fire. They are taught as My own being, i.e. that of the All-Creating One. My, the All-Creating One's, compassion becomes manifest and is known as the five forms of the self-originated pristine awareness. Whatever appears as the six categories of sentient beings, it is known as My, the All-Creating One's, own being. From My own being, i.e. that of the All-Creating Sovereign, everything originates—in short, all that appears and exists as animated or inanimated. I make everything and therefore [all] originates from Me. For this reason there is not a single thing that is not encompassed in Me. From Me, the teachers' three forms of manifestation also emanate, and thus My, the All-Creating One's own being is declared to be the three teachers. Also the Buddhas who dwell in oneness in the three aspects of time, i.e. past, present, and future, abide in My own being, the All-Creating One's, which is without past and future. Also the bodhisattvas, freed from [thinking in] subject/object [dichotomy], are My, the All-Creating One's, own being as I have created them as bodhisattvas. Also, if you have entered the state of balance by means of the four yogas, you will rest in tranquil balance in Me, the All-Creating One. As everything is made by the All-Creating Sovereign, likewise, everything is encompassed in the All-Creating Sovereign Herself."

Such She said.

This is the eleventh chapter of *The All-Creating Sovereign, The Mind of Perfect Purity,* in which is said that the root of all things is encompassed in the intrinsic self of the All-Creating Sovereign, mind of perfect purity.

12

{p. 48} After that the All-Creating Sovereign, mind of perfect purity, proclaimed this sutra about the source of all things.

"Listen, great bodhisattva! I am the source of all sacred instructions. Likewise you must know that all and each thing in the way it appears, that everything emanates from Me! Listen to this [exposition on] the general and great origin of [all] things! I shall instruct you on how all things [come to exist]. As I, the All-Creating Sovereign, mind of perfect purity, am the sovereign of all great sacred instructions, the teachers' three [forms of manifestation] first emanate from Me.

'Sacred instructions' are called the teachers' words. As I am the root of all instructions, I, the All-Creating Sovereign, did not teach the Buddhas of the three times and the sentient beings of the threefold world any other teaching besides that which comes forth from the mind. All the tantras and sutras are general comments. The tantra and sutra sections are the teachers' teaching and they have emanated from My, the All-Creating One's, own being. [These scriptures] comment on both, teacher and teaching. I, the All-Creating Sovereign, mind of perfect purity, am declared to be the climax of all teachings. Although from Me [have emanated] the teachers' three forms of manifestations, their teachings of the vinaya, sutras, abhidharma, and tantras—organized into their appropriate sections of a hundred thousand, are still associated with striving and achieving [associated with the practice of] generative, consummate, and secret [meditations]. But you will proceed towards Me only after transcending all striving and achieving. You will not see Me unless by transcending striving and achieving. This explains the climax of all teachings.

I, the All-Creating Sovereign, mind of perfect purity, am declared to be the quintessential vigor of all vehicles. Three vehicles exist with regard to the three [manifestations of the] teachers, but only one vehicle exists with regard to [the truth of] certainty. {p. 49} This one [vehicle] is the 'earth' (*bhûmi*), the universal vehicle, the mind of perfect purity. This is explained as the quintessence of all vehicles.

Oh, I let appear the great wisdom after the darkness of ignorance was cleared away. Further, if you ask [Me] to explain how does this come, [I answer]: the darkness of erroneous reflections darkens [one's mind] as one does not understand that all existent things are in their suchness the perfect purity. But because the All-Creating mind of perfect purity makes all things just as they exist, one should understand the All-Creating mind of perfect purity [in this way].

Then also the self-originated great pristine awareness will arise and spread after the darkness of discriminative appreciation (*so sor rtog pa*) has been removed with regard to how all things have come to appear. Therefore it is said that after the darkness of ignorance is removed, [awareness] will rise and spread. Oh, great bodhisattva, to tear apart this web of discursive thinking, one should sever the chain of obscurations (*klesha*).

Some of the followers of the vehicle of causation see all things which exist as poison, and they think [these things] ought to be abandoned; others see [the same things] as objects of the mind's attachment and think they have to scrutinize this attachment by means of the two truths; others see [the same things] as objects of purification and they think that by means of the three purifications and blessed miracles in the way of 'lord and servant' (i.e. deity yoga) [the purification of the world is brought about]; others think that they want to achieve the purification of the nature of their mental flux by means of the four forms of service and worship. [The practitioners of Atiyoga] cut the chain of obscurations, that is the discriminative appreciation, after they have rid themselves of such thinking that there is nothing else but the mind, because of Me, the All-Creating mind of perfect purity."

{p. 50} Such She spoke.

"Oh great bodhisattva! I, the All-Creating Sovereign, mind of perfect purity, taught you to understand My own intrinsic being as to the point that all existent things, just as they are, are nothing else but Me. You will instruct the hosts of attendants, [gathered] around you, in My teaching so that they will understand My, i.e. the All-Creating One's, intrinsic being, and become transfigured into My own being. When they are transfigured as My intrinsic being, they will not engage in [such doctrines as] the two truths, nor [in such practices as] giving up and obstructing all existent and apparent things, nor will they engage in blessing [these things] by means of the three purifications, nor will they engage in achieving or seeking the contemplation on bodhicitta. They will understand that everything has been created in Me, the All-Creating; therefore everything is the same with regard [to its groundedness in] Me, the All-Creating One. As I am sameness, there is no need to generate sameness. Previously, I already taught that this sameness does not need to be generated."

Such She spoke.

This is the twelfth chapter of *The All-Creating Sovereign, Mind of Perfect Purity,* in which is explained the source of the lore of certainty.

13

{cont'd p. 50} Then the All-Creating Sovereign, mind of perfect purity, proclaimed the ways of explanation (*bshad lugs*) which explain the general instructions (*spyi lung*) regarding all things, because She is the sovereign of all teachings.

"Listen, oh great bodhisattva! Because I am the general instructions on the things I am proclaiming the five ways of explanation which explain the meaning of their definitions by means of the five general meanings (*spyi don*):[44]

(1) The instruction explaining the meaning of accounts of transmission (*lo rgyus*);

(2) the instruction explaining the meaning of "root";

(3) the instruction explaining the meaning of yoga; {p. 51}
(4) the instruction explaining the meaning of the intended aim;
(5) the instruction explaining the meaning of the word.

First I shall teach the explanation of the meaning of accounts of transmission because they provide the basis for faith. I shall teach the meaning of the root because the root of all things is encompassed in the mind. I shall explain rudimentarily the meaning of yoga because the particularity of each vehicle needs to be detailed. I shall explain that there is a need for the meaning of purpose because it is taught that there is no purpose in striving or achieving. I shall explain the meaning of the word in accord with the letter because the meaning of non-discursive thinking (*mi rtogs*) should be understood.

(1) Oh great bodhisattva, now to the explanation of the meaning of the accounts of transmission! First, because it is taught to be a basis for faith, the explanation of the meaning of the accounts of transmission is taught, the explanation as to the blessing [coming from] the own being, the explanation as to the teaching about My own actuation, the explanation as to the integration of meaning with word. Also you ought to believe [this] because of the way in which the source originated, that from Me, the All-Creating One, the teachers' three manifestations originated by means of My own being, actuation, and words.

(2) Listen, oh great bodhisattva! The explanation of the meaning of "root": Because everything which is encompassed in what appears and exists as animated or inanimated, such as everything that belongs either to the Buddhas or to the sentient beings, is made by Me, the All-Creating Sovereign, mind of perfect purity, there is no other thing {p. 52} from the primordial, nor anything outside of the mind of perfect purity. Because the entirety [of what exists] is taught to be Me, the mind of perfect purity, this explanation of the meaning of 'root' is given.

(3) Oh, great bodhisattva, listen now to the explanation of the meaning of yoga! What I, who transcend cause and result, teach is the essentials of Atiyoga, the great perfection, despite the fact that the teaching of the manifestations of complete communal joy and that of truth [maintain] that there are individual peculiarities in the different tantra and yoga classes. It is taught to be the consummate lore, distinct from [all other] vehicles. For this reason, this teaching is called the stipulation of the meaning of yoga.

(4) Oh, great bodhisattva, listen to the explanation of the meaning of purpose (*dgos ched*). Those Atiyoga adepts of propitious karma who have had faith in Me, the All-Creating Sovereign, [mind of]

perfect purity, for countless kalpas in the past, they will know that there is no doctrinal view to contemplate, no vows to observe, no salutary acts to strive for, no path to proceed on, no *bhûmi* to be practised, neither cause nor result nor the dichotomy of absolute and conventional Reality, neither meditation nor achievement. Because they realize that bodhicitta cannot be generated [through striving], and that there is no antidote [to the three poisons], they will see the own being of the all-creating mind. This is the explanation of the meaning of purpose."

Such She spoke.

"(5) Oh, great bodhisattva, listen to this explanation of the stipulated meaning of the word! It is taught that all things, just as they appear, are suchness, that is Me, the All-Creating mind of perfect purity. If the nature of suchness, the all-creating [mind], is not proclaimed with words and letters, the sentient beings with a capable mind {p. 53} will understand it, and thereby the nature of suchness will appear unveiled. If thereby words and letters are proclaimed, it is known as the stipulated meaning of the word.

(1) Oh great bodhisattva, whatever accounts of transmission are told, they are the accounts of transmission of the teacher, the teaching, and the retinues.[45] The nature of the retinues emerges as the teacher's three manifestations from the three aspects of the teacher's all-creating own being. There are three ways to proclaim the teacher's three manifestations: these are the accounts of transmission of the teacher's three teachings.

(2) Whatever is proclaimed as root, it is so, due [to the fact] that the teacher's three manifestations emanate from Me; therefore whatever dharma is proclaimed, it is taught to have its root in the mind of perfect purity. This explains the definition of the meaning of root with regard to the teacher, the teaching, and the retinues.

(3) Although My own being is one in its suchness, the four yogas have their yogic particularities as to [their related] doctrinal views, practice, vows, and [ways of] achievement. Thus they are not in accord as to their individual particularities. To overcome striving and achieving at the Atiyoga stage is the explanation of the meaning of yoga.

(4) The explanation of the meaning of the purpose: if one sees one's own mind as suchness and as the stipulated purpose of all sentient beings in the threefold world, one will not dwell at a stage [where one clings only to] the words of the Buddha. By virtue of this [insight] one will gain the Atiyoga. However, those of narrow faculties and without proper predisposition will not understand what is

unveiled and obvious. They are like those who search for a precious gem {p. 54} by working away on a piece of wood. Those of good faculties and proper disposition will recognize that with regard to the Atiyoga there are neither doctrinal views, nor vows, nor salutary acts, nor bodhisattva stages (*bhûmi*), nor paths [to enlightenment], that neither the generation of bodhicitta, nor [the reflection on] causation, nor meditation or achievement provide an antidote [to the three poisons], and that the absolute and conventional are not two different [things]. Thereby they will see the mind's own being; such is the stipulated purpose."

Such She spoke

"(5) The definition of the meaning 'word' is such that by pronouncing the word, i.e. the non-existent word and sound of the meaning, which [also] does not exist, inactivity is seen as the meaning. By realizing that the All-Creating [Mind] is not in need of any activity, the teaching of the meaning of 'word' is given."

Such She spoke.

This is the thirteenth chapter of *The All-Creating Sovereign, Mind of Perfect Purity,* in which the ways of explanation pertinent to the mind [are discussed].

14

{cont'd p. 54} Then the All-Creating Sovereign, mind of perfect purity, gave this noble instruction about Herself being secret.

"Oh, great bodhisattva! I, the All-Creating One, am also the secret one who [is] in all. From Me, the teachers' three forms of manifestation come, but the three aspects of My own being cannot be taught and [remain] secret [therefore]. In Me, the Buddhas of the three times dwell, but My own being cannot be taught and should be kept secret. In Me, all the hosts of retinues are united, but My own being cannot be taught and should be kept secret. I make all the sentient beings in this threefold world, but My own being cannot be taught and should be kept secret.[46] {p. 55} If the teaching about My own being is not kept secret, the teachers' three forms of manifestation will not arise from Me. If the teachers' three forms of manifestation do not arise from Me, the three teachings, the three vehicles, and the three retinues, they all will not appear. If the three teachings and the three vehicles are not perfect, all [retinues] will not understand the matchless perfect purity pertinent to the three jewels, i.e. Buddha, teaching, and community. If My own being [in its relationship to] the Buddhas of the three times is not kept secret, but is taught, a loss will occur as to the teachers' three manifestations, although [essentially they are] non-existent. If My own being, in terms of the hosts of the three retinues being united in Me, is not kept secret, but taught, the vehicles of the three teachers will not be detailed in their peculiarities. If My compassionate nature as [apparent in] the sentient beings of the threefold world, whom I have created, is taught, the teaching of the three teachers will not remain. If the teachings of the three teachers do not exist, who then will call all things, made by Me, the All-Creating One, perfect? For this reason, I Myself, the All-Creating Sovereign, teach My own being after I caused it to become apparent. I teach My own being with regard to Me. The teachers' retinues, that come forth from Me, I, the All-Creating One, do not inspire them with My teaching. [Who know that] I, the All Creating One, am Atiyoga, to them I shall reveal My own being."

Such She spoke.

This is the fourteenth chapter of *The All-Creating Sovereign, Mind of Perfect Purity,* in which [is explained that the All-Creating One remains] secret to those of deficient talent.

15

{cont'd p. 55} Then the All-Creating Sovereign, mind of perfect purity, proclaimed this evident instruction about Her great message. {p. 56}

"Oh great bodhisattva! I, the All-Creating Sovereign, teach the evidence [of My being] under three aspects because My own being is [also] taught under three aspects:

(1) the teaching of the meaning 'teacher';

(2) the attendants who wish to understand this meaning; and

(3) the certain, unerring meaning.

These three issues are made evident by Me, the All-Creating One.

(1) Now the evidence of 'teacher' who teaches the meaning: The three forms of manifestation as that of truth, perfect communal joy, and incorporation, are taught as the first retinues and also as the teachers' three forms of manifestation. This is the teaching of the meaning 'teacher'. [My own] nature free of subject and object, the

teaching as to My actuation, and the nature of compassion—these three [facts] evidence the three aspects of My own being for the good [of all sentient beings]. [These three facts] are also known as the evidence of the three [forms of the] teacher.

(2) [Now] the evidence as to those who wish to understand this meaning, in particular [that] of the teaching about the three retinues of the three teachers! The teaching in its detail is as follows: The Buddhas dwelling in the three times, and all sentient beings living in this threefold world, abide in a non-reflective state of balance. I, the All-Creating, am evidenced through them as retinues. Those who do not understand that the obscurations (*klesha*) pertinent to the sensory objects are not generated through the sensory faculties, and who reflect upon their own mind of perfect purity in terms of it being a thing or [the thing's] Reality, these people will remain obscured [and divorced] from [their entry into] the first bodhisattva stage (*bhûmi*) up to the tenth. My actuation will become apparent under the dual aspect of teacher and retinue to the bodhisattvas of the tenth stage who are seen to enjoy the five sensory objects.

(3) By reflecting upon the nature of suchness with an understanding mind {p. 57} they will gain a notion of having understood. Some will understand [this notion] as eternal, and others will understand it as separate from the empty. When the four kinds of non-Buddhists, who see causation in a wrong way, become converted (literally blessed) they are taught causation. [As a consequence] they will give up their sins and [develop] the four virtuous attitudes. For three great eons I shall be evident as teacher and retinues who are existent. As to the pristine awareness which has intelligence as its object, it will become evident in terms of the certainty of the pure.

Oh, great bodhisattva, what is called evidence is evident by whom, what [is evident], and to whom [is it evident]? By whom is it [made] evident?—by Me! What is evident?—the mind in itself is evident! To whom is it evident?—It is evident to the retinues who envisage it as their individual goals.

To some it becomes evident for the purpose of giving up; to others for the purpose of obstructing; to others for the purpose of practising; to others for the purpose of purifying; to others for the purpose of rejecting and acquiring; to others for the purpose of itself. Some see it as an object to be given up; some as an object to be obstructed; some as an object for cleansing; some as an object for purifying; some as an object for rejecting and acquiring; some as an object for gathering [the retinues] under [one's] supremacy. The retinues following the teaching of causation see it this way.

Oh great bodhisattva! As to My own being, becoming evident, I teach the following with certainty: I am actuating you, which is the revelation of My own being, and which comes forth as your own being {p. 58}. By virtue of your own evident nature, you ought to know your own being; you ought to understand your own actuation, thereby you teach this message to the retinues [receptive to the teaching] of causation."

Such She spoke.

Then Sems-dpa' rdo-rje gave this sermon to the retinues about causation:

"Oh, attendants who should be instructed in causation, the teacher of the teaching, the All-Creating One, has made everything in a perfect manner. The perfectness becomes evident; it becomes evident as my own being. Therefore I understand that I am [Her] own nature. I understand I am Her actuation. Nothing else is to be recognized as existent. I recognize that She Herself exists in all.

If you do not recognize Herself as existent [in you] by not understanding that She Herself is in the very object, whereby you consider the objects as great enemies, then you will not see your own mind in its Reality (*chos nyid*) for as long as a hundred eons because you have abandoned your own being. If you do not see your own mind in its Reality you are about to abandon your own [nature of] perfect purity for as long as a hundred eons, and you will not obtain the bliss of the deedless (*bya med*). But if you do not understand the object as your own self, you will consider the object as an enemy because of its conditions. This [view] obstructs your own nature, and for a hundred eons you will not see your own mind in its Reality. If you do not see your own mind in its Reality, your own perfect purity will be obstructed for a hundred eons, and because of that you will not obtain the great bliss of the deedless. By not understanding the object as your own self, you will consider the object as an object for purification. Thus if you attempt to purify your own being, you will be unable to see your own mind in its Reality for as long as three great eons. {p. 59}

Not to see your own mind in its Reality is to be without the confidence [to see] your own mind as not in need of purification. If you see filth in subject and object with regard to the objects which are of perfect purity and simplicity (*rang dag*), you will attempt to cleanse them through the three purifications, i.e. inner, outer, and mental, as well as through bathing and [other] purifications.

By not seeing your mind in its clarity, you are deprived of the clarity of your own mind. For seven lifespans you will not see your own mind in its Reality. If you consider the objects as [something which is] either to be accepted or rejected, although they are of perfect purity where accepting and rejecting is not [applicable], you practise accepting and rejecting with regard to the self-originated itself! You exercise accepting and rejecting as to your own selves! For a duration of three lifetimes, you will not see the non-duality of your own mind. If you view the objects as something which can be accomplished through striving, although they are self-perfected, of consummate purity, you will appropriate and subjugate everything by means of the three *samâdhi* of bodhicitta. Because you wish to accomplish through striving what is your own [mind's] perfect purity where striving is not [applicable] you will assume the form of a joy manifestation at the sixteenth of every month, or for a duration of 1,106 years, and you will consider [the practice of] endurance with regard to your own self-perfected mind. For those of you who [attempt to] accomplish [enlightenment] through striving, it is of no use to consider what is evident as your own mind in its Reality as cause and result. But for those of you who are endowed with the right karmic disposition it will evidence itself in its meaningfulness."

Such Sems-dpa' rdo-rje said.

Then the All-Creating Sovereign gave this sacred instruction:

"Oh great bodhisattva! The evident Reality is your own mind. Those who adhere to the vehicle of causation {p.60} will not recognize their own mind as evidencing [Reality]. Therefore, for eons, they will remain [in a state of mental] obstruction because of their abandoning [such insight]. By [thinking of] progressing [on the path] through purifications they will stay [in samsara] for three eons. With purifications like bathing and other purifying [rites] they will spend seven lifespans, and another three lifespans with [exercising] blessing, and acquiring and rejecting. By wishing to gather retinues for themselves, they spend 1,106 years [to generate] the visualization of joy manifestations, thereby cognizing it as their own mind. [But] when they gain infallible insight (*rtogs pa*) they will obtain without effort the great bliss.

Oh, great bodhisattva, listen! You ought to comprehend My sacred instruction, which is the All-Creating One's, because [this instruction] is unlike the Mahâyâna [which teaches] causation. Likewise, you ought not to ponder on the system of causation because, from the primordial, everything, in the way it appears, is one with the Reality of your own mind.[47] By understanding your own mind in its suchness your own perfect purity will appear as actuation. Although [many] do not understand this, they apply individual terms, such as 'the appearance of the conventional' or 'the non-appearance of the absolute'. [But] absolute or conventional, these are not two, but only one truth. Through such statements, whether or not the pure truth is truly existing, I become also obscured as they [attempt to] define the pure.

The desire for bliss is a sickness of attachment, and for this reason, you will accomplish bliss [only] by not desiring it. By performing Buddha sâdhana you will not realize [buddhahood],[48] but you will be self-perfected by abiding in your own being which cannot be sought. Contemplate without reflection on the own being which cannot be sought.

I do not teach that the pure Buddha exists in words [claiming] to define *(bla dags)* the essence of 'Buddha'. Whoever sees the Buddha as existent will not realize {p. 61} the Buddha [who is not different] from the dimension of Reality (*chos dbyings*), but if [some people] do not theorize the Buddha, they will cognize their own mind as deedless (*bya med*). If no [theoretical framework] is applied their own mind will shine forth as [it has been] from the beginning. [This mind] does not actually appear but their own mind is all-encompassing. This appearance is the actuation of existence.

To those who follow the vehicle of causation, and who do not think this way, the deedless Reality of their own mind will be obstructed due to [their concerns] for giving up obstacles, purging, and various blessings. [This is like somebody] who leaves things in their place, but then searches for them in the far distance. After giving up the bliss of the deedless, they take to striving—there is no weariness[49] other than this.

The samâdhi of no-agitation (*ma yengs*) is a hitching post [binding the mind instead of freeing it]. Since beginning the [own being] is without agitation or loss. The great vehicle of causation, which is a teaching in need of interpretation (*drang ba'i lung*), is taught by impostors in hope for an un-agitated samâdhi. Since beginning [own being] is without agitation and without loss; it is the antidote of all striving and achieving, and destroys them. If I, the All-Creating One, would expound such a teaching to the retinues by teaching a doctrine of causation [it would mean] to exercise praise and dispraise in saying 'result comes from causes'.

Those who adhere to a samâdhi and a yoga in the pursuit of buddhahood give up the genuine (*ma bcos*) yoga due to their desire for samâdhi. The genuine balance is the entirety of Reality, and apart from this Reality there is no Buddha. To apply a name to the Buddha is [just] a word (*bla dags*). What is called Reality is nothing else but one's own mind; the genuine own mind is explained as manifestation of truth. What is genuine is birthless from the primordial. The gist of the birthless is to be without striving and achieving. {p. 62} Trying to achieve [spiritual progress] through striving will not bring about the deed-less achievement.

Oh great bodhisattva, listen! The teachers in their three aspects as manifestation of truth, joy, and incorporation, the teachings of the one vehicle, of the two vehicles, and of the three vehicles, were brought forth by Me, the All-Creating Sovereign. I am the origin from which all teachers emanate. They come forth from the three aspects of My own being.

The non-reflective, well-poised manifestation of truth comes forth from My nature, which is free of subject and object, and it does so [for the good of] the retinues who are non-conceptual, unborn, and joyful. The retinue of the manifestation of truth is indivisible as it is taught that it is in balance and unborn. This is declared as the [true] dharma without remainder (*lhag ma med pa'i chos*).[50]

As My own being appears in everything, therefore My manifestation of joy comes forth as hosts of retinues who enjoy the sensual pleasures in a purified [manner]. Thereby the actuation is perfected as to doctrinal views and practice. What emanates from My playful (*rol pa*) actuation is not the common vehicle.

The corporeal manifestation and the four retinues work the weal of whatever students are to be disciplined by means of these corporeal manifestations that come forth from My compassionate nature. [These manifestations] also come forth as [My] compassion in accord with [the teaching on] causation.

Oh great bodhisattva! In short, what is called evident instruction is taught as being My own nature. This is explained as the evident instruction. As My, the All-Creating One's, own being is one, the perceivable objects appear in three aspects, and from them come forth all things, such as the Buddhas, sentient beings, the animated and inanimated world—everything. {p. 63} My, the All-Creating One's, own being becomes evident [in this way]. Who discern anything else to exist beside this will not meet Me, the All-Creating One, for the duration of eons. Therefore My first retinue, the three manifestations, are the retinues [following] the vehicle of causation and gradual purging.

Oh great bodhisattva! I am this evidence; there is no other evidence. I Myself am evident; one's own mind is evident; the nonerring is evident; the firm is evident; and the suchness is evident.

Oh great bodhisattva! My evident nature evidences the Buddhas of the five great [elements]. This is how the Buddhas of the five great [elements] are. My actuation is evident as this Reality because of all that appears and exists as animated and inanimated world. It is evident in all that exists. Because it does not need any deeds, it exists since the beginning as Buddha. Because it is without striving and achieving, it is since the beginning known as great. What is known as the revealed Buddha is this evidence of My own being. Because it has become the centre, the central vigor, it is the self of everything. As it does not need any deeds, it is the Buddha since the beginning. As it is free of striving and achieving, it is since the beginning known as great. The great self is known as the great Buddha (*bdag nyid chen po sangs rgyas che bar bshad*). This evidence which is unborn and non-conceptual is the dimension of Reality because, since the beginning, it is free of subject and object. As it is not in need of deeds, it is the Buddha since the beginning. As it is not in need of striving and achieving, since the beginning, it is known as the great. It is known as the dimension of Reality and the great Buddha.

I am surely evident. Simile, meaning, and investigation are taught as three aspects. The sky is taught as a simile [giving] meaning to Reality. Certainly, those who investigate the mind of perfect purity, and certainly those who have doubts will say this is the Buddha by means of simile, meaning, and investigation. This suchness, My own being, will not appear to anybody, although it is evident. 'This' (*de*) is the non-erring nature; 'such' (*bzhin*) is the genuine (*ma bcos*) own being; '-ness' (*nyid*) is called the actuation in itself.[51]

Do not overvalue the existence of the Buddhas in the three times with regard to suchness and the own being as such. But do also not undervalue the non-existence of the threefold world and its sentient beings. I do not explain the Buddha's non-existent greatness because they who apply analytical and discursive thinking will not be able to grasp it."

Such She spoke.

This is the fifteenth chapter of *The All-Creating Sovereign, Mind of Perfect Purity,* in which the evidence as to the three aspects of Her own being is explained.

16

{cont'd p. 64} Then the All-Creating Sovereign, mind of perfect purity, gave this sacred instruction to Sems-dpa' rdo-rje:

"Oh great Sems-dpa' rdo-rje, listen! Since the beginning, I, the All-Creating Sovereign, have created the teachers, the teachings, the retinues, and the time [appropriate for their instruction], but I also created the teacher of the teachers. The teachings are taught to be My own being. Also the retinues have emanated from My actuation, and time and locale as My own being are in this way taught to be My own being, i.e. the All-Creating One's. Beside of this, I did not teach a single issue which is not Me. {p. 65}

Also your self, oh great Sems-dpa' rdo-rje, is taught to be My own being, i.e that of the All-Creating One. Therefore, also you have come forth from Me and by Me. Contemplate upon Me, the All-Creating One, as the core of all things. I, the All-Creating One, am [the one who has everything] perfectly created, thus, I do not teach all [the retinues] that there needs still something to be done. If I would teach the retinues that still something needs to be done, they would be afflicted by a sickness of striving, and a damage would occur in negating the self-originated pristine awareness. There would be a damage done as to altering (*'chos pa*) the mind of perfect purity. There would be a damage as to altering suchness. Such damage will be contrary to the good qualities. If lies spoil the truth with deceit, then one cannot achieve what is deedless because [the mind of perfect purity] is free of striving.

You, oh Sems-dpa' [rdo-rje], should know Me, the All Creating One! All things which I have created are since the beginning the self-originated pristine awareness and suchness. The three [manifestations of the] teacher are My self-originated pristine awareness. The three teachings are My suchness in itself. Also, all the retinues, the same way as you, Sems-dpa' rdo-rje, are perfected as are time and place,[52] that is everything is Me, the All-Creating Sovereign, mind of perfect purity."

Such She spoke.

This is the sixteenth chapter of *The All-Creating Sovereign, Mind of Perfect Purity,* in which an instruction is given to Sems-dpa' rdo-rje.

17

{cont'd p. 65} Then the All-Creating Sovereign, mind of perfect purity, talked about how to uphold the relics of Her own manifestations.

"Oh great bodhisattva, grasp this! If one always upholds the relics and bones, one has to say that they are equal to the progenitor {p.66} of the Victorious One (*jina*), that is to Me, the All-Creating One."

Such She spoke.

Sems-dpa' rdo-rje addressed this question to Her:

"Oh progenitor of all Buddhas of the three times, teacher of the teachers, All-Creating Sovereign! One who always upholds the relics and bones, how should this person understand 'manifestation', of what Victorious One, and what manifestation? What bones of what Buddha, and what relics?"

[The All-Creating Sovereign:]

"Listen, oh great bodhisattva! These manifestations are My sons, the manifestations of the three Victorious Ones. My mind is known as 'bones', as present in the Victorious Ones of the three times. If one upholds these beings as eternal and non-temporary, they are the base for worshiping all the Buddhas of the three times. This is known as the bones and relics of the manifestations."

[Sems-dpa' rdo-rje:]

"Oh teacher of the teachers, All-Creating Sovereign! Although the bones and relics of the manifestations are in such way well explained, then [tell me] how does one worship the Buddhas of the three times? What are the good qualities [acquired] through this worship?"

Such he asked.

[The All-Creating Sovereign:]

"Oh great bodhisattva, listen! The bones and relics of My manifestations are to be worshiped by constantly contemplating the mind as the Buddhas of the three times! One will not be divorced from their good qualities, but will gain them, and after that one will become mighty like the everything-making All-Creating Sovereign."

Such She spoke.

This is the seventeenth chapter of *The All-Creating Sovereign, Mind of Perfect Purity,* in which [the explanation of the] bones of the manifestations is given.

18

{cont'd p. 66} Then the All-Creating Sovereign, mind of perfect purity, proclaimed that the Reality of all things is "My self:"

"Oh great bodhisattva, listen! The entirety of what appears and exists as animated and inanimated appears as an appearance of My actuation. The pure is pure in the dimension of Reality. {p.67} The various teachings[53] about the features of disciplining, and the origin of the various forms of the three manifestations are taught as the essence of the three vehicles. This makes the followers [of the vehicles] of causation content.

By not depending on past objects, [the practitioners of Atiyoga] will not desire the result nor the completion of the cause. Through an attitude free of desires, [they will understand that] nature is self-perfected. From the primordial it is [like that], and there is no need for [certain] activities, as likewise, the essentials are unagitated, and therefore don't need to be achieved. Because the nature of all things is self-perfected there is no instruction given to achieve [anything] by striving, even if some [claim] to realize the Buddhas of the three times. If some seek what is sought by meditation, then this is a crucial point in a meditation which achieves nothing.

Oh great bodhisattva! Although all the teachers, besides Me, perceive whatever perceptible objects there are, such as the various actions and deeds, the stages of analytical contemplation (*bsam pa'i ting 'dzin*), and various lights radiating, [the fact is that] actuality (*ji bzhin pa*) is unagitated. It cannot be achieved through acts and deeds. The analytical contemplation will diminish; the radiating lights will calm down; there will be no seeing of whatever object of perception. Thereby there is no activity of striving carried out.

Oh, great bodhisattva, the teaching of achieving through striving for the objectives [of the spiritual path] is taught for the followers of the vehicle of causation. However, with regard to the Reality [as taught] by the Mahâyâna [which asserts] cause and result, [one should know that] it divides things and their reality into two [categories]. But there is no instruction to be obtained and no Reality to be sought through [categorizing] things [in such a way]."

Such She spoke.

This is the eighteenth chapter of *The All-Creating Sovereign, Mind of Perfect Purity,* in which [is explained] {p. 68} that there is no achievement by means of striving.

19

{cont'd p. 68} Then the All-Creating Sovereign, mind of perfect purity, proclaimed the chapter about achieving through non-striving:

"Oh great bodhisattva, listen! The three manifestations of the teacher, emanating from Me, have taught the teachings of the three vehicles. The three teachers do not teach a lore of non-striving, but I, the All-Creating One, teach the one vehicle, and I do not expound an instruction of achieving trough striving.

Oh great bodhisattva, listen! From the the All-Creating [Sovereign, mind of] perfect purity, from My nature, [comes] the spontaneously self-perfected nature, free of striving. This is the central vigor of the manifestations of the three Victorious Ones. My own being is realized as the perfect and genuine manifestation of truth; My actuation is perfected as the genuine manifestation of joy; My compassion is evident as corporeal manifestation. There is no teaching about a result achieved through striving."

Such She spoke.

"Oh great bodhisattva, listen! The three manifestations are encompassed by Me, the All-Creating One. All things which appear just like that, i.e. [My] own being, [My] actuation, and [My] genuine compassion, are taught to be the teacher's three forms of manifestation as My suchness. Besides Me and My suchness, there is not even praise for the good qualities of what is called 'Buddha', and there is no dispraise for the faults of what is called 'sentient beings'. There is nothing else than abiding just like that in balance, without conceptual thinking.

The Buddhas have not received any instruction beside this one from Me, the All-Creating One. {p. 69} Not even I, the maker and All-Creating Sovereign, have a trace of a teaching on suchness, the balance, free of conceptual thinking in Myself or by Myself."

Such She spoke.

This is the nineteenth chapter of *The All-Creating Sovereign, Mind of Perfect Purity,* in which [is explained] the self-perfection through non-striving.

20

{cont'd p. 69} Then the All-Creating Sovereign, mind of perfect purity, talked about the origin of all things as coming from Herself:

"Oh rDo-rje, who encompasses all things, listen! I, the All-Creating Sovereign, mind of perfect purity, am the central vigor of all things. I am the seed of all things. I am also the cause of all things. I am the stem of all things. I am the ground (*gzhi ma*) of all things. I am the root of all things.

I am called the central vigor because all things, which appear just like that, are permeated [by Me]. I am the seed because all existent things, which appear just like that, are born [from Me]. I am the cause because all things, which appear just like that, arise [from Me]. I am the stem because all things, which appear just like that, branch out [from Me]. I am the ground because all things, which appear just like that, abide [in Me]. I am said to be root because all things, which appear just like that, are Me.

Oh great bodhisattva, listen! I, the All-Creating Sovereign, mind of perfect purity, teach that the three manifestations come from the three aspects of My genuine nature only as designations. Certainly, the teachers in their three manifestations do not depart from suchness. Only by designation [it is said] do the unborn truth manifestations come from Me, the All-Creating mind of perfect purity, who is free of subject and object, and [consequently] unborn. {p. 70} Certainly, as 'truth manifestation' is a mere designation, it does not depart from suchness.

I, the All-Creating mind of perfect purity, am evident as actuation but only as mere designation. As 'manifestation of perfect joy' is a mere designation, the manifestation of joy does not depart from suchness. I, the All-Creating mind of perfect purity, am evident in My compassion as corporeal manifestation. The corporeal manifestation arises only by mere designation from [My] compassion and genuine own being. Certainly, also this corporeal manifestation does not depart from suchness. The three manifestations do not depart from the nature of suchness.

Likewise, the dharma taught by the three manifestations, and the retinues gathered around the three manifestations do not depart from the entirety of things. Those who define the unagitated Reality as cause and result exercise achievement through striving, and thus are in error as they desire cause and result, and they are far from transcending cause and result, which [in actuality] were made by Me, the All-Creating One."

Such She spoke.

"Oh great bodhisattva, listen! The teacher in Her three manifestations, originating from Me, the Buddhas of the three times, originating from Me, the retinues, place and time, etc. also originated from Me—if all these things are Me, the mind of perfect purity, then you ought not to investigate them through investigation, oh Sems-dpa' rdo-rje. I am from the primordial the All-Creating mind of perfect purity, and also all that I created is the mind of perfect purity. My own being is from the primordial utterly pure. {p. 71} It is perfect because from the primordial it encompasses all that exists through Me. It is from the primordial the mind because My own being is luminous (*gsal ba*). My own sky-like being, the mind of perfect purity, which exists from the primordial, [creates] the world as illusion, such as [saying it consists] of momentary particles. The teachers in their three manifestations and the Buddhas of the three times opt for a method [to discipline] the retinues, sons or nephews, and give instructions on the non-erroneous truth: they are teaching such as the mind of perfect purity is like the sky, and the All-Creating One as the origin of all is like the sky."

Such She spoke.

This is the twentieth chapter of *The All-Creating Sovereign, Mind of Perfect Purity,* in which is explained the mind of perfect purity, the All-Creating One, as origin of all things.

21

{cont'd p. 71} Then the All-Creating Sovereign, mind of perfect purity, proclaimed these words which come from Herself because [She] is the sovereign and the origin of all Buddha-teachings:

"Oh you great bodhisattva, rDo-rje, listen! By being the Sovereign who has made all things, I am father and mother of the teachers in their three manifestations, and the progenitor of all the Buddhas of the three times. I am illuminating (*sgron ma byed*) the teachers of the retinues, as well as place and time. The teachers in their three manifestations have emanated from Me, the All-Creating One, from the three aspects of My nature. Due to the three ways of explaining [exercised] by the three manifestations the dharma is also explained in three ways. This is also explained by Me, the All-Creating One.

Because My nature, i.e. that of the All-Creating Sovereign, excels {p. 72} in worthiness all the teachers, I am teaching the source of non-erring accurate statements (*nges pa'i gtan tshig*) through five systems of explanation which give the gist of these statements.[54]

Oh great bodhisattva! I am the All-Creating Sovereign, mind of perfect purity. This mind of perfect purity is from the primordial perfect and grand. The great perfection (*rdzogs chen*) transcends causation from the primordial. Two different systems of explanation are taught: [one is] taught as the explanation of transcending cause and result, and [the other is] the explanation system which stems from the teachers in their three manifestations which emanate from the nature of the All-Creating Sovereign, mind of perfect purity.

Now the system of explanation of the All-Creating Sovereign, mind of perfect purity: Because the mind of perfect purity is beyond cause and result the gist of the accurate statements is given in five systems of explanation.

The three systems of explanation [affiliated with] the teachers in their three manifestations: among the five aspects of perfection, the truth manifestation is explained through blessings, the [manifestation] of perfect joy is taught through its own actuation; the corporeal manifestation is affiliated with the verbal expressions of meaning. These are the three explanation systems of the teachers' three manifestations. The three aspects of My nature constitute [the individual] explanation systems. I, the All-Creating One, am beyond causation. And because[55] I am beyond causation, I am beyond the scope of sensory activity. The mind of perfect purity, Reality, transcends all. The mind of perfect purity is the central vigor of everything. Because it is the central vigor, it is also taught to be the source of confidence. The mind of perfect purity is the root of all things; and because it is the root it encompasses the gist of all. The mind of perfect purity excels everything in worthiness; and because of this excellence in worthiness, it is distinct from [the other] vehicles.

{p. 73} To understand the mind of perfect purity [is to understand] Reality as the entirety of the Buddhas. For this reason I am teaching [this lore] for the benefit of the talented ones. The mind's nature cannot be expressed in words. The inexplicable nature of the mind does not appear. For this reason, if I would say that because of its non-appearance, it cannot be pointed at, all [the retinues] would not see their own mind but engage in achieving through striving. For this reason I do explain its (i.e. the mind's nature) meaning in words although it is inexplicable. Therefore, through the five systems of explanation pertinent to the gist of the statements, the meaning of the All-Creating Sovereign, mind of perfect purity, was fixed in a non-erring and correct manner. As there is neither cause nor result, it was fixed [in this way].

As everything is the mind of perfect purity, confidence is established. Because of the mind of perfect purity being existent, confidence is there from the primordial. As there is no striving [directed] towards the mind, one is confident. As there is no striving, [the practitioners] are confident from the primordial. For this reason they abide in great bliss, [which can] not [be reached through] striving. In this way, they abide in My nature, i.e. in that of the All-Creating One. There is no other Buddha besides Me, the All-Creating One."

Such She spoke.

This is the twenty-first chapter of *The All-Creating Sovereign, Mind of Perfect Purity,* in which is treated the explanation systems of the firm statements.

22

{cont'd p. 73} Then the All-Creating Sovereign, mind of perfect purity, proclaimed this great origin of the deedless (*bya med*) teaching of perfection, in order to place the mind in [a state of] balance.

"Oh great bodhisattva, rDo-rje, listen![56] As to the deedless objects, which are non-existent like the sky, [some claim] that they come forth as part of [previous] pledges from subtle objects, i.e. the path of dharma, while [these people] do not understand that the objects they perceive do not exist. As investigation and meditation are particularly pointless [for realizing] {p. 74} the manifestation of truth, [the follower of Atiyoga] remains just so, and does not at all investigate the self-originated pristine awareness. To seek the essential goal by means of religion and its branches, is to enjoy in this through a method which does not [entail] any understanding, as there is no remedy to cure the non-existent, i.e. the goal of the deedless. Outside of the rise of the own being of central vigor, there is no other truth manifestation. By dissecting an atom, one part will remain totally free from [being oriented towards] the cardinal directions. The good awareness, which is non-existent yet purposeful (*don nyid*), originates by itself. You will achieve the mastery of balance after entering this pure path with regard to the broad essence which does not at all immediately recognize [things]. There is no place for being attached to because nothing is becoming, and nothing has become. Likewise, there is no place for the mind to grasp what is not an object. If one wishes for obtaining manifest [results] one will always ponder upon their causes, [but] one will not realize the aim of balance because of being happily attached to meditation.

Because the one manifestation (i.e. the *dharmakâya*) encompasses everything, there are no things which are to be augmented. Because the destination (i.e. nirvâna) cannot be reached, the dimension of Reality knows no loss. As things dwell in enjoyment (*rol*) there is no place for lowering or elevating. As to the aim of the great self-origination, everything is poised just as it is.

The eye which sees the no-object, sees the wonder. Who separate themselves from what they hear and what people talk about, they will remain in a state of union with things and Reality, and will be inseparable from them.[57] There is no explanation in addition to calling it the ultimate Reality (*don dam chos*). If they deliberate as to whether or not the path of perfect purity is erroneous,[58] they will not realize it. Also the self-originated pristine awareness is free of the limitations of the word. As to the apparent existence of the true self and the eternal Buddha {p. 75} you ought to understand it like the simile of the body and its shadow.[59] The essence of negating negation and non-negation rests with the issue of voidness which is void and not void [at once]. [Such notion] is born as a recognition of what arises from the sky's own being.[60] You will receive the deedless by not desiring the bliss to capture it. This awareness is about to come forth from what is not an object of enjoyment.[61] Indeed, you will be entirely engulfed by suffering due to the [spiritual] pursuit by placing your heart on being attached to the previous sages.[62]

Those who, motivated by the wish to enter this path to nature, constantly meditate on the notion of how the omniscient one is, are sick from attachment due to their longing for the great bliss. If they don't apply the great medicine of abiding in stillness the cause for proceeding to celestial realms will be seized by obscuration (*klesha*). It is a great sickness to enter a path which is no-path. Those who wish to proceed on it are like a deer pursuing a mirage.[63] [Abiding in stillness] is not an object of gain, nor does it arise from the threefold world. A state where they gaze at the ten bodhisattva stages (*bhûmi*) is an obscuration of perfect purity.

The truly acute awareness is free of all thinking; like a precious jewel it arises amidst spiritual friends. Those who are not fixated on an issue which is imperceptible and unchanging, such people will have fulfilled all their hopes due to their own being. [Such awareness] will well arise in its grandeur if they contemplate what cannot be investigated. To all, it is a teacher of the different forms of passion, which does not materially appear; it is a master teacher free of [such concepts as] oneself and others—a treasure of jewels. It teaches selfless compassion which is known as the objective of all achievement. {p.76} It does not move in its inner [being] nor is there room for searching it in its inner [being]. It is imperceptible to those who take on the [bodhisattva] vows whose objective is the attachment to external objects.

It is the selfless compassion which cannot be entered upon, nor can it arise. It exists from the primordial and for all future time; there is no other jewel [than this]. By desiring this bliss they will turn their back towards this bliss. Being grasped by bliss means to seek bliss by means of bliss. To thirst for the taste of the dharma is to err from the perfect purity.

Likewise, no such subject as the Buddha can be seen. As there is no Buddha, there is no name 'Buddha' to be given. It is an error [to assume] that the teacher carried the name 'Buddha'. This is a wrong path as it aspires to achieve Buddha[hood] through something else.

There is not the slightest trace of a teaching that all things are formless. [This self-originated pristine awareness] is calm and free of attachment and grasping; it is not a thing and totally abandoned (*rnam par spong*), because its nature is the great nectar, but there is no sensation of a way to enjoy it.[64] It is broad (*yangs*), grand, the great dharma. It is the antidote to all smallness. If they make equal the parts of what they perceive as great, they will be freed from the concepts of small and big.

The teaching, the expanse, the perception, and the appearance[65] are like scenes [created by] a magician. Such things come forth because the awareness is befogged [by such concepts as] emerging and entering. It is superior to all vehicles. Let it go, let it rest—it is the nature which cannot be coveted, nor can it be obtained. There is not a trace of eagerness; it is like the great eagle soaring in the sky. It knows neither expansion nor contraction. There is no need [of fearing] that it gets lost nor can it be consumed. Like the ocean it makes the various things arise from the primordial. The limitations of its qualities are like those of the sky. {p.77} The place of its contraction is not certain. It arises as the great king of samâdhi at once from the central vigor of perfect purity. Its appearance is like the great ocean. It expands like the unknowable boundaries of the sky: There are no such things as birth and demise as it is the realm of sensory perception of All-Good (Samantabhadra).

It is explained that through praise the twelve limbs of causes and conditions are bound. But the wise should know that this is only an entrance to delusion. The appearance of the six categories of sentient beings should first be known as path. Those who, in the pursuit of desires, are saturated with compassion, may pursue the perfect purity by whatever [means] they like.[66] Butchers, whores, offenders of the five limitless sins, and covert sinners are abandoned by the world. But the wholly perfected one, due to the honey of the dharma, [knows these acts] not different from the great bliss. In this way they should see the yield of all things, because of the nature of the things.[67] [To claim] that Reality is dependent on others is like [a person] searching for Reality by means of the things, or for the sky by means of the sky, like one who extinguishes fire with fire—these [accomplishments] are difficult to do. The imperceptible essence is not hidden to the mental flux of all [creatures]. Those who live in accord with perfect purity, which they don't appropriate, dwell entirely in their own being."

Such She spoke.

This is the twenty-second chapter of *The Ten Teachings on the Deedless Perfection,* in which the non-existent no-objects [are treated].

23

{cont'd p. 77} Then the All-Creating Sovereign, mind of perfect purity, gave this talk on what is not an object of doctrinal views.

{p. 78} "Oh great bodhisattva, listen! Because all the existent things are one's own mind of perfect purity, consequently no objects of doctrinal views are given. Those of non-conceptual thinking (*mi rtog pa*) will have a mental attitude equal to the sky—i.e. one of balance. Yoga means to do this. Those who do not reflect upon that which appears to the five sense faculties in terms of being self-illuminating (*rang gsal*), they, too, have a mental attitude equal to the sky. These practitioners of yoga dwell in suchness. Those who speculate about the meaning of words and letters, they, too, dwell in a mental attitude [equal to] the sky [due to] the non-speculative balance or suchness. The main point of not thinking (*bsam du med pa*) is to abide from the primordial in a sky-like [state]."

Such She spoke.

This is the twenty-third chapter of *The Ten Teachings on the Deedless Perfection,* in which is explained the sky-like thinking which is not an object of doctrinal views.

24

{cont'd p. 78} Then the All-Creating Sovereign, mind of perfect purity, taught the chapter of the ways of abiding, that is the seal of the lore of deedless perfection (*bya med rdzogs pa'i lung*).

"Oh great bodhisattva! The teaching about how the mind itself, the All-Good (Kun-tu bzang-po, Samantabhadra) is abiding, is as follows: when you only abide in the mind of perfect purity, you abide in the central vigor of all things. Such knowledge is the All-Creating Sovereign. The All-Creating Sovereign is without becoming, thereby She is taught to be without becoming.

When you only abide in the truth manifestation you will abide in a state free of conceptualizing subject and object. To be free of [conceptualizing] subject and object, is to be without becoming.

When you only abide in the manifestation of perfect joy, you will abide in the perfect saturation of desires by being endowed with the pleasures arising from the five sensory objects. {p. 79}

When you abide in the corporeal manifestation only, you will abide in the fulfillment of all needs by being embodied in whatever [form] is required in accord with the time for disciplining and by whom.

You will abide without becoming in the three times. This is the characteristic of the sky, the seal of all things. The sky's characteristic is suchness. The characteristic of the three manifestations is to abide just as they are, that is to abide in the suchness of all. All the existent things are genuine, just as they are. [Among] all who want achievement by striving there is not one who has arrived [at that goal] through previous progress [on the path]. There is not one who has received [the result] by what she or he has done in the past. There is none who achieved [what he or she had aspired to] in the past through striving for achievements. There is no becoming as everything is just as it is."

Such She spoke.

This is the twenty-fourth chapter, [taken from] *The Ten Teachings on the Deedless Perfection,* in which an instruction is given on the deedless perfection, the seal of non-becoming.

25

{cont'd p. 79} Then the All-Creating Sovereign, mind of perfect purity, gave an explanation about one's own mind being the teacher for the sentient beings in the threefold world.

"Oh you sentient beings of the threefold world! If I taught that this, your own mind of perfect purity, is the teacher for the duration of 100,000 eons (*kalpa*), you will not be able to see your own mind as teacher. For this reason, I, the All-Creating Sovereign, have become present in your own mind as the teacher.

Listen to this lore of one's own mind [being] the teacher! {p. 80} I, the All-Creating Sovereign, am the cause of everything, and from the mind of perfect purity come forth the five great elements as the mind's actuation, and from them come forth the five teachers as the mind of perfect purity.

Manifestation is taught as the manifestation of perfect joy; 'truth' (*dharma*) is explained through the actuation of one's own [nature], and 'teacher' is declared to be one's own nature. The teachers in their manifestations of perfect joy [teach] not to speculate on thinking itself,[68] nor to speculate on other doctrinal issues. The five teachers of the mind of perfect purity teach likewise that all is Reality.

The pristine awareness (*ye shes*) of the mind of perfect purity, coming forth as teachers in the manifestation of [the element] 'earth' do not teach words or letters, but teach [through] one's own nature,[69] so that one does not speculate on self and other. They teach a non-speculative thinking of balance. All sentient beings of this threefold world, by understanding this, are equal to the Buddha. They will achieve through non-striving the Reality which [others] zealously seek.

The pristine awareness of the mind of perfect purity, coming forth as teachers in the manifestation of [the element] 'water' does not teach words or letters, but teaches through one's own actuation, so that one does not speculate on self and other. They teach a non-speculative thinking of balance. All sentient beings of the threefold world, by understanding this, are equal to the Buddha. They will achieve through non-striving the Reality which [others] zealously seek.

The pristine awareness of the mind of perfect purity, coming forth as teachers in the manifestation of [the element] 'fire' do not teach words or letters, {p. 81} but teach this lore through its actuation, so that one does not speculate on self and other. They teach a non-speculative thinking of balance. All sentient beings of the threefold world, by understanding this, are equal to the Buddha. They will achieve through non-striving the Reality which [others] zealously seek.

The pristine awareness of the mind of perfect purity, coming forth as teachers in the manifestation of [the element] 'wind' do not teach words or letters, but teach this lore through its actuation, so that one does not speculate on self and other as being [two] different [entities]. They teach a non-speculative thinking of balance. All sentient beings of the threefold world, by understanding this, are equal to the Buddha. They will achieve through non-striving the Reality which [others] zealously seek.

The pristine awareness of the mind of perfect purity, coming forth as teachers in the manifestation of [the element] 'sky' do not teach words or letters, but teach this lore through its actuation, so that one does not speculate on self and other as being [two] different [entities]. They teach a thinking of non-differentiation. All sentient beings of the threefold world will be instructed in this lore by their own actuation because of these evidences (i.e. the elements). In this way they ought to understand all.

Oh, all you sentient beings of this threefold world! Because I, the All-Creating Sovereign, have created you, you are My children and equal to Me. Because you are not second to Me, I am present in you. The five teachers related to My actuation teach that the five aspects of [My] nature are just one. As this One is Me, the All-Creating One, consequently, you ought to have confidence [in this truth].

Oh all you sentient beings of this threefold world, if I were not, you would be non-existent. If there was a time where you did not exist, the five teachers would not come forth. Also the non-speculative lore would not be taught."

Such She spoke.

This is the twenty-fifth chapter of *The Ten Teachings on the Deedless Perfection,* in which the coming forth of one's own mind as teacher [is covered].

26

{cont'd p. 82} Then the All-Creating Sovereign, mind of perfect purity, gave the assurance that the unborn, the mind of perfect purity [will appear] as teacher as a sign of the teacher originating from the five great elements, which come forth from the mind.

"Oh great bodhisattva, listen! The mind of perfect purity, which is beyond thinking and inexplicable, is much praised by others as it became a lamp for the teachers. As it became the central vigor of [all] things it is Manjushrî himself. It dwells in the self-perfected bliss which is deedless and self-perfected. It became the ground of an ocean of [diverse] religious practices, such as morals, etc., and it is taught to be the path of whatever form of liberation. It became the mother of the *tathâgata,* and likewise the path of all [*tathâgata*].

If [this mind of perfect purity] was not, nothing would originate, therefore I am the best path of liberation. It is a path, subtle and difficult to understand, which is non-speculative and beyond thinking. It is non-existent (*mi gnas*), imperceptible, and non-conceptual (*spros med*), it is free of all thinking. It cannot be captured in words, free of form and colour, it is not an object of the sense faculties. It is firm, difficult to comprehend, and totally inexplicable.

Those who enter upon the path of the previous sages will be caught by a sickness, that is a path attached to meditation. When they consider this path to lead towards the goal in accord with Buddha's word, they are following a sequence of speculations and are similar to those who pursue a mirage.

The truly pure path cannot be pointed out in words. To teach it as the truly pure in itself makes Me obscured: the pure and the impure are not two [different entities] but like an amalgam. Also, pristine awareness and ignorance are not at all to be distinguished. One should be free of all these thoughts such as [the All-Creating Sovereign] is like a lamp which illuminates from the primordial. [The inexplicable mind of perfect purity which transcends all thought] dwells as the master of meditation [covered by] the fog of being unagitated by its very nature. {p. 83} It is the eye which sees directly, but does not see due to the direct seeing. Therefore it is called the eye of the omniscient one. It is a natural knowledge, broad and without boundaries or a centre. It dwells as the mastery of balance that neither acquires nor rejects. It is like an amalgam whereby the mind and its karmic inheritance (*bag chags*) are not two [different entities]. All the existent things which are cognized due to perception, are neither rejected nor abandoned as they appear as a beautification of Herself. One rejoices in them due to a method of not-at-all thinking. One reaches the mastery of balance by dwelling in this truly pure path of the five obscurations (*klesha*) and the five limitless offenses—things which are abandoned by everybody because they are in disagreement.[70]

One should not give up everything like women, etc. When one places the two meanings of the transmittance (*lo rgyus*) on a valid cognition (*tshad ma'i blo*) one will proceed towards the goal of achievements after stabilizing the three samâdhi. This is called a deviation from the lore of non-striving, and it obscures [the mind]. [This mind of perfect purity] dwells in the bliss of self-perfection which is totally perfected and deedless. This is the central vigor of the great self-originated pristine awareness which is free of all designations, non-agitated and unchanging. It has overcome the ill of striving with the nectar of having achieved eternal perfection (*zin pa*).[71] It dwells just like that in the objects which have been eternally perfected with regard to doing and striving.

Oh great bodhisattva, listen! As all things are the own being of the perfect and pure mind, they are the great empty circle (*thig le chen po*). Therefore they are neither conceptual (*spros med*) nor encompassed, neither born nor ceased. [This pristine awareness] dwells just like that and cannot be deprived. This central vigor of non-thinking abides from the primordial like the sky in total transcendence of thinking and articulating such reflections."

{p. 84} Such She spoke.

This is the twenty-sixth chapter of *The Ten Teachings on the Deedless Perfection*, in [which is explained] that the deedless perfection is not to be contemplated.

27

{cont'd p. 84} Then the All-Creating Sovereign, mind of perfect purity, gradually taught the great lore in accord with Her own instruction.

"Oh great bodhisattva, listen! As all things have come forth from Me, all things, which appear just like that, are taught to be from the primordial within the dimension of the very pure. The dimension of Reality consists from the primordial in all the inner (i.e. animated) and outer (i.e. inanimated) things. Because the Buddhas and the sentient beings are not different as to their field of perception, which is pure from the primordial, how then could one attempt to alter that through antidote and [following] a path? If one does not wish to stir with vehement actions the unachievable, then this is the point earlier made about the deedless and spontaneously self-perfected.

To what end should the dimension of Reality, where reflection and the pure are not two, be enticed by the habits of ordinary people [characterized by] wrong reflections? It is not different from the earlier explained great path even if one calls it an erroneous path by confusing the habits of the sentient beings with the non-dual great bliss. For this reason, and because [the follower of Atiyoga] knows balance, [this person] will be the lord of the Buddhas. To speculate on the I and the mine is the wrong path of the unbelievers. Enticed by ordinary people you may feel compelled to enter a path of speculating on the practice of religion, although there is no path on which to proceed, and no time [appropriate] for speculation. How could one find Reality by searching for a thing! Certainly, through such speculations you will seize a wrong path and you will rely on a teaching of a monkey-like *acârya* who lacks valid cognition. {p. 85} Instead it is suitable to pay a limitless price for a treasure of jewels that is an *acârya* with authentic teachings, as this is like applying a certain salt[72] to gold."[73]

Such She spoke.

This is the twenty-seventh chapter of *The Ten Teachings on the Deedless Perfection*, in which the lore of the dimension of deedless purity is explained.

28

{cont'd p. 85} Then the All-Creating Sovereign, mind of perfect purity, talked about Her own nature as immutable.

"Oh great bodhisattva, listen! My own being is within the dimension of the immutable. My pristine awareness is immutable like the sky. My Reality is of immutable nature. My mind is the immutable central vigor of all things. Likewise, everything is immutable but the teachers in their three manifestations, although emanating from Me, they teach through their embodiments a doctrine which defines things as causes and results. [Thereby] they make [their followers] to renounce the sensory objects with their senses.

I do not teach those sentient beings who embrace [the idea] of the five obscurations to be conditions for their own existence that there is a self-originated Reality. If one taught 'the evil life forms are a great offense', and that one should give up the offenses [committed] through body, speech, and mind by engaging in the ten precepts, for many eons [such a person] will not meet the self-originated pristine awareness because he or she would exercise acquiring and rejecting with regard to the self-originated Reality.

Listen, oh great bodhisattva! If I taught the host of retinues, although they are [My] manifestations and united in Me, to renounce the things through the five self-originated pristine awarenesses, to give up and to subdue them like enemies through the five awarenesses, the [retinues] will not recognize that these five enemies (i.e. the sensory objects) are the self-originated pristine awarenesses. But I do not teach to give up one's own mind.

{p. 86} Oh great bodhisattva, listen! If one claims that the results stem from causes and if one applies ultimate and conventional truths as two [separate] concepts to Reality which comes from one's own mind, and if one continues to do that for three eons, one will not be able to change one's self through vows and [the performance of] the ten perfections (*pâramitâ*). I do not teach that the mind in itself is mutable.

Oh great bodhisattva, listen! [Some] hope to gain supranormal abilities (*siddhi*) [from the deity they propitiate] by being blessed with a samâdhi of the Reality of one's own mind, by purging with purification rites [the mind which is] like the moon in the water, and by visualizing the lord (i.e. one's chosen tutelary deity) and making offerings to please the [god]. But [these people] will not cognize their own mind because[74] it is not like the moon in the water. Therefore I am not teaching that within the duration of seven lives the self-originated pristine awareness will not exist.

Listen, oh great bodhisattva! Those who meditate upon the blessed wonders of their own mind, may hope to be bestowed with whatever supranormal abilities they wish for themselves because of the friendship and accord between the [visualized] deities[75] and themselves as meditators. But, for three lifespans, they will not meet their own mind of the deedless which cannot be obtained by desiring the self-originated Reality. Such [lore] I, All-Creating [Sovereign], do not teach.

Oh great bodhisattva, listen! By transfiguring Reality which originates from itself into a deity, by [performing] the four seals,[76] and by emitting and condensing the sacred mantras[77] they achieve only to make the immutable Reality change. To think that one can obtain [reality] by virtue of [performing] a samâdhi of the mind, and that thereby anything will be obtained—such, I do not teach.

Listen, oh great bodhisattva! I do not teach that the dimension of Reality is mutable because as the dimension is the ground, it is immutable. The three manifestations, in subjugating the dimension [of Reality], {p. 87} teach their own retinues a samâdhi of seeking calm abiding (*samatha*). Thereby they are teaching a doctrine in need of interpretation.[78] Likewise, the immutable sky, this sky in itself, cannot be altered through the sky. Likewise, the immutable Reality, this very Reality, cannot be altered through any thing. Likewise, the immutable mind, this very mind in itself, cannot be realized through one's own mind. This would be a meditation making the immutable change. To place one's hope in pledges (*pranidhâna*) and the duration in carrying out a *samâdhi* fixated by the time, this is exasperating. Such is not taught by Me, the All-Creating [Sovereign]."

Such She spoke.

This is the twenty-eighth chapter of *The All-Creating Sovereign, Mind of Perfect Purity,* in which the deedless perfection is explained as immutable, and not to be found through striving.

29

{cont'd p. 87} Then the All-Creating Sovereign, mind of perfect purity, talked about the mind resting in balance.

"Oh great bodhisattva, listen! I, the All-Creating Sovereign, mind of perfect purity,—all things are Me. From the primordial, My entire nature is resting in balance.

It is taught that My own being should be known as of five aspects (*rang bzhin rnam pa lnga*): teacher, teaching, retinue, place, and time. These five aspects are poised in My own being. But the teachers' own being also rests therein. In their truth manifestations, they rest in genuine balance and are poised as My own being. In the manifestation of joy, they rest in the genuine actuation, and are poised as My own being. In their corporeal manifestations, they rest in genuine compassion, and are poised in My own being. {p.88} The self-originated pristine awareness is poised. Place is where anything is put in place; this also rests in balance. Time is the time which combines past with future. Being in balance is associated with time.

Oh great bodhisattva, listen! The totally perfected has five aspects. There is not anything else called 'thing' besides what rests in genuine balance. Oh great bodhisattva! It is also not said that there is even one thing which is not encompassed in the totality of the perfected. Oh, because everything is poised in Me, all things are liberated in their Reality. The teachers are liberated in genuine Reality. The teaching is liberated in genuine Reality. Also the retinues are liberated in genuine Reality.

Oh you, who accept that all things are liberated, do not falsify your own body by contemplating [upon it as] a deity! Do not falsify spoken words or speeches. Do not practise samâdhi so that you don't falsify the mind! By falsifying one will not attain the state of balance, and by not being in balance one will not be liberated.[79] Without liberation one will not attain identity with Reality.

Oh great bodhisattva, it is like this: the All-Creating Sovereign, mind of perfect purity, rests from the primordial in a state of balance and transcendence, but the [followers of] various doctrinal views do not know how to rest in balance. The great perfected, the All-Creating One, rests from the primordial in balance, but if the hearers and solitary awakened ones hear or learn about it, they would say 'this produces poison', and they will abandon their own mind [by assuming it] constitutes an obstruction. They will also not know how to poise the doctrinal views, and they remain for many eons not knowing how to be poised.

{p.89} If [the followers of] the Mahâyâna-sûtras hear about the Great Perfection, they will not understand the suchness of their own mind. Likewise, they will not know how to rest in balance. They will continue for three eons [to think that they] progress by cleansing.

If the followers of yoga (the first level of the four) hear [about the Great Perfection] they will not understand that all things which appear just like that are the suchness of their own mind, and they will not know how to rest in balance. They will continue for seven life-spans to sanctify their mind by [practising] the limbs of bodhicitta and various miracles (*cho 'phrul*).

If [the followers of] the Mahâyoga hear about it, they will try to achieve through striving something new, although it is from the primordial, as they are [in accord with] the nature of causation. For 2,600 [years] they will not know how to rest in balance, and they will remain at the stage of the three samâdhi.

If the followers of Anuyoga hear about it, they will apply such designations as causation to what exists from the primordial. Likewise, they will not know how to rest in balance. As cause they [want to] achieve the dimension of pure Reality, and, as result, the mandala of pure pristine awareness. Uninterrupted they remain like this for one lifetime.

If the followers of Atiyoga hear about it, they will abide in the realm of Buddha from the primordial. They will gain the deedless great bliss. As [they realize that] there is nothing to achieve, thereby they will gain buddhahood.

Sentient beings, either humans or gods, are not of the same mental abilities. Some use their abilities, but only partially. Some also [know] that their abilities are definitive from the primordial. {p. 90} Therefore there is a reason [to teach these people,] and I am teaching [this lore]. The Great Perfection of Atiyoga is [to understand] like this: *'ati'* will be explained by the letter: *'a'* is the unborn Reality which is poised. *'Ti'* is explained as the non-striving self-perfected. Those who claim that the Great Perfection of Atiyoga is connected with causation will not reach the goal of understanding the Great Perfection. Those who claim that the ultimate and the conventional are two entities, use words of praise and dispraise. For this reason, they will not understand what is the non-dual. But the understanding of all the Buddhas of the three times is such that it does not see a duality, that it rests in balance, and understands oneness."

Such She spoke.

This is the twenty-ninth chapter of *The All-Creating Sovereign, Mind of Perfect Purity,* in which the mind resting in balance is covered.

30

Then the All-Creating Sovereign, mind of perfect purity, expounded to rDo-rje sems-dpa', who is the central vigor of Herself, this talk which is like an imperishable banner of victory on the lore of Sems-dpa' rdo-rje's own being as the deedless perfection.

"Oh great bodhisattva, listen! I shall explain your own being to yourself. Your self is Me, the All-Creating [Sovereign]. From the primordial, I am the mind of perfect purity.

The mind of perfect purity is like this: It[80] is, oh rDo-rje sems-dpa', like the big sky; it is All Good (Kun-tu bzang-po, Samantabhadra),[81] broad, the dimension of Reality. This all-pure, great path is unproduced, unobstructed, and inconceivable as it liberates all [sentient beings]. To actualize its final purpose, love should not be practised as great compassion. {p. 91} This greatness (i.e. the mind of perfect purity) does not praise any good qualities of this profound greatness. Its final purpose is unagitated in itself. It is liberated through a deedless liberation. As the self-originated pristine awareness is free of striving, it has been liberated, and is thus taught as path of liberation.

The elements are the Victorious One (Bhagavan) who abides in the nature of all beings. Even what is called wrong is nothing else but the liberated, self-originated [awareness]. To achieve this great awareness, which is so difficult to obtain, by relying on wisdom and skill-in-means,[82] is nothing but words saying to rely on others, while the true bliss arises from one's own [mind].

The great wonders are not difficult [to see]. Through subtleness the understanding of suchness as to all good qualities and forces immediately arises from its own. This non-apparent Reality is to be contemplated not by means of searching for it, but by leaving it. If one searches for it therein, its suchness will not arise from it. The most secret Reality cannot be heard by anything, how then by the ear faculty? Likewise, the faculty of the tongue cannot at all proclaim it.[83]

By perfectly understanding the beings' suffering as mind of perfect purity, one dwells in joy. One will not be upset by it, but dwell in balance, just like the horizon of the sky. Although the particularities are identical, some may still say 'it is due to karma'. If one is under the influence of such karma thinking, one will not be in the self-originated pristine awareness. The causes are the same as the conditions for the immutable (literally diamond), and therefore what is unborn is imperishable. One will not advance to the dimension of Reality by striving for the [mind of] perfect purity, which is the vigor [of the universe] from the primordial. A contemplation of the great good qualities cannot be achieved through contemplating them by means of contemplation itself.[84]

From intuitive insight (*rnam rtog nyid*) arises pristine awareness as to its Reality which is unthinkable, and not to be practised. This is called the subtle door. If the mind searches for the path of solitude, one grasps the solitude amidst the wilderness. If one reflects, one should contemplate the process of reflecting.[85] Applying designations like 'cause' and 'result'[implies] a cleansing of both, virtues and offenses. Who says 'I want to leave this world' will generate an eagerness for acquiring and rejecting. Attachment and detachment are a path of [mere] words and, similar to the Middle Path, they are like an echo. But the lord of all beings explained to the sentient beings (*sems dpa'*) that happiness and suffering have the same cause. Also from attachment, hatred, and ignorance, the great path of perfected purity stems. [The lord of all beings] also said that the five good aspects of habits are an adornment of the dimension of Reality.[86]

The intuitive understanding of the sky is unborn, and this intuition is like the sky. From pledges, detached [and unselfish like] the sky, a self-fulfillment comes [as great as] the sky.[87] The truth manifestation in its [state of] sameness and non-reflecting is like the moon in the water, which cannot be grasped like an object.

The profound [system] of vowels and and consonants is taught as a play of All-Good (Samantabhadra). There, the *A* is adorned with *TA* and *PA* radiating [light] from their parts.[88] The profound teaching of the Buddha arises as a field of sensory activity of the entire world.[89]

Emaho! The field of Buddha's sensory activity is not a place which can be gained through zealous striving, and as it is not an object of the six sensory perceptions. [A person attempting to gain it through zeal] is like a blind person pursuing the sky. A path which is more and more holy (according to the progress made) is not in accord with the lore of the deedless.

{p. 93} But if one proceeds on this path, one cannot reach [its destination] like [one cannot reach] the end of the sky. Likewise, because That[90] is like such: That is taught to them (i.e. the retinues) so that they will obtain That. Because That is the central vigor of That, That comes forth from That—o great wonder! That of the past, That of the present—likewise great in its being placed in That. That likewise is also the path to That. That is That's very nature. Like this, all the paths rely on a support which comes from the moon.[91]

As all is this balance one will not achieve anything by looking only into one direction. Like [to distinguish between] present bliss and future bliss, apparent [bliss] and concealed [bliss] is also a fault on which one should not rely. The three times are one; there are no particularities, they arise from the primordial not as past or future. As the truth manifestation encompasses [all], it is one, and therefore rests in the greatness of the great. Also the religious practice [done] in the threefold world is just a name and appears as illusion. Even a great place [created and ruled] by a universal monarch (*cakravartin*) is [just] a place of [another] illusionary practice. Those who rely on the time factor for their practice will not achieve [their goal] within that time. If one practises free of any desires, this is declared an empty sign in itself. As [the ultimate] is one, there are no particularities whatsoever. Thus the yogi abides like in the sky, the birds' pathway.

How could all things be, if one makes false claims about the central vigor [of all things] which is unoriginated and unborn? Both, outside and inside, are the inside of the outside itself. The parts of the profound are not the object of cognition. The mere word 'existence' gives a wrong thrust because it lacks the balance of meditation. {p. 94}

As to applying such designations as outer and inner [to the pristine awareness, you ought to know that] it equally dwells in the nature of the five aggregates and the sensory fields. [But] it is improper to apply any name or designation to it as it is inseparable from the three times. Its inagility is the seal of the manifestations; its unwavering [nature] is pristine awareness. As it cannot be appropriated, it is of no-self. It cannot be abandoned, is without verbalization (*tshig med*). It is balance.

What, by what, and in what comes forth—although all retinues and all forms of behaviour come from itself (i.e. pristine awareness)—to call it woman or man—such is not at all taught by the sovereign of balance.[92] There is no place to apply to it such names as penance and fear.

If one joins the *A* with the *PA* one wishes to bring forth [what is truly known as] the bliss of illusion. As the nature is surely not simple it may appear according to one's views.

As to a bliss whose appearance is desired by a striving mind it is a great fault and an obscuration of It (pristine awareness). [To claim] that meditating on the appearance [of a deity] is the door to all the aspects of enlightenment (*byang chub yan lag*) is like [reaching] for the moon in the water. Such meditation is like a child's playground, although [by its nature even such meditation] arises undefiled and detached. Even if one assumes the form of a great lord of wrath by appearing with frowned forehead in the middle of a mandala, and if one lets come forth the letters [of the mantra], one will not realize the calm in itself.

It is taught that by being under the power of obscuration (*klesha*) a person will not be subdued by it, even if he or she cuts off the tip of the palm tree and burns the seed in the fire.[93] Even by a hundred thousand times practising whatever [one wishes to do] only the flower will arise.[94]

Due to the lack of defining characteristics (*mtshan ma med pa*) nothing will come forth from any source. {p.95} The yogis who dwell free of words[95] are of good fortune. As they do not distinguish between what is of purpose for themselves or for others, they rejoice in a goal of bliss which is an illusion.[96] Without a remainder they are fully perfected. Immutable they dwell firmly. The limitations of [these yogis] are equal to those of the sky.

There is not one thing which is dependent on another. This great self-perfected bliss will intuitively be understood by the strength of the self which is incomparable pristine awareness. Because of that, things do not originate from anything else.

This is difficult [to understand] because it is easy, yet in its easiness it is difficult. It is not apparent, yet encompasses all. By teaching [about it] That becomes a mere name, oh rDo-rje sems-dpa'. One cannot point at That. This miraculous and wonderful joy rests like the sky in the deedless. If you do not perceive That as being different from ignorance, instantly, That comes forth by itself. This is the path where all is equal; it rests as nature in all beings. Because of the fault [stemming] from mingling with a child, it is like the medicine searching for the physician.[97] The goal of intuitive understanding is the great bliss.

This is the pure world where the light of the cardinal directions gathers. Therefore the four cardinal directions, the intermediary directions, zenith and nadir, are perfected. From a rainbow oscillating in [different] colors, the [Buddha] families become apparent. At the same time [this pure world] is greater than the five elements with their atoms moving in their immobility. It is not placed on such designations as past, present, and future. By cognizing It as free of beginning and cessation, Itself rests in the three times in their great form (i.e. time in its timelessness).

Due to balance there is no gradual [progress]. {p.96} Because of Its oneness, It is free of wishing for particularities. Although in Its ornamenting the accumulations [constituting this universe] It is spread out, by resting in Its nature It is not scattered. There is nothing to be desired because It is perfect. It is nectar—pure from the primordial. It cannot be grasped by a special way of thinking (*lhag pa'i bsam pa*), particularly not by the twelve [limbs] of decreasing and increasing. It is the lord of good qualities because It thinks through the individual mind (*yid*). The viewing scatters the accumulation. By seeing It one will be perfected in balance as to the supranormal abilities. By grasping It for a short period and being united with It, joy will be generated—this is the vow. One makes an offering by unified oneness because one takes joy in skill-in-means [like] in a dance performance. By letting go the non-appropriating (*mi gzungs*), this is the 'throwing' (*gtor ma*) [of the sacrificial cakes].

The ritual acts will remove, without any doing, the obstacles of the non-speculative pristine awareness, and the mantric words are unspoken and poised. Even if all meritorious [acts] such as *gurupûja* and generosity are not done with a detached and non-agitated attitude, their performance will become a great fetter. Therefore this lore will become an obscuration for so many as they mix it with that [zeal]. If one understands this in this (i.e. the right) way then there is nothing with regard to That that is to be achieved."[98]

Such She spoke.

This is the thirtieth chapter of *The All-Creating Sovereign, Mind of Perfect Purity,* which is "the indestructible nature of rDo-rje sems-dpa' as a banner of victory."[99]

31

{Cont'd p.96} Then the All-Creating Sovereign, mind of perfect purity, spoke about the All-Creating One's nature—the deedless, consummate, and spontaneously self-perfected.[100]

{p. 97} "Oh great bodhisattva, listen! [My] own being [even] in its variety is not two, but also each part in itself is not to conceptualizable (*spros bral*).

Although they may not understand [things] in their suchness, they ought to give up the sickness of striving because whatever is made to appear is all good and thus consummate (*zin pa*).[101] Then they will be poised in balance by abiding in the spontaneously self-perfected."

Such She spoke.

This is the thirty-first chapter of *The All-Creating Sovereign, Mind of Perfect Purity,* i.e. the Six Vajra Verses.

32

{Cont'd p. 97} Then the All-Creating Sovereign, mind of perfect purity, taught Sems-dpa' rdo-rje this chapter of four definitive statements about the lore of the deedless as realization of the quintessence.

"Oh great bodhisattva, you ought to understand the quintessence in this way: Whatever appears is one in its suchness. It cannot be falsified by anyone. The sovereign of unconceptualized sameness dwells in the spirit (*dgongs pa*) of the truth manifestation which cannot be cognized."

Such She spoke.

This is the thirty-second chapter of *The All-Creating Sovereign, Mind of Perfect Purity,* i.e. the four definitive statements.

33

{Cont'd p. 97} Then the All-Creating Sovereign, mind of perfect purity, taught about the difficulties of understanding Her nature as the self-originated pristine awareness which, like a sovereign, makes all things intelligible. But also this Sems-dpa' rdo-rje is called the pristine awareness in terms of his intellectuality as Reality which stems from Her (i.e. the All-Creating One).

"Oh great bodhisattva, grasp these words with your mental capacity (*yid kyi dbang po*). These words let you understand the quintessence. If the place (*gnas*) of all is the dimension of Reality, {p. 98} how then can the quintessence of the word 'dimension' (*dbyings*) be understood (*rig par byed*)? If the object of all views is the realm of the sky, how then can the quintessence of the word 'sky' be understood? If the five elements are apparent in their luminous nature, how can the quintessence of 'apparent' be understood? How can the quintessence of the sentient beings in this threefold world, who have originated from these [elements], be understood? Listen to Me, because you yourself are the sovereign of intelligence (*rig pa'i rgyal po*)!"

Such She spoke.

[Sems-dpa' rdo-rje:]

"Oh teacher of the teachers, All-Creating Sovereign, I understand Your own being which is so difficult to understand in terms of these four words: (1) I understand [Your own being] as not diversified because of the word 'dimension.' (2) I clearly understand that it is without obscuration because of the word 'sky.' (3) I understand it to be the central vigor of all [things] because of the word 'element.' (4) I understand it to be the quintessence [of the universe] because of the word 'sentient being'. By understanding this [situation], I do understand that [You] create all, [a fact] so hard to recognize. It is not taught that there is anything else than the All-Creating One Herself."

Such he spoke.

Then the All-Creating Sovereign again addressed the sovereign of intelligence:

"If you understand My nature, which is so difficult to grasp, then you will understand the buddha-dharma in its abbreviation and in its extensions. Who could otherwise be called 'sovereign of intelligence'?

[Sems-dpa' rdo-rje:]

"Oh creating sovereign, All-Creating [Sovereign], mind of perfect purity, Your own being is like that: it is Reality, mind, and primordial awareness, and the intelligibility of Reality. This is how I see Your own being. The word Reality is [another] word for the nonconceptual mind itself. [The word] realm of the sky is [another] word for the mind itself in its stainlessness. The word essential element (*snying po 'byung ba*) is [another word for] the mind's own actuation. The mind of the sentient beings is an intelligence which understands distinctiveness (*so sor rtogs pa*). {p. 99} Nothing exists besides the mind's own being; nothing is besides the mind—the All-Creating Sovereign."

Such he spoke.

[All Creating Sovereign:]

"Oh great bodhisattva, if you understand this nature you will also understand My, the All-Creating's, own being. You understand

Me, understand the one, understand all, understand everything! Oh, great bodhisattva rDo-rje, I shall give you the name Sovereign of Intelligence (*rig pa'i rgyal po*). If you, oh Sovereign of Intelligence, understand it this way, how then do you understand these things: that the vehicles, which are taught by the teacher's three forms of manifestations, who emanated from Me, come forth in three aspects, and that whoever has the three [kinds of] wishes for [obtaining] results from causes will achieve the three results (i.e. the three forms of nirvana) by means of performing the different activities [related with] doctrinal views and religious practice?"

Such She spoke.

The Sovereign of Intelligence replied:

"Oh All-Creating Sovereign, the teachers' three forms of manifestation emanate from You as Your threefold actuation.[102] In an enigmatic way (*ldem dgongs*) You taught these three teachings as three aspects and as the mind being of discriminative intelligence. With what intention did You teach in such enigmatic manner? Is it because of the intention to strive for calm abiding in non-agitation? In an enigmatic way you introduced us to whatever subjects [You felt] appropriate. The teachers' three forms of manifestation taught [the doctrine] as a teaching that requires interpretation (*drang lung*). Some of them taught the result [coming from practising] the bodhisattva stages and the paths, some that the result is without substance, like the moon in water, and some that the result is the achieving in itself. The teaching of the three forms of manifestation is declared to be an enigmatic teaching; it is taught not to be a definitive lore but one that demands interpretation. It has a meditation [system] which zealously strives for a non-agitated calm abiding (*mi 'phro zhi gnas*). {p. 100} The Mahâyâna of causation is taught to be a system in need of interpretation."

Such he spoke.

[All-Creating Sovereign:]

"Listen, oh Sovereign of Intelligence, you great bodhisattva! The ultimate is taught to be of a definitve [meaning]. You, Sovereign of Intelligence, understand this, or don't teach! There is no point in manipulating (*bya ba'i yul*) what is perceived, as it is non-existent (*mi gnas*). The true nature which is non-intelligible and transcends intelligibility is neither an object of *samâdhi* nor of non-contemplative thinking. It is not a desiring mind, and not a coveted result. It abides in [a state of] as-it-is, free of intelligibility. This leads to buddhahood via a path which cannot be walked on. Do not engage in intellectualizing, and you will find the self-originated pristine awareness. Do not seek salutary acts, as nature is spontaneously self-perfected (*lhun gyis grub*).[103] Do not observe the vows as the true nature is entirely pure. Objects and sensory faculties are lucent in their suchness.[104] Do not regard the Buddha and the sentient beings as being two [different entities]. You ought to view everything as one in suchness. Suchness is one, and not many. How could one apply designations, like giving praise, to the central vigor of the immutable and unborn?"

"Oh great bodhisattva, Sovereign of Intelligence! Buddhas, sentient beings, what appears and exists as animated and inanimated world—all this is as My nature, i.e. that of the All-Creating, [and] free of praise and dispraise. My own being and suchness are one, but the teachers' three forms of manifestation nevertheless teach their individual teachings, in which they teach a doctrine of suchness that requires interpretation."

Such She spoke.

This is the thirty-third chapter of *The All-Creating Sovereign, Mind of Perfect Purity,* in which is explained the definitive teaching and the teaching that needs interpretation.

34

{p. 101} Then the All-Creating Sovereign, mind of perfect purity, proclaimed this sutra on Herself as the integration of the intentions of all Buddhas.

"Oh Sovereign of Understanding (*rtogs pa'i rgyal po*) listen to these words! I, the All-Creating Sovereign, integrate in Me the quintessence (*yul*) of the intentions of all the Buddhas [existing] in the three times. In this, i.e. My own being, their manifestations are integrated, their teachings are integrated, their intentions are integrated. Listen to My word on integrating [the Buddhas'] intentions."

Such She spoke.

[Great bodhisattva:]

"Oh teacher, All-Creating Sovereign, is it that in You the intentions of the truth and joy manifestations, of Samantabhadra, Vajrasattva, Vipashyin, Ushnisha, etc. up to the seventh [Buddha] Shâkyamuni, and those of the 1,022 Buddhas, the truly perfected ones, numberless like atoms, are integrated?"

Such he asked.

Then the All-Creating Sovereign said:

"So it is. Oh Sovereign of Understanding, listen now!"

[Great bodhisattva:] "Ho ho, yes, so it is."

[All-Creating Sovereign:]

"I shall teach you the essentials of integrating [the Buddhas'] intentions with regard to simile (*dpe*), quintessence (*don*), and characteristics (*rtags*).[105] My own being is like the sky. The quintessence of Me is Reality. My actuation is the mind of perfect purity. (The explanation of simile:) Oh, I am without obscuration, but unknowable (*mi rtog pa*). The unknowable is the sky[-like] truth manifestation. I am not to be known, and there is no acquiring or rejecting. As there is no acquiring or rejecting, [I am] like the sky. Like the sky which is without acquiring and rejecting so is All-Good (Samantabhadra) without acquiring and rejecting. What is free of acquiring and rejecting is integrated in Me.

Oh great bodhisattva, listen! Oh, I am unborn like the sky. Like the unborn sky, the diamond mind is unborn. {p.102} What has the intention of the unborn, that is integrated in Me. Also all the perfected Buddhas, like Vipashyin and Shâkyamuni, the seventh one, the 1,022 [Buddhas] and all the numberless and perfected [other Buddhas]—their intention is of the sky's nature: unborn, unknowable, without acquiring and rejecting. By means of a simile, I taught how [everything] is integrated in Me.

(The explanation of quintessence:) Oh great bodhisattva, listen now to how the quintessence of the intention of all the Buddhas who have previously taught is integrated [in Me]: It is taught that the unborn Reality is integrated [in Me] because all Buddhas are unborn, likewise the teaching is unborn and so is the All-Creating One's own being. The explanation of what is integrated:[106] As to the All Creating Sovereign's own being, Reality is unobstructed. Likewise, the Buddhas who have taught in the past, are unobstructed with regard to Reality. Therefore it is taught that [the Buddhas] are integrated [in Me] because of Reality [which permeates everything].

(The explanation of characteristics:) Oh great bodhisattva, listen! The explanation of [the Buddhas] being integrated by virtue of their characteristic: As to the characteristic—the perfectly pure mind is the characteristic of all. By virtue of the All-Creating Sovereign's mind, the truth manifestation and Samantabhadra, Vajrasattva, etc. and all the Buddhas of the three times, without exception, are integrated in [My] mind because of their essential characteristic. Therefore [this is known as] the integrating due to the three categories of simile, quintessence, [and characteristic].

In Me, the All-Creating Sovereign, the general things are integrated, the intention is integrated, and the one who cultivates the intention is integrated. The general integrates simile, quintessence, and characteristic as integrals. The distinct encompasses five integral aspects: (1) the intention of the truth manifestation is integrated [in Me]. [The truth manifestation] has the ability to send forth the wonder of immutability, and is integrated because of its non-speculative [nature] and its sameness. (2) The intention of the joy manifestation is integrated [in Me]. {p.103} It is integrated because it bestows the fullness of all desires and makes the nature apparent. (3) The intention of All-Good (Samantabhadra) is integrated because of the ability to make the All-Creating Sovereign evident in so far as all existing things are neither good nor bad, neither to be acquired nor rejected. (4) The intention of the Immutable Being (Vajrasattva) is integrated as it subsumes the unborn, unobstructed intention. (5) The seventh [Buddha, i.e.] Shâkyamuni and the [other] 1,022 [Buddhas], numberless like the atoms [in the universe], and their individual form, utterance, and spirit carry out their purpose; but also from their form, utterance, and spirit come forth the Reality of form, utterance, and spirit which is the way of fulfilling the purpose of form, utterance, and spirit. These are also integrated in the All-Creating Herself.

In the palace of the dimension of Reality (*dharmadhâtu*) is not a single thing which is not integrated in Me. In the mansion of the sky's expanse is not a single thing which is not integrated in Me."

Such She spoke.

At this moment, Sems-dpa' rdo-rje was frightened and fainted. After he awoke from his swoon he asked:

"Oh great Sovereign who is integrating all! If all created things are integrated [in You], are then all non-created things also integrated, or all things which have not yet come forth? With regard to the dimension of Reality and the expanse of the sky, the unbelievers have a false view that both are eternal or transitory. If this is your unerring intention, how then are Buddhas and sentient beings [distinguished by] their names? What characterizes an unbeliever and what a Buddhist?"

Such he asked.

Then the All-Creating Sovereign, mind of perfect purity, the all-integrating sovereign declared:

"Oh great bodhisattva, listen! {p.104} If you, oh great bodhisattva, want to understand My own being and if you have confidence that all is also integrated [in Me] then it is unlikely that you do understand My own being. Because of the unlikeliness of understanding there is no confidence. You must understand the all-creating perfectly pure mind. If you have understood the all-creating perfectly pure mind then the limitations of eternity and transitoriness will shine forth due to the certainty [obtained] as to the self-originated mind of perfect purity. As it is unborn and free of [such concepts as] object and subject, the limitations of an 'eternal substance' will shine forth, and because the self-originated pristine awareness is immutable , the limitation of transient non-existence will shine forth.

'Mu' (i.e. the first part of the Tibetan word *mu stegs,* unbelievers) is for the dimension of Reality, and *'stegs'* for the place of knowing. Who sees the Buddhas and the sentient beings as different will not see the All-Creating Sovereign, mind of perfect purity."

Such She spoke.

This is the thirty-fourth chapter of *The All-Creating Sovereign, Mind of Perfect Purity,* on the lore of integrating [the Buddhas'] intention.

35

Then the All-Creating Sovereign, mind of perfect purity, gave this central tractate on the Great Perfection which is not a place to practice anything else than Her own teaching, and She taught that it is beyond striving and achieving and causation.

"Oh great bodhisattva, this, My own being, is difficult [to grasp]. Entrance [to the Buddhist path], doctrinal views, vows, salutary deeds, progress on the path, stages of accomplishment, pristine awareness, and Reality—these eight topics are not in accord with doctrine and practice of any other vehicle of the five [taught by] the three manifestations.

'Entrance': one enters through the door of non-striving;

'Doctrinal views': [I am] teaching [them] as not to be contemplated;

'Vows': [I am] teaching [them] as not to be observed;

'Salutary deeds': [I am] teaching [them] as not to be sought; {p. 105}

'Path': [I am] teaching that there is no path to be proceeded on;

'Stages of accomplishment' (*bhûmi*):[107] [I am] teaching not to practice them;

'Pristine awareness': it is non-speculative (*mi rtogs*) and immovable;

'Reality': [the state] of as-it-is which is unaltered (*bcos su med*).

Oh great bodhisattva! If these essential points are expounded to the followers of the vehicle of causation, the people will [still] say that the world is the cause and the Dharma the result, and likewise the results come from causes, and that the cause consists in the acts achieved by the sentient beings in the threefold world, while the result consists in the Buddhas of the three times whose appearance the people so much desire. By making the [study of] doctrinal views and [the performance of] meditation a cause, they aspire to achieve the result of their meditations. But by means of such meditation, they will not obtain the result. Because all things exist just like that, what great fault is it then to alter what is like that by enticing the truth with lies! Once they have cut off the diversion [provided by] such sensory objects as zealously striving for doctrinal views, meditation, and vows, etc., and once they are guided by the right method, and once they have retreated into solitude, I teach them by means of a method of non-conceptual cognition and equipoise."

Such She spoke.

This is the thirty-fifth chapter of *The All-Creating Sovereign, Mind of Perfect Purity,* where the lore of the Great Perfection is explained.

36

Then the All-Creating Sovereign, mind of perfect purity, explained that the nature of all things is integrated in Her own form, utterance, and spirit.

"Oh great bodhisattva, know My own being like this: I am the own being of the mind of perfect purity; the mind of perfect purity is the All-Creating Sovereign. {p. 106} The All-Creating Sovereign's own being [unfolds into] form, utterance, and spirit, and there is not one thing not created by [My] form, utterance, and spirit. The Buddhas of the three times are created by [My] form, utterance, and spirit. But also the sentient beings of the threefold world as to their body, speech, and mind, are created by the All-Creating Sovereign's form, utterance, and spirit. Also the entirety of what exists and appears as animated and inanimated world in its unaltered Reality and likethatness is created by form, utterance, and spirit of Me, the All-Creating [Sovereign]."

Such She spoke.

Sems-dpa' rdo-rje again asked:

"Oh All-Creating Sovereign, sovereign of creation (*byed pa'i bdag po*)! Please explain the main point of ignorance (*ma rig*) and non-understanding (*ma rtogs*)! How was [the whole] created, this explain to me!"

Such he asked.

[All-Creating Sovereign:]

"Oh great bodhisattva, listen! The nature of My form, utterance, and spirit [produced all]. The form as the evidence of Reality created the wonder which Samantabhadra sports.[108] The utterance as the evidence of the words teaches the understanding of the essence of Reality through words. The spirit created the teacher as a lamp of pristine awareness because of the self-originated pristine awareness' ceaselessness.

The actuating essence as the focus of Reality is non-erring. Oh great bodhisattva, you ought to understand this essential point: besides whatever appears as animated and inanimated as it does, and besides Me actuating My form [utterance, and spirit], nothing else exists. I teach and explain through My own actuation. You, great bodhisattva, will teach others who have not yet understood [Reality].

Oh great bodhisattva, listen! The sounds of earth, water, fire, wind, sky, and the words of the six forms of sentient beings {p. 107} are nothing but My, the All-Creating Sovereign's utterance. You should apply an explanation uniting the letter of the words with their meaning. You, Sems-dpa' rdo-rje, will teach others who have not yet understood [Reality].

Oh great bodhisattva, listen! As to all the six forms of sentient beings living in this threefold world, the elements in their incomprehensible sameness and as to the unborn, incomprehensible, ceaseless Reality, nothing exists which is not in My spirit, that is, in that of the All-Creating Sovereign. You, Sems-dpa' rdo-rje, will teach others who have not yet understood [reality].

If you, great bodhisattva, don't teach them this lore it will be very difficult for them to know My own being. If it will not happen that they understand and meet Me,[109] then even all the representatives of the lineages of all the Buddhas of the three times, all the sentient beings living in this threefold world, those who crossed nine passes and nine valleys[110] [to arrive] at the tenth bodhisattva stage, and the representatives of such lineages as that of the three wisdom-holders, i.e. 'control of life', 'seal', and 'perfection', will for a long time not meet Me, the All-Creating [Sovereign]. If I, the All-Creating [Sovereign], am not met then all the six forms of sentient beings living in this threefold world will not understand their own being nor their own actuating force. The bodhisattvas dwelling on the tenth bodhisattva stage, even if they are waiting for three endless eons, they will not come to meet Me, the All-Creating [Sovereign]. Even the three wisdom-holders in control of the body (*lus la dbang bsgyur rigs 'dzin*) {p. 108} will not be able to know their own being. Even after their bodies assumed the appearance of the Buddha's manifestation of communal joy, they will not see that their own mental faculty is their own mind [of perfect purity]. Therefore they will not see that I, the All-Creating Sovereign and their own being are not different. As they don't see this, they are seized by a hopeless disease. For this reason, you must teach My own being."

Such She spoke.

This is the thirty-sixth chapter of *The All-Creating Sovereign, Mind of Perfect Purity,* in which is explained the integration [of all things] in [the All-Creating Sovereign's] form, utterance, and spirit.

37

{cont'd p. 108} Then the All-Creating Sovereign, mind of perfect purity, taught that the great and perfect Reality is not to be meditated upon.

"Oh, you great Sems-dpa' rdo-rje, and [you others],[111] the wisdom holders who dwell at a certain stage of accomplishment (*bhûmi*), the bodhisattvas who dwell at a certain *bhûmi,* and the sentient beings in this threefold world whose karma has matured, they all ought to understand not to meditate upon My own being, the Reality, the mind of perfect purity, [their] mind as Reality, because I, the All-Creating Sovereign, am for the good of all. Intuit that Reality, as mind cannot be contemplated upon.

But the teachers of causality, i.e. the three forms of the teachers' manifestation, will proclaim that this world, in accord with the fact that things and their aims [arise] as causes and results, comes into existence due to result stemming from cause, and although My own being as Reality is not to be meditated, they will teach their individual systems of meditation. When they say that all misery arises according to the four truths and that the bad forms of existence (*durgati*) are the cause for the arising of misery, they are about to abandon Reality, i.e. the mind of perfect purity. [They do so] despite the fact that Reality and the mind of perfect purity are one in their actuation. Thereby they don't see Reality and give it up. {p. 109} By progressing on the path through practising the ten stages of accomplishment—such as [considering] the ultimate and the conventional truth as different, [or carrying out] the ten perfections such as generosity and ethics—they will not see Reality, but stay on the level of practising, despite the fact that Reality is the actuation of the mind of perfect purity (called bodhicitta in the sutra system which is criticized here).

Although Reality is the actuation of the mind of perfect purity, they will bless with good words all things, which appear just like that, by virtue of the five enlightening insights and four wonders (*byang chub lnga dang cho 'phrul chen po bzhi*) at a time auspicious as to the position of planets and stars, and they will contemplate on [these things] as manifestation of a deity. Thereby they don't see that one's own mind is not to be contemplated. Although [all] things and the actuation of the perfectly pure mind are one, it will not happen that [they see] the nature of the apparent existence if they contemplate the aggregates in their diamond fashion which are a transfiguration of their (i.e. the practitioners') own personality as deities by engaging in the three *samâdhi* and five rituals by means of the four religious practices (*bsnyen bsgrub bzhi*). In their striving for achievement they degrade their own mind to a deity, and therefore they will not see their own mind in its deedlessness. As to Her own Reality, the All-Creating Sovereign, mind of perfect purity, the teacher of the teachers, does not teach the teachers' three forms of manifestation to meditate on their own mind which is liberated in its own Reality from the primordial. If one strives to achieve something through meditation, one's own mind is then abandoned."

Such She spoke.

"Oh great bodhisattva, if they desire to realize their own mind they do not dwell in the imperceptible balance because the realization happens only due to non-desiring. But those who abide in nature with regard to the objects which they neither want to acquire nor to abandon, and who abide by virtue of nature in the immovable nature, they will realize that the mind is the actuation of suchness, and they will realize suchness in all things. They ought not to alter suchness! {p. 110} They cannot realize anything else than the actuation in itself. They should not strive for anything because nature is [itself].[112] If they seek it they will not find it outside the dimension [of Reality]. They shall not disturb it by doing because it has been perfect since it was created. They shall not work on its realization because it has been always realized. They shall abide in balanced stillness (*mnyam pa*) and ought not to speculate nor think about it in any way.

Oh great bodhisattva, listen! Even the Buddhas of past generations did not strive for a lore other than that of their own mind. They did not alter suchness. They did not meditate by investigating *samâdhi*. Realization will come by not speculating on one's own mind. Where you now live and where you will go in the future, the imperceptible stillness will be realized."

Such She spoke.

This is the thirty-seventh chapter of *The All-Creating Sovereign, Mind of Perfect Purity,* in which the lore and sutra on no-meditation [is covered].

38

{Cont'd p. 110} Then the All-Creating Sovereign, mind of perfect purity, taught how the teaching of the retinues' teachers becomes an error and a fault.

"Oh great bodhisattva, listen! The three teachings of the three teachers [instructing] the retinues are erroneous and faulty. If you ask, how can that be? [I reply:] the six vehicles of obtaining [results] are an error as to the Great Perfection. If you ask how can that be? [I reply: the followers of] the bodhisattva sutras, in their desire for the [eleventh stage called] 'all light', assert that Reality is empty like the sky because they have examined it with the two truths, but as to the great bliss of Atiyoga, the mind of perfect purity is beyond such examination. These sutras are at fault with regard to transcending such examination. {p.111} In order to transcend such examination, the sutras are the wrong [instrument]. In order to understand and examine the Great Perfection, the sutras I declare to be the wrong [instrument].

Those who desire to gain the diamond-like Kriyâ[-yoga] will continue to purify the three doors (i.e. body, speech, and mind), and to maintain [the notion] of purifying the objects, and of subject/object [dichotomy]. But the great bliss of the Atiyoga is the mind of perfect purity, which is beyond a subject-object [oriented concept]. In order to overcome the subject-object [oriented concept], the Kriyâyoga is at fault. In order to grasp the Great Perfection by applying a subject-object [oriented concept], I declare the entire Kriyâyoga to be an error.

[Those who pursue] the doctrinal views and practices of Upayoga try to achieve the [aim of] yoga by carrying out rituals (*krîya*). But they will fail to intuit the issue of non-duality because this issue is not associated with doctrinal views and religious practice. With regard to the great bliss of Atiyoga [you must know] that it is the non-dual mind of perfect purity. With regard to its non-duality, the Upayoga is at fault. As to distinguishing the Great Perfection [in terms of] duality, the Upayoga I declare to be at fault.

Those who desire to be solidly established in the Yoga may enter the door [of investigating] whether or not characteristics do exist, and [they may] make the four seals (*phyag rgya bzhi*) their main point, but they will not be capable of entering that which is beyond acquiring and rejecting. The great bliss of Atiyoga is the mind of perfect purity which is without acquiring and rejecting. As to [realizing] to be without acquiring and rejecting, the Yoga is at fault. As to applying [a philosophy of] acquiring and rejecting to the Great Perfection, the Yoga I declare to be at fault.

Those who desire [the transfiguration into] Vajradhara by means of Mahâyoga, may enter the door [of practising] method and wisdom; they may successfully perform the four religious services (*bsnyen bsgrub*) in the mandala of their purified personality. But as to the great bliss of Atiyoga, the mind of perfect purity is beyond striving and achieving. For this reason, Mahâyoga is at fault when it comes to transcending striving and achieving. As to applying [a philosophy of] striving and achieving to the Great Perfection, Mahâyoga I declare to be at fault.

{p. 112} Those who desire the stage of unspecified Anuyoga may enter the door to the dimension [of Reality] and to pristine awareness, but they will still view the transfigured pure dimension of Reality as cause for all existent things, and the mandala of pristine awareness as their result. The great bliss of Atiyoga is the mind of perfect purity which is beyond cause and result. As to transcending causation, the Anuyoga is at fault. If a view of causation as two distinct [concepts is applied to] the Great Perfection, the Anuyoga I declare to be at fault. I teach that [considering] causation and fruition as two different things is an error and a fault.

Oh great bodhisattva! As to any practice or theory [applicable] to the Great Perfection, there is nothing which resembles an achievement [based on] causation. As to a practice or theory [applicable to] the mind of perfect purity, it should be of the nature of the sky—and the sky transcends all theorizing. Those who engage in theorizing will not achieve [the mind of] perfect purity which is like the sky. Those who are occupied with [such concepts as] subject and object with regard to the sky-[like] own being and to doctrinal views and practice will not achieve the sky[-like mind of] perfect purity. They will be at fault and wrong [by assuming that] subject and object originate as two [different entities].

Those who consider theory and practice as two [things] will not realize the perfect, sky-like purity for the reason that they distinguish as two things whatever exists, be it the sky which actually is not two, or the [mind of] perfect purity which actually is not two. They will be at fault and wrong [by assuming that] subject and object originate as two [different entities].

As [the mind of] perfect purity is of a sky-like nature, and as there is no striving nor achieving with regard to the sky, those who engage in striving and achieving will not realize the sky[-like] perfect purity [of the mind]. They will be at fault and wrong [by assuming that] adopting and rejecting emerge as two [different things].

As [the mind of] perfect purity is of a sky-like nature, and as there is no striving nor achieving with regard to the sky, those who {p. 113} engage in striving and achieving will not realize the sky[-like] perfect purity [of the mind]. They will be at fault and wrong [by assuming that] that achievements are made due to striving.

As [the mind of] perfect purity is of a sky-like nature, and as there is no cause or result of the sky, those who consider cause and result as two things will not realize the sky[-like] perfect purity [of the mind]. They will be at fault and wrong by considering cause and result as two [things].

Oh great bodhisattva, the nature of all things is like the sky, but as to the sky, it does not have this nature. There is also no simile which could apply to the sky. There is also no measure which could apply to the sky. All things without remainder should be essentially known this way.

Oh great bodhisattva, you ought to intuit this! Each vehicle has its own doctrinal view. As to the central vigor of a doctrinal view, there is no other [essence] than that about Reality, i.e. the mind of perfect purity, but such central vigor does not exist in other doctrinal views. Therefore what is called doctrinal view is declared [by Me] to be a doctrinal view of error.

Each vehicle has its own vows, but they don't take you to the path of perfect purity. Because the perfect purity is free of subject and object, and because there is nothing else to be observed, the vows also don't need to be observed. Observing the vows, I declare, is an error.[113]

Each vehicle has its own salutary deeds. Because the perfect purity is perfect in itself, there is nothing to be sought through salutary deeds. Through activity nothing will become perfected in itself. Seeking [results] through salutary deeds, I declare, is an error.[114]

Each vehicle has its own stages [of spiritual progress]. Because the Buddhas of the three times, the teacher's present three manifestations, all the sentient beings of this threefold world, and whatever appears as animated or inanimated, is in the mind of perfect purity, [the state of] the Great Perfection, there is no progress by practising the bodhisattva stages. Progressing by practice of the bodhisattva stages and the paths, I declare, is an error.[115]

{p. 114} Each vehicle has its own [perception of] Reality. In the Great Perfection, Reality is the mind of perfect purity. As there are no things except the mind, all doctrines of the [different] vehicles are the mind of perfect purity. [Attempting] to perceive Reality, I declare, is an error.[116] In the Great Perfection, the self-originated pristine awareness should not be made an object of speculative thinking. No speculation, no movement: pristine awareness!"

Such She spoke.

This is the thirty-eighth chapter of *The All-Creating Sovereign, Mind of Perfect Purity,* in which is explained the errors and faults as to doctrinal views and religious practice.

39

{cont'd p. 114} Then the All-Creating Sovereign, mind of perfect purity, taught that She is the central vigor of the Buddhas, and that Her nature in all its totality is without error or fault.

"Oh great bodhisattva, listen! I am the mind of perfect purity of all, and therefore I am called the central vigor of all. As to the teachers' three forms of manifestation, the Buddhas dwelling in the three times, the wisdom-holders (Vidyâdhara), and bodhisattvas, all the sentient beings of this threefold world, and all that exists as the animated and inanimated world, they are nothing but Me, the central vigor of all that is emanated.

Now when you ask, how does that come to be, [I answer] that from imperceptible stillness itself the unborn truth manifestation emanates. From [My] own actuation itself, the wish-fulfilling manifestation of communal joy emanates. From compassion, the great [mind] of perfect purity, the corporeal manifestations emanate for the good of the sentient beings.

If all the Buddhas of the three times, as well as the previous Buddhas, understand the imperceptible, i.e. the self-originated pristine awareness as mind as such, the previous Buddhas dwell also now in a state of imperceptibility. [But] the present Buddhas by not intuiting the self-originated pristine awareness as mind as such, work for the good of the sentient beings. The Buddhas who will come in future {p.115} are prophesied not to intuit the perfect purity, the self-originated pristine awareness. They will certainly come for the good of the sentient beings. If the wisdom-holders and other people do not see the self-originated mind of perfect purity by theorizing it, how then can they meet the central vigor of [their] own mind?

As the self-originated pristine awareness is not obscure to the sentient beings of this threefold world, it illuminates as recognition (*rig pa*) the sensory faculties and their objects. The genuine mind of perfect purity is explained as [this awareness'] pure central vigour.

Among all the things which appear and exist as animated and inanimated, there is not one which is not born from Me. All causes stem from Me, therefore [I am] declared to be the central vigor of all. I excel everything; I am excelling even the three forms of manifestation. I am excelling the Buddhas of the three [times].

I have created the wisdom-holders, the bodhisattvas, and all the sentient beings living in this threefold world, as well as all that appears as animated and inanimated, and I am excelling them in entirety. I, the All-Creating Sovereign, mind of perfect purity, have established in the past the teaching of the mind of perfect purity as a universal teaching. This teaching of the mind of perfect purity cannot be established by all. If you ask how it was established, [I answer]: Because there is nothing which ought to be done with regard to things, one enters [this teaching] through the door of non-striving. Because there is nothing beside the mind of perfect purity, Reality is the mind of perfect purity, and because the mind should not contemplate [a doctrinal view], [this teaching] was established as free of doctrinal views and meditation. As Reality is beyond [the distinction] of subject and object, {p. 116} [this teaching] was established as being without observing the vows. As [Reality] is self-perfected from the primordial, [this teaching] was established as being without striving for any salutary deeds. As the mind of perfect purity abides in all, [this teaching] was established as not practising the bodhisattva stages. As to an opportunity of proceeding toward the mind of perfect purity, I teach that there is no proceeding on a path because there are no stages of the mind toward which one may proceed. Because Reality is the mind of perfect purity you should not engage in a doctrinal view other than Reality. But the pristine awareness, i.e. the self-originated awareness, is not the awareness which perceives [sensory] objects.

Because I, the All-Creating Sovereign, mind of perfect purity, excel the goal of [all] doctrinal views and religious practices, and because I am the central vigor of all created thing, I am called the central vigor of the Victorious One."

Such She spoke.

This is the thirty-ninth chapter of *The All-Creating Sovereign, Mind of Perfect Purity,* in which the central vigor of the Victorious One is explained.

40

{cont'd p. 116} Then the All-Creating Sovereign, mind of perfect purity, taught this teaching [which says] that the mind of perfect purity is Her own being.

"Oh great bodhisattva, listen! Because I have established this teaching, I am teaching all Buddhas of the three times, the wisdom-holders and bodhisattvas, and all sentient beings of this threefold world that by not engaging in any striving or achieving they are Buddhas from the primordial. The three teachings which [advise] to strive and achieve and which [are inaugurated by] the three forms of the teacher of the retinues will diminish because of the errors and faults [contained in these teachings]."

Such She said.

{p. 117} Then Sems-dpa' rdo-rje again asked:

"Oh teacher, All-Creating Sovereign, Your teaching is that of the mind of perfect purity. If this mind of perfect purity is Buddha, are then all sentient beings of this threefold world [also] Buddhas? If all sentient beings in this world are Buddhas, why then do they circle in this threefold world?"

Such he asked.

Then the mind of perfect purity, the All-Creating Sovereign, replied:

"Oh great bodhisattva, listen! All things which appear just like that and which originate from the mind of perfect purity, evidence Reality. Reality, although being one in its suchness, appears in five aspects. If [some] say that because of the desire and dislike for these five [aspects which are the five sensory objects], obscuration and suffering arise, then they are ready to give up the Reality in the five sensory objects. Although the self-originated pristine awareness shines forth [in all things] they will be unable to give up the threefold world and will continue to circle in this three[-fold] world.

Reality, which is one in its suchness, appears as the five sensory objects, and if they say that because of desire and disliking, these five sensory objects are the cause of the samsara, then they are bound to obstruct Reality in the five sensory objects. Although the self-originated pristine awareness shines forth, they will be unable to obstruct the threefold world for many eons, and they will continue to circle in the samsara.

Reality which is one appears in the five sensory objects, [but] desire for and disliking of the five sensory objects arises. If [some] say that these [sensory objects] are the place where attachment exists, they are bound to purify Reality in the five sensory objects. Although the self-originated pristine awareness shines forth [in all things], they will be purifying the threefold world for many eons and continue to circle in the samsara.

{p. 118} Reality which is evident and one in its suchness shines forth as Reality in the five sensory objects. And if [some] say that because desire for and disliking of these five objects arises, they are a place [in need] of blessing, they are bound to perform blessings of the outer and inner worlds, and purify Reality in these five sensory objects. Although the self-originated pristine awareness shines forth they will continue for seven lifespans to perform their blessings and circle in this threefold world.

Reality which arises from the mind of perfect purity is evident. As it is one in suchness, Reality shines forth in the five sensory objects. If some say that because of desire and disliking, the five sensory objects are the cause for celestial and evil rebirths, they will apply [an attitude of] acquiring and rejecting to suchness. Although the self-originated pristine awareness shines forth, such an [assumption] is not suitable for rejecting [the five sensory objects] because of their own conditions. [These people] are about to reject what is unsuitable for this (i.e. becoming aware of the mind of perfect purity), and therefore they will circle in the samsara.

This Reality, evident as it comes forth from the mind of perfect purity, is one in suchness, and therefore Reality shines forth in the five sensory objects. Desire for and disliking of the five sensory objects should be unobstructed as to [the Buddha's] form, utterance, and spirit [being present in these objects]. [But these people] will try to achieve even more with regard to [the Buddha's] form, utterance, and spirit. As they attempt to achieve what is existent from the primordial, they will circle in the samsara because of this 'achievement'.

Oh great bodhisattva, therefore, since they have given up the mind of perfect purity, the self-originated pristine awareness, existing from the primordial, will be non-existent [to them]. Since they [want] to give up the samsara, there is nothing to call nirvana. Since they [want] to give up the perceiving of things (*chos can*), Reality, which exists from the primordial, will be non-existent [to them]. Everything is one in suchness. Therefore [the attempt] to alter suchness, although all is one in suchness, is an error.

{p. 119} [The etymology of suchness (*de bzhin nyid*):]
de ('this'): a name of the non-erroneous;
bzhin ('such'): has the meaning of un-altered;
nyid ('-ness'): is understood as a self-determining characteristic.

Do not attempt to alter this suchness! Those who attempt to alter this suchness will try to alter the mind of perfect purity. Those who try to alter the mind of perfect purity will actually only achieve the samsara."

Such She spoke.

This is the fortieth chapter of *The All-Creating Sovereign, Mind of Perfect Purity,* in which the nature of the mind of perfect purity is explained.

41

{cont'd p. 119} Then the All-Creating Sovereign, mind of perfect purity, taught that "I am the nature of all things."

"Oh Sems-dpa' dam-pa rdo-rje! You must know My own being like this: I am a lamp for the teachers; [I am] the mind of perfect purity. I am the central vigor of all the Buddhas of the three times. I am father and mother to all sentient beings of the threefold world. Also, I am the cause for all that exists as animated and inanimated. Not one thing is that does not emanate from Me. Because I am not abiding [in one place] (*gnas*), I am all-integrating.[117] From the primordial, I am the Buddhas of the three times.

Because I am dwelling in imperceptible stillness I am the primordial Buddha (*ye sangs rgyas*) in imperceptible stillness and truth manifestation. Because My actuation is the joy manifestation, I Myself am the primordial Buddha in the communal joy manifestation. Because I

Myself appear as self-originated pristine awareness, {p.120} I Myself am the evident Buddha in compassionate corporeal manifestation. For this reason, I am declared to be the central vigor of all the Buddhas of the three times. I am the pristine awareness which shines forth as mind of perfect purity. The self-originated pristine awareness in its five aspects (i.e. the five sensory consciousnesses) [brings forth] the six categories of sentient beings. Thus I am the father and mother to the sentient beings of this threefold world. I am also the actuation of whatever exists as animated or inanimated. What appears as 'earth'[118] comes forth from My actuation. I Myself am the eternally existent [earth] Buddha. Because of all its integrating quality, the mind in itself is the element water. I am not two, but an integral one, and therefore the element water. I am the stillness of all, and its warmth—the element fire. Because it equally dwells in everything—the Buddha of fire. I, in My beginningless nature, am agility—the beginningless agility evident as the Buddha of the element wind. I am faultless and all-illuminating, therefore the designation sky is used. [I] am the Buddha [of the element sky]. There is nothing in the universe (samsara) [made of the five] great elements which is a Buddha and is not coming forth from Me. It is taught that the five elements are My own being. In [this] one[ness] the nature of the twenty-five [subelements] are completed. In what appears as earth, water is existent in a nuclear way. In the stillness of fire, the agility of the [element] wind shines forth. Because of its faultlessness and illuminating ability, it is the sky's nature. In [this] one[ness] the twenty-five [subelements] are completed. The good qualities of the five great elements are shown by the mind of perfect purity. The [existent] things are non-dual and one in the mind of perfect purity. By the one all is made, made by the All-Creating Sovereign."

Such She spoke.

This is the forty-first chapter of *The All-Creating Sovereign, Mind of Perfect Purity,* in which is covered the oneness of [Her] actuation.

42

{p. 121} Then the All-Creating Sovereign, mind of perfect purity, taught this: that all existent things, i.e. the mind of perfect purity, are in themselves enlightened.

"Oh, great bodhisattva, listen to [how] the truth manifestation [correlates with] the mind of perfect purity! From the mind of perfect purity the truth manifestation comes; nobody has altered it, not even an iota of it. Therefore there is no Buddha besides the mind [of perfect purity].

[Listen to how] the manifestation of communal joy [correlates with] the mind of perfect purity! From the mind of perfect purity the manifestation of communal joy comes. There is no other manifestation than that of communal joy as a form manifestation (*rûpakâya*) of the mind of perfect purity.

[Listen to how] the corporeal manifestation [correlates with] the mind of perfect purity! There is nothing else to work for the good of the sentient beings than the corporeal manifestations of the perfect and pure mind. There is nothing else than the mind of perfect purity, not even the Buddhas of the three times.

The Buddhas of the past previously saw and understood that one's own mind must never be altered. The Buddhas of the present are likewise recognizing that the genuine mind must not be altered. The Buddhas who will come in the future to work the good of the sentient beings will teach not to alter this self-originated mind as such. Thus during meditation one should not try to alter the mind. Go and enter a path of non-alteration!

Those who do not recognize that all existent things are in the mind of perfect purity, will achieve nothing due to [their attempt to] achieve [spiritual progress] through alteration [of the mind]. They pretend to achieve something only by altering their non-understanding; for as many as countless eons they will not meet {p. 122} the bliss which cannot be sought. Ho! Although the three manifestations cannot be alienated from the mind, in the sutras and shastras of the teachers' three manifestations the performance of altering [the mind] is given as goal. As to this, the teachers of the three manifestations do not teach this in accord with their own being. Whatever a teacher teaches which asks to alter this suchness, is only a kind of truth. It is not a lore of definitive meaning but a lore which requires interpretation."

Such She spoke.

This is the forty-second chapter of *The All-Creating Sovereign, Mind of Perfect Purity,* in which [the topic] "non-altering" is covered.

43

{cont'd p. 122} Then the All-Creating Sovereign, mind of perfect purity, personally taught that all things are the teacher Herself.

"Oh great bodhisattva, listen! I am the teacher of all things. From the three aspects of My own being come the teachers who are taught to be of three kinds. Also the teachings are of three aspects, [such] I teach. Given that, the hosts of retinues are also threefold, [such] I teach. Whatever the teachers in their three forms are proclaiming, it is a lore that teaches the nature of things, a lore that teaches the actuation of things, and a lore that teaches the meaning of words. The lore that teaches the nature of things comes forth as a blessing from the unborn. It is taught that all things, which appear just like that, are the suchness of things.

The lore that teaches the actuation of things [says that] all things, which appear just like that, emerge as manifestations of the teachers themselves. It is taught that nothing is beside the actuation of things.

The lore that teaches the meaning of words: the meaning of all things is transformed {p. 123} and condensed so that the ignorant and unknowing sentient beings of this threefold world may be taught by combining the meaning [of words] with their sound. Thereby the teachers' nature is taught. The retinues who accept this are taught to be of three kinds: (1) the retinues who have overcome striving for the achievement of Atiyoga, and who abide in buddhahood by virtue of their confidence that they have entered the door [to liberation]. (2) The retinues of the level of wisdom-holders or of [those at the stage] of the first to the tenth bodhisattva stages, and who abide at a stage of meditation close to the achievement of buddhahood (*ma thob nye reg bsgoms pa*). (3) The retinues who vowed to aspire to bodhicitta, who abide at a level of suppressing the poison of [striving for] results from good causes. These are explained as the teacher's three retinues."

[Sems-dpa' rdo-rje:]

"Oh teacher of the teachers, All-Creating Sovereign! If the three teachers and the hosts of retinues are like this, then how are the threefold teachings taught?"

Such he asked.

[All-Creating Sovereign:]

"Oh great bodhisattva, listen! The teaching of the truth manifestation is taught to be suchness. This suchness has no particularities. All things, which appear just like that, are the mind's actuation—that is suchness. Who meditates on this will be made to alter [the primordially existent suchness]. Who does not understand this teaching about the truth manifestation, will not recognize the imperceptible Reality as [mind of] pure perfection in its unerring suchness. Who alters this [mind of perfect purity] will meditate on it. Therefore they will not intuit that their own mind is unalterable.

The things which appear and exist, and the mind of perfect purity which does not appear, come forth from the mind's suchness as suchness. If suchness is not understood [as one] but viewed as diversity, {p. 124} then suchness will be sought apart from the dimension [of Reality]. By seeking [liberation] through the Buddhas of the three times, one will not find it.

Oh great bodhisattva, listen! The teaching of the communal joy [manifestation] is such an enjoyment: the five aspects of enjoyment are, as to Reality, only one enjoyment. The enjoyments are five—that of form and so on (i.e. the five sensual objects). Each of them [is divided] into five, thus twenty-five [forms of enjoyment] are experienced. The twenty-five enjoyments are transfigured as five manifestations (*sku lnga*). This transfiguration is explained as the actuation itself of the actual Reality. I teach the wisdom-holders of the tenth bodhisattva stage that My form as manifestation of communal joy cannot be enjoyed in the enjoyment of the Buddhas and all sentient beings."

Such She spoke.

"Oh great bodhisattva, listen! The teachings of the corporeal manifestation are in accord with the intention (*don*) of compassion. [The corporeal manifestation in its] three aspects of form, utterance, and spirit, teaches the sentient beings of this threefold world, who are of differing thoughts, to give up these differing thoughts for the sake of following [the Buddhas'] form, utterance, and spirit. Because [the corporeal manifestation] teaches what is suitable for those who [stay] at places of solitude after they have turned away from relishing sensory objects, My compassion is thereby made into a teaching in need of interpretation.

Oh great bodhisattva, listen! Because I am the teacher of all things, I even teach the Buddhas My nature, and I also teach the sentient beings My nature.[119] By teaching My nature it is put into the teachers' mouths, but My nature must be intuited. Buddhas, teachings, and retinues are nothing else but the three aspects of My own being. The teachers' own being is Me, and therefore ceaseless.[120] The teaching as My own being is unalterable. {p. 125} The retinues who grasp this, are grasped by My actuation."

Such She spoke.

This is the forty-third chapter of *The All-Creating Sovereign, Mind of Perfect Purity,* in which She personally talked about the teacher.

44

Then the All-Creating Sovereign, mind of perfect purity, expounded the meaning of the deedless with regard to Herself.

"Oh great bodhisattva, the meaning of the deedless is like this: All-creating is My own being, but I am deedless. As I am from the primordial consummate in My existence (*byas zin*), I am the Reality of the deedless. As Reality is My own being, there are no deeds [related] to this being. I am of a non-alterable nature, such is the nature of the deeds [pertinent] to [My] nature. This non-alterable perfect purity—do not [attempt to] alter it, oh Sems-dpa' rdo-rje! If you [attempt to] alter it, oh Sems-dpa' rdo-rje, then you will [attemtp to] alter Me, the All-Creating One. Likewise, all things, existing as they do, are My, nature, i.e. that of the All-Creating One.

Oh great bodhisattva, listen! My nature is immutable. If [the followers of the other vehicles] meditate [on this nature], they [will try to] alter and transmute it. From the primordial beginning I am spontaneously self-perfected. If they attempt to achieve [results], they will [try to] alter Me. If they [wish to] proceed towards Me, they will never arrive [at the goal]. If they search for Me, they will never succeed in it. If they practise [to realize] Me, they will never be pure. Do not theorize Me, as I am no object [for speculations]. Do not proceed towards Me as there is no path. Do not purify Me as I am faultless. Not abiding [in existence] (*mi gnas*) I am not an object of perception. Unconceptualized I am beyond being an object of thinking. All things named through perception are taught to be My actuation. {p. 126} Those who indulge in abandoning and obstructing this [teaching] will not meet with Me, the All-Creating [Sovereign], for a duration of three eons. Those things which [they think ought] to be abandoned are taught to be My actuation.

Oh great bodhisattva! The mind of perfect purity is the All-Creating Sovereign. The All-Creating [Sovereign] creates through the mind of perfect purity. Outside of the mind of perfect purity, nothing is creating. The mind of perfect purity is from the primordial without error. As it exists from the primordial, it also is without error from the primordial. The ways of lies and truth do not apply to what is without error. It is beyond all [such distinctions] as cause, conditions, results, striving, or achieving. If [the sentient beings] do not understand that [the mind of perfect purity] is beyond [the dichotomy of] subject/object, and striving/achieving, they will look out for success after they have meditated on carrying out acts of striving and achieving—

and there is nothing more severe than to obstruct the mind of perfect purity in this way. [However] they will abide in nature and non-conceptual balance by having not the slightest inclination towards the non-existent and the non-conceptual. With regard to what from the primordial is of consummate existence, no attitude of striving should be generated. Those who abide in this great bliss will become the central vigour of all things! Therefore [such distinctions as] 'I' and 'others' do no good. This central vigour which comprises the one and all illuminates even the mind of the Buddhas of the three times with no-doctrine, and it lets shine forth the mind of all sentient beings as faultless.

Oh great bodhisattva, listen! I, the All-Creating One, am the fulfillment of all sentient beings, yet My fulfillment is not generated by anything else. A teaching which depends on others is not My lore. I am all-perfected; from the primordial I am consummate in My being, perfect. As I am consummate in My being from the primordial, doctrinal views and religious practice are not needed. {p. 127} As I am utterly pure from the primordial, there is no need for observing any vows. As I am abiding in the state of perfect purity, there is no need to practise the state of a wisdom-holder or of the tenth bodhisattva stage. As from the primordial I am self-perfected due to non-striving, there is no need for any act of striving from the primordial. As the self-originated pristine awareness is not an object of reflection, there is no need for the intuitive awareness to be illuminated by some objects. As the great bliss and the truth manifestation are one in the mind (*sems*), the three times—like past, future, [and present]—do not exist but are an all-permeating one. Because totally perfected [retinues], time, place, and all these things are just one, and as all is one, I am the all-perfected one. [The system of] Great Perfection [is so-called] because of Me, the all-perfected one. For this reason you should not [try to] achieve [results] through striving, as was previously taught with regard to doctrine, religious practice, good acts, vows, bodhisattva stages, and [the five] paths.

If in such manner [the nature] is not intuitively understood, and if they engage in striving and achieving, they will be isolated from the goal which transcends causes and results. They will not meet with the great bliss. They, who are without intuitive insight, will be captured by the sickness of striving and achieving. Therefore, the Great Perfection which is beyond cause and result, is not a suitable field of practice for those of no talent. They will practise a doctrine of cause and result."

Such She spoke.

This is the forty-fourth chapter of *The All-Creating Sovereign, Mind of Perfect Purity,* in which is expounded that the Great Perfection is meaningless to those without talent.

45

{cont'd p.127} Then the All-Creating Sovereign, mind of perfect purity, expounded that the lore of the Great Perfection is without contemplating a doctrinal view.

"Oh great bodhisattva! Not to contemplate one's own doctrinal views [means] I am the All-Creating One, and I ought not to be contemplated upon. {p. 128} I, the All-Creating One, am not an object of contemplation. I am unalterable and dwell as nature in all.

The teachers' three manifestations, stemming from Me, say with regard to Reality, which becomes apparent through Me, that what is not to be meditated, the abiding in nature, is the ill of the five passionate desires. They don't lead [their disciples] into the unaltered [nature] but force them to contemplate abandoning and obstructing. Such teachings are in contradiction to the central vigor of the unaltered. The bliss of the deedless will not be obtained by [those who claim] that the four groups of non-Buddhists were established as retinues after being blessed by the manifestations of compassion. Oh great bodhisattva! When, with regard to Reality which emanates from Me, they say that it is the ill of the five passionate desires, they theorize and apply the two truths to the bodhisattvas of the first to the tenth stages. Thereby they will contemplate on the theory and practice of the manifestations' teaching of whether the ultimate is not, or whether the conventional is. This obstructs My central vigor, i.e. the unalterable 'as-it-is'.

Oh great bodhisattva! From Me, Reality emanates. The manifestations of communal joy instruct the retinues on the unalterable, the 'as-is', the Reality, but they do not understand [what is implied by saying] 'as-is' and 'unalterable'. Thus [their followers] bless the outer and inner, the animated and inanimated world through purging [rituals]. They evoke the wisdom deities of meditation by means of the limbs of enlightenment (*bodhyanga*, Tib. *byang chub yan lag*)[121] and all kinds of rituals. At one moment they make offerings, [at the next moment] they dismiss [the visualized deities], and interrupt their meditation. Again they meditate, and again they interrupt it—it's like a child's [toy] house [made of] clay! This obstructs My central vigor, the 'as-is', the unalterable.

{p. 129} Oh great bodhisattva, listen! Due to the teachers' teaching, emanating from Me, they enter upon an inquiry as to whether or not the defining characteristics of meditation exist with regard to the apparent Reality which emanates from Me. They apply acquiring and rejecting to the one Reality. When they contemplate the wisdom deities and themselves, who took the vows, as separate [entities] they hope that [the deities as their] friends give them supernatural abilities. A meditation which views the one as two is an error! As My actuation is one there are not two to be gained.

Oh great bodhisattva, listen! My nature is evident, yet they transfigure their own person, purified with regard to the psycho-physical aggregates, elements, forms of consciousness, sensory abilities, and sense objects, into a diamond deity. They perform meditations through the rituals and the four types of religious service. They work for the good of the beings by mentally radiating and contracting [the visualized mantras] and by [making] offerings to the noble ones. They hope to gain supernatural abilities by combining [the practice of] radiation and contraction [of mantras]. They concentrate on obtaining such supernatural abilities for themselves through themselves. But this will make the meditating mind feel exhausted.

The lore of the Great Perfection, not to be meditated upon, is a good quality of My mind, i.e. that of the All-Creating One. There is no need to exercise austerities to achieve [results] through striving because of the great qualities of the mind of perfect purity. There is no need for acts of striving because [all] is without cause or condition. There is no need to achieve anything else than the nature of the result (i.e. nirvana). There is no need to carry out meditation as Reality is oneself. There is no substance which could decay as nothing is born. Do not seek a place for meditation, do not depend on others. Those who meditate on Me will never meet Me through this meditation. Because I am evident as Reality there is no need to give up suffering, [which is] the unborn. As the self-originated [pristine awareness] is being in itself, there is neither birth nor cessation, therefore {p. 130} there is no need to obstruct the dependent arising, such as ignorance and so on, or the sense faculties. There is no need to purge Reality—the self-originated and pure one. There is no need for cleansing as from the primordial It is pure. There is no need for striving or achieving something as It is from the primordial self-perfected. There is no thing which is cleansed through applying doctrinal views. Suchness and [the five Buddhas such as] Vairocana ('Diverse Appearance') and Samantabhadra ('All Good'), and even the things which appear to the six sense faculties are nothing else than what exists from the primordial. Those who perform meditation in [attempting] some achievements with regard to That are like someone chasing behind the shape of the sky [in an attempt to catch it].

My nature is truly beyond the scope of sensory perception. My nature should be truly intuited as the things which are apparent through Me because My actuation is made visible to all [retinues] and is taught with regard to the [retinues'] different capacities. If they don't see My nature this way, I shall not teach them My vehicle, i.e. that of the All-Creating One.

As they are of no talent [to understand] the spirit of the Great Perfection, they will embrace a lore which needs interpretation, i.e. the vehicle of causation. From the primordial, I am beyond the scope of sensory perception. If I would teach those of no talent and in favour of [the vehicle of] causation, they would repudiate the mind itself when [listening to this] teaching because they would be driven to praise and dispraise. For this reason they will be born into the six categories [of sentient beings] and will stay forever in samsara.

Oh great bodhisattva, intuit this quintessential point! Because I am totally beyond the scope of sensory perception, I am beyond the scope of the senses and I do not come through words. My nature is comprehensive and dwells in the empty circle (*thig le*). It is explained as non-conceptual, non-dual, and one from the primordial.

There is no need to carry out deliberations in order to preserve the vows. There is no need to carry out deliberations as to striving for salutary deeds. The bodhisattva stages should not be practised as there is no path to proceed on. {p. 131} Do not search for Reality in anything else than yourself. The self-originated pristine awareness is imperceptible and non-agitated; this is My lore, i.e. that of the All-Creating One. There is no other lore. Do not engage in achieving and striving as [I] am beyond causes and results. Do not meditate on any concrete item as it is non-originated. There is no need for decay as it is unborn. As I am imperceptible do not meditate [on Me] as if I were perceptible. In the middle of the great dimension of the all-encompassing great bliss, the nature of this unreflected great balance rests. Do not engage in meditation, and do not try to understand intellectually the imperceptible nature, i.e. Reality.

Oh great bodhisattva! If they meditate—and on whatever they may meditate—it is a sickness to Me. There is not an iota to be meditated upon as the mind of perfect purity is without [such concepts as] subject/object, and the mind of perfect purity is the central vigor of all. A meditation as explained before will not produce any results. Likewise I am teaching right now that [no result] will be obtained through meditation.

Oh great bodhisattva, rely on Me! I am the All-Creating Sovereign, mind of perfect purity. The All-Creating One has created [all], and the entire creation is created in Herself.
'All': is a word meaning 'without remainder'.
'Creating': its central thrust is to make everything.
'Purity': it is not grasped.
'Perfect': because it is the central vigor of all, it is perfected in its central vigor.
'Mind': the self-originated wisdom is the mind in all."

Such She spoke.

This is the forty-fifth chapter of *The All-Creating Sovereign, the Mind of Perfect Purity,* in which is expounded "no doctrine should be meditated upon."

46

{cont's p. 131} Then the All-Creating Sovereign, mind of perfect purity, expounded that the Great Perfection has no vows to be observed. {p. 132}

"Oh great bodhisattva, listen! I am teaching that there are no vows of the Great Perfection which ought to be observed. The nature of the All-Creating Sovereign, mind of perfect purity, is unborn and of a non-conceptual nature, and from it the various objects come forth as the wonders of origination. By knowing the own being of these objects and not reflecting upon them, you will transcend them as objects of reflection. As there is no perceiving of the objects, nor rejecting them, or accepting them—nothing, it is only perfected in the oneness of stillness.[122] Then you are totally separated from the regulations and vows and the acts [required for] observing them.

The three teachers, emanating from Me who does not observe [any vows], bless with their compassion the four segments of non-believers, and then they discipline them [and they become] the four retinues. The rules which they should observe are like this: the numbers of the basic [rules] and the supplementary ones are 250 and 550. However, they don't know the true purpose, nor the number or [right] time for observing [the vows]. For this reason they don't have a method to preserve the vows, nor are they able to do it.

The Great Perfection is beyond any reflection and common practice. The vows are limitless and immeasurable like the sea. [The vows] are subsumed under body, speech and mind. [They say:] Suffering comes from the senses and their objects, but the body cannot find a spot to put its foot on to stay or walk;[123] truth becomes evasive when its meaning should be expressed in words, and the mind's thinking is total obstruction of truth. It is not the case that through non-erring thinking everything can be achieved. Because of body and speech being firmly bound with the vows, it is very difficult to grasp the central vigor of truth itself. By not preserving [the vows] and not damaging [them] [these people] will not meet [the truth]. Not to preserve [the vows] {p.133} nor to damage them—this is the lore of the All-Creating One.

Oh great bodhisattva, listen! The teachers stemming from Me, deliver a teaching that at an auspicious conjunction of the stars and planets, the outer and inner realms should be cleansed through clean ablutions. They promise that vows and morality are for the good of the sentient beings. But whatever pledges [are made] and whatever moral [conduct is observed] no [results] will be achieved. Atonement for not fulfilling the pledges does not mix well with the mind. This impairs Me, who does not observe [any vows], far and wide.

Oh, you of secret indestructibility, with regard to the three vows [you ought to know]: there are three basic pledges, and five supplementary ones. The three basic ones are subsumed under Buddha's form, utterance, and spirit. The 'form' [related vow] is to meditate upon a deity's corporeal form, but it is the body's bond. The 'utterance' [related vow] is to utter mantras as [a form of meditation], but this does not give peace. A mental absorption comprised of radiating and contracting [seed syllables] does not promise [insight in] the imperceptible ground, nor is it endowed with bliss.[124]

The five supplementary vows are as follows: First, the vow regarding what should be known, i.e. the five aggregates, the five elements, consciousness, sense faculties, objects, etc., but also the nature of the deities and mandalas should be known. Those who do not see that there is neither anything to be known (i.e. an object) nor anyone who knows (i.e. subject or agent), they will enjoy in a clever way the five vows of enjoyment—uniting and freeing,[125] stealing, abusing sexuality, and lying. They will enjoy therein after they have come to understand that not enjoying them would be seen as a loss. But as That is imperceptible, they will be isolated from [the state of] stillness.

As to the five vows which ought to be readily taken: [These yogis] claim that they will achieve the corporeal form of a Buddha by the five ingredients [relevant] to these vows, i.e. excrements, urine, etc.[126] { p. 134} When they emit and contract the five seed [syllables] of the hero's [mantra],[127] they are made to believe that they readily acquired the five corporeal forms of the Buddha. They think that they would not achieve these five forms, if they did not readily accept [these practices]. However, they will not achieve what transcends reflective thinking and what is free of acquiring and rejecting.

As to the five vows which should never be given up: Attachment, hatred, etc. are the five poisons. In taking the great vows of the secret diamond, the five obscurations (*klesha*) will be transformed into the five wisdoms. [They believe] that if they don't give up the five poisons they will obtain the five wisdoms. However, with these [methods] they will not achieve the bliss which is without acquiring and rejecting.

As to the five vows of successful achieving: [They claim] to achieve successfully the mandala through [control over] the five aggregates, five elements, consciousness, and sensory objects. When they complete the three *samâdhi* and the five *pûja* [they assume that] they have achieved the mandala of the Buddha pentade (*pañcatathâgâta*). They attempt to seek the mind by means of the five *pûja* and *samâdhi*. However, they will obstruct spontaneous self-perfection which in its imperceptibility cannot be sought.

These corporeal forms of the Buddhas [as seen] in meditation are like an evanescent rainbow, and even the reciting of *pûja* and the uttering of mantras is like a pale paint. They will not be spontaneously perfected because of their engagement in striving and achieving. If one tries to achieve something that is not existent, no achievement of anything whatsoever will happen.

There is no vow to be observed with regard to Me, the All-Creating One. As there are no causes and conditions there is no need for achieving something by striving. As [all] is spontaneously perfected there is no need for carrying out any religious practice. As [only] pristine awareness is existent, there is no need for factual knowing (*shes par bya*). As [all] is self-originated, there is no need [for the concepts of] cause and condition. As there is neither good nor bad, there is no need for acquiring or rejecting [anything]. As there are no things which could exist as substances, [this situation] is explained as non-existence. Not to engage in [the assumption of] things as substances, is not to obstruct the pristine awareness. Such a person is said to be in stillness.

{p. 135} Oneness is taught as all being one in the mind. Because all things which appear just like that, are perfected as the mind of perfect purity due to one's profound trust, I declare such a person to be spontaneously perfected.

[To see] Reality as heat or cold, hunger or thirst, dumbness or stupidity [is like seeing] the retinues of the three manifestations as enemies, or the six *pûja* as a means of escape. There is no need to achieve anything by striving as explained before.

Because the cause itself is the self-originated pristine awareness, they will not gain control over the conditions of their acts. As the nature of Reality is not caused by conditions, I am not teaching that they will achieve something through striving. [If they assume that] the self-originated pristine awareness is not identical with all, they will not realize this self-originatedness through cause, conditions, and acts. It cannot be captured by [the concept of] two truths. How can they teach with certainty the oneness when [they proclaim] a teaching of doubts and uncertainty, i.e. the two truths, although with certainty [all] is one. People who practise yoga and covet religion and who say that they rely on the teaching of causation [as given by] the three teachers, for them the two truths and the four syllogisms (*pramâna*) may be necessary. Because I, the All-Creating One, have made all things, there is no need for two truths with regard to the things I made. If there is no need for the two truths with regard to the things I made, how then could everything, made by Me, be made in the mind of perfect purity? The mind of perfect purity does not have an ultimate and a conventional truth."

Such She spoke.

This is the forty-sixth chapter of *The All-Creating Sovereign, Mind of Perfect Purity,* in which is explained that there are no vows to be observed.

47

{cont'd p. 135} Then the All-Creating Sovereign, mind of perfect purity, expounded on the Great Perfection {p. 136} in terms of there being no seeking of salutary actions.

"Oh great bodhisattva, listen! I, the All-Creating Sovereign, the great consummate one, teach that from the primordial salutary actions ought not to be sought because the Great Perfection is perfected in itself. A lore is taught that salutary actions ought not to be sought, yet the teachers in their three manifestations, coming forth from Me, advise their individual retinues that they should aspire to salutary actions.

Each [manifestation] advises in an individual way which actions ought to be aspired to. The corporeal manifestations direct [their followers] as to what actions, based upon which causes, they have to pursue. When [the followers] embark upon the three limitless meditations (i.e. love, compassion, and mercy) in terms of bodily, vocal, and mental [actions], they vow to give up killing, stealing, and adultery by means of the body; they vow to give up gossip, rough and deceitful words, slander and so on by means of speech; [and they vow] to give up greedy and hostile thoughts by means of the mind. When they have established this performance of the ten moral acts as cause, then they desire to achieve the [ten] bodhisattva stages and the stage of full enlightenment by practising generosity, morality and the [other] of the ten perfections, and they perform these exhausting actions for three eons. But this is not what I, the All-Creating Sovereign, teach.

The manifestations of communal joy teach the retinues that salutary actions should be carried out in accord with [the concept of] causation. The mental performance of meditation is like this: purification of the inner and outer realms by means of ablutions and purifying rites. The blessing through miraculous actions is thought to consist of a mind [characterized by] wisdom and vows. Afterwards they perform *pûja* and send [the evoked deities] back by means of a contemplative mind. Such salutary actions may be continued for seven lifespans.

The manifestations of communal joy are built upon the manifestations of truth and teach the retinues the Mahâyoga. {p. 137} [These retinues] are taught that a great self exists and that they should meditate on deities endowed with their individual colours and families as being within a mandala which is [the retinues'] own mental flux. The peaceful deities are the agents of peaceful works; the deities of abundance are the agents of works of abundance; the deities of might also let [the retinues] enact deeds of might and control; the deities of coercion also let them do works of exorcism. Thereby [these retinues] may achieve [the state of] wisdom-holders of [the categories] 'staying in life' (*tshe la gnas pa*) and of 'seal' (*phyag rgya*). But these four [kinds of] exhausting works will not lead to any [true] achievements; and certainly [those who follow this system] will not achieve the non-striving [state] of deedlessness. As the Great Perfection transcends causation from the primordial, the deedless cannot be achieved through striving. A teacher of a view upholding causation, and who has made the assumption that the given phenomena (*dhar-*

ma) are the world's defining characteristics, may teach a doctrine [saying] that [the followers] will achieve the result after they have sought after the cause.

The mind is without cause, and thus is from the primordial without a result. Despite [the fact that] also the mind of perfect purity is without birth, they have no doubts that decay comes from birth, once they adopt the simile that the world arises as given phenomena. While they do not understand that the self-originated is without causation they proclaim that results arise from a sought cause, after they have assumed [the opinion that] the phenomena are the world's defining characteristics. This makes the vehicle of causation a doctrine in need of interpretion (*drang lung*).

Oh great bodhisattva, listen! A teaching saying 'pristine awareness, pristine awareness' consists of this incomparable pristine awareness which does not stem from any cause, i.e. the self-originated pristine awareness which is unobstructed and all-permeating. As [this awareness] generates everything, from nothing else the phenomena (*dharma*) arise. {p.138} By adopting the causal phenomena of this world as norm (*tshod*) [for establishing philosophical conclusions], they will never generate a result which is without striving.[128] The mind of perfect purity is not generated, neither by causes nor conditions. You ought not to adopt the phenomena of origin and cessation, i.e. this world, as a norm [for inferring its final value]. As the mind of perfect purity is not generated from any condition it is improper to take the conditioned phenomena of this world as a normative example (*dpe*).

Oh great bodhisattva, if they desire the greatness (*che ba*)[129] they will actively strive after meditation and evocation (*sâdhana*). But by seeking after meditation and evocation, they will not realize the infinite greatness. This infinite greatness is self-originated and is great from the primordial. If you engage in meditation you will adulterate Buddha's spirit. Who adulterate Buddha's spirit will abandon all the Buddhas. But even if they do not abandon the Buddhas, yet abandon their own mind of perfect purity, they will be unable to meet their own being for eons.

Oh great bodhisattva, have the mind not engage in *samâdhi* or meditation! Do not try to conceptualize the pristine awareness as an object! With your voice you ought not recite [the mantras] or utter the heart-[syllables], nor should you perform *mûdra*s with the gestures of your hands. With your mind you should not carry out a meditation of radiating and contracting [the visualized deities or mantric syllables]. Those who dwell in their inner being are unagitated and spontaneously perfected. Who abide in their own being cannot be adulterated by anybody. Abiding in suchness, which is not sought, is taught to be the utmost deed of deedlessness. Those who understand this final point do not carry out any deeds. As they do not carry out any deeds, they abide in suchness. Whoever abides in suchness will realize the non-erring, unadulterated [balance]. This unerring nature is unadulterated. {p. 139} This in itself is called the unerring actuating nature itself (*ngo bo nyid*). Outside suchness there are none of the [eighteen] special characteristics of a Buddha."[130]

Such She spoke.

This is the forty-seventh chapter of *The All-Creating Sovereign, Mind of Perfect Purity,* in which is said that salutary works should not be sought.

48

{cont'd p. 139} Then the All-Creating Sovereign proclaimed in person that the ground of all things is the All-Creating One Herself.

"Oh great bodhisattva, listen! I, the All-Creating [Sovereign], am the mind of perfect purity of everything. This mind of perfect purity is the ground of all things.

From the three aspects of My nature, i.e. that of the All-Creating One, [comes] the fullness (*phun sum tshogs pa*) which fulfills all needs. The three aspects of My nature are to be known as follows: (1) unborn (*skye ba med pa*), (2) without termination (*'gag pa med*), and (3) the source for the wonder of ceaseless creation (*mi 'gag skye ba'i cho 'phrul*).

The fullness is taught under three aspects: (1) the fullness which [stems] from the unborn nature, free of birth, reveals (*bstan*) the ground of [all] things; (2) the fullness of the own being of the teacher's three manifestations who stem from the stainless, unobstructed nature; (3) the fullness of the three retinues' own being who stem from the actuation of the unborn wonder of creation.

Oh great bodhisattva, listen! My own being is the sole Reality. I am the wonder of creation from which arise the three retinues due to the teacher's ceaseless three forms of manifestation. I am one in Reality and suchness, and pertinent to [this truth] there are six bases (*gzhi ma drug*) which are methods you ought to understand: {p. 140}

(1) As to making doctrinal view a basis for cognizing Reality [you ought to know that] it is just a means to let you see [Reality]. As the

unborn is not an object which you can perceive, you will never gaze at suchness by means of a doctrinal view.

(2) As to making vows a base for purging one's own faults, [you ought to know that] it is just a means for removing the hindrances. As suchness is not an object which you should observe, suchness will never be mastered by means of observing [any vows].

(3) As to making rites a base for spiritual realization, [you ought to know that] they are just a means for letting you make this realization through striving [for it]. As suchness is not an object which you could strive for, suchness can never be realized through striving.

(4) As to making the path a base for progress by means of proceeding [on it, you ought to know that] it is just a means for progressing towards the goal. As suchness is not a path on which you may proceed, suchness will not be reached through proceeding.

(5) As to making the bodhisattva stages a base for abiding [in them, you ought to know that] they are just an unnecessary means of religious practice. As suchness exists in everything and all, there is no stage to be practised so that you could abide [in them].

(6) As to making the pristine awareness a base for understanding, [you ought to know that] it is just a means to understand Reality. As suchness is never an object of cognition, the self-originated pristine awareness cannot be cognized as an object.[131]

Oh great bodhisattva, listen! The mind of perfect purity is the ground of all things, but [the followers of the system of causation] will never encounter the unaltered ground of their own mind due to the fact that striving will adulterate suchness. This is so because each vehicle has its individual set of six practices and six doctrinal views which teach the retinues to consider causation. Then each [disciple] has to think what [vehicle] is suitable [to him or her]. But suchness is never an object of striving even if they engage in striving by means of taking the six practices and six doctrinal views as base. {p. 141} They will never meet their own mind as the unaltered ground [of the universe] as this striving adulterates suchness.

Oh great bodhisattva, listen! As to the teaching which says 'no contemplation of doctrinal views' [you ought to know the following]: I do not teach that the objects are unrelated to the self (*rang*) because the root of all things is nothing else but one self, and therefore it is impossible that the self looks at itself in terms of a doctrinal view. Therefore it is [known as] the teaching 'no contemplation of doctrinal views'.

As to the teaching which says 'no observance of vows' [you ought to know the following]. The observance [of the vows] cannot obstruct one's own mind, which is the self-originated pristine awareness, consequently you should not observe [the vows].

Ho, as to the teaching which says 'no striving after salutary acts' [you ought to know the following]. Because the Great Perfection is beyond causation from the primordial, those who desire the results after they have accomplished the causes in forms of salutary acts [will never realize the Great Perfection].[132] This teaching is called 'no striving after salutary acts' because the Great Perfection cannot be desired as a result and because the salutary acts, free of striving, are spontaneously perfect.[133]

As to the teaching which says 'no proceeding on the path' [you ought to know the following]. Oh, all the Buddhas of the three times and the sentient beings of this threefold world proceed on a path towards the mind of perfect purity. With regard to this mind [of perfect purity] the Buddhas and sentient beings are not different. Consequently, there is no proceeding on a path towards this mind by means of this mind.

As to the teaching which says 'no practice of the [bodhisattva] stages (*bhûmi*)' [you ought to know the following]: as this sole stage of the mind of perfect purity is the dimension of Reality (*dharmadhâtu*), those who attempt to realize it by means of practising are bound to causation and fruition. I do not teach[134] a lore [claiming] that there is a realization of this stage of the mind of perfect purity, i.e. the dimension of Reality, by engaging in practising and adulteration.

As to the teaching which says 'no understanding of the pristine awareness as object' [you ought to know the following]: regarding these objects, they are from the primordial the self-originated awareness. Consequently, the pristine awareness {p. 142} cannot be an object to the pristine awareness."

Such She spoke.

This is the forty-eighth chapter of *The All-Creating Sovereign, Mind of Perfect Purity,* in which She personally proclaimed that the ground of all existing things is the All-Creating Herself.

49

{cont'd p. 142} Then the All-Creating Sovereign, mind of perfect purity, taught "I am the place (*sa*) in which all existing things abide."[135]

"Oh great bodhisattva, I am the All-Creating Sovereign, where the central vigor of the entire [mind of] perfect purity abides. The own being of the mind of perfect purity is the palace of the dimension of Reality. All the Buddhas of the three times and all the sentient beings of this threefold world abide in the the vast dynamics (*klong chen*) of the mind. There is not one thing that does not abide therein. Luminosity is wherein everything abides, and all rests therein by being neither coagulated nor separated. There is no need to cleanse it in order to progress spiritually. If you cleanse it to make spiritual progress you would adulterate your own mind. But with adulteration you cannot cleanse your own mind. This is the universal place (*spyi sa*) in which everything abides.

Oh great bodhisattva, listen! The teachers in their three forms of manifestation, who emanate from Me, teach the gist of the bodhisattva stages under three aspects to those retinues who are attracted to [the concepts of] causation: the bodhisattva stage of generation (*bskyed pa'i sa*), the bodhisattva stage of practice (*spyod pa'i sa*), and the bodhisattva stage of realization (*sgrub pa'i sa*); these three they are teaching. At the bodhisattva stage of generation [a realization of] the mind [is aspired to] by generating the four [religious services]. At the bodhisattva stage of practice [a realization of] the mind [is aspired to] by practising the ten ways of living (*spyod bcu*). At the bodhisattva stage of realization [a realization of the mind is aspired to] by desiring achievement. Because this is taught as a teaching of a meaning in need of interpretation I do not teach that it is a pure lore of definitive meaning.

Now listen to My lore which is pure and of definitve meaning! {p. 143} Because the mind of perfect purity has neither cause nor condition, the mind of perfect purity cannot be generated at the bodhisattva stage of generation. If the mind of perfect purity were produced at the bodhisattva stage of generation, it would be in conflict with the mind of perfect purity being [limitless like] the sky and [identical with] the dimension of Reality. Those who are under the influence of remembering good and bad acts will attempt to abandon the external objects, which are [nothing else but] the dimension of Reality, which cannot be abandoned. [However] they can obstruct [the shortcomings of this transitory world] only by not obstructing the self-originated pristine awareness. By not understanding that the self-originated pristine awareness [abides] in the objects, they cannot annihilate such statements as 'subjects and objects exist'. Thereby the mind of perfect purity is not generated.

By practising the ten [aspects of] enlightenment at the bodhisattva stage of practice all the existent things are removed from the mind of perfect purity. This leads to the exhaustion of the apparent dimension of Reality which is like the sky. There is not even an iota which is in motion with regard to the sky, likewise nothing changes as to the mind of perfect purity.

As to the wish to achieve enlightenment at the bodhisattva stage of realization, there are the following names given to the bodhisattva stage of realizing enlightenment: (1) All-light (*kun tu 'od*), (2) Non-craving lotus eye (*ma chags padma spyan*), (3) Diamond holder (*rdo rje 'dzin*), (4) Solidly built (*stug po bkod pa*, Skr. Akanishta), (5) Wheel great-assembly Vajradhara (*'khor lo tshogs chen rdo rje 'chang*), and (6) All-Good inseparable from cause and result—these are the six bodhisattva stages. But because the mind's own being is free of causes and conditions, I do not teach that one can achieve the result by spiritual realizations.[136]

Now I am going to teach you the six forms of the mind's own being. The six [forms] of the mind's own being are as follows:

(1) The characteristic of the self-originated pristine awareness is indestructibility which is known as 'the place where all is light' (*kun tu 'od kyi sa*) as it is total luminosity present in the five sense organs {p. 144}.

(2) As there is no desire [directed] towards the imperceptible objects, [this stage] is called the non-craving lotus eye.

(3) As the mind of perfect purity is without becoming or ceasing, I call it the diamond holder.

(4) As your own being is limitless Reality and as the imperceptible self-originated pristine awareness is poised in balance, I call this stage the place which is firmly established (*stug po bkod pa*).

(5) The own being of the mind of perfect purity, in its mandala configuration (*dkyil 'khor*), abides as perfect purity in the things themselves. As mantric letters (*yi ge*), clustered in the mandala configurations, [the mind] is without origination or cessation in its [symbolic representation of] divine form, utterance, and spirit (*sku gsung thugs*) [I] call [this stage] the place of diamond-holder (*rdo rje 'chang gi sa*).[137]

(6) The mind of perfect purity is without cause and result, and therefore all things which arise from this mind are from the primordial dissociated from good and evil, or from acquiring and rejecting. For this reason I call it a place of no-distinction. For this reason [you ought to know the following] about the pure and perfect mind's dimension of Reality: The Buddhas of the three times and all the sentient beings of this threefold world who originate from this [mind of

perfect purity] abide therein; therefore the perfect pure mind's dimension of Reality is known as a place of universal practice (*kun spyod sa*).[138]

Such She spoke.

What is called the place of achieving buddhahood (*sangs rgyas sgrub pa'i sa*) is taught to be a place where there is no practising because what stems from the own being of the mind of perfect purity that abides in the mind of perfect purity as was explained before."

This is the forty-ninth chapter of *The All-Creating Sovereign, Mind of Perfect Purity,* wherein is explained that the Great Perfection is not a place of practice.

50

Then the All-Creating Sovereign, mind of perfect purity, taught that the self-originated pristine awareness, the mind of perfect purity, is without any fault. {p. 145}

"Oh great bodhisattva, listen! The pristine awareness is called so because the pristine awareness is pristinely aware [of all]. The self-originated pristine awareness is from the primordial [in a state of pure] awareness. If some understood this pristine awareness as an object [it would implie that] it could not be self-originated because it would come from objects. But because it isn't an object at all, it cannot be illuminated (i.e. recognized). For this reason, this self-originated pristine awareness is a pristine awareness which is intrinsically aware [of everything] from the primordial. This is called 'pristine awareness'.

The pristine awareness [present in] the teachers of the retinues is called a pristine awareness pertinent to objects. Who understands the objects (*rtog byed*), this person is called one who cognizes (*rig byed*). This object which ought to be cognized emanates from the mind of perfect purity. Therefore the mind of perfect purity cannot be an object. As the pristine awareness emerges from itself it cannot be contemplated in meditation. Who does not engage in meditation will not have karmic imprints [leaning] towards meditation. A dimension of Reality with no latent tendencies is explained as the intention of the Buddhas of the three times. The intention of all the Buddhas of the three times cannot be recognized like an object but abides in balance from the primordial.

Oh great bodhisattva, listen! Because the people do not understand that from the primordial the self-originated pristine awareness of all the Buddhas of the three times is in their mind, the Buddha's intention does not become manifest in them. [This self-originated pristine awareness] is absolutely no object of cognition. A practitioner of the Atiyoga who abides in a state of non-conceptual thinking and who [thinks] 'whatever is, is right', this person manifests the Buddha's intention.

Oh great bodhisattva, listen! The self-originated pristine awareness {p. 146} enacts the Buddhas' intention. Because the self-originated pristine awareness cannot be conceptualized as an object it is not associated with karmic imprints (*bag chags*) of conceptual thinking. The enacting of inherited karmic imprints is called meditation, but I do never proclaim that the non-conceptual is of such inherited karmic imprints. The non-conceptual and self-originated pristine awareness [unfolds into] five aspects, and they originate in the five sensory faculties which are the mind's own being. This self-originated pristine awareness is ceaseless (*'gag pa med*). The mind of perfect purity is apparent in its actuation. The ceaseless self-originated pristine awareness appears in individuality but as such it is not to be abandoned as it appears due to a condition which is itself. A meditation which is non-conceptual will not accumulate such karmic imprints but is in accord with the intention of the Buddhas of the three times. Who abides in this [state of] not conceptualizing whatsoever, they will not abide in Me, and not in a state which benefits sentient beings, but they will be integrated with the mind of perfect purity which is the manifestation of truth. This is the summation of the intention of all the Buddhas of the three times.

Oh great bodhisattva, you must understand the meaning of this word which is an application of cognition (*rig pa*). The self-originated pristine awareness abides fivefold in the sensory objects. [As such it is called] the fivefold pristine awareness which is not an object-oriented desire, but which appears as the fivefold object-oriented desire (*yul 'dod lnga*). Because these objects are from the primordial pristine awareness, I do not teach that objects and pristine awareness are two different entities. On this account I also explain the objects as self-originated pristine awareness. Except for the sole self-originated pristine awareness nothing exists.

The retinues' teachers, emanating from Me, may use [the term] 'pristine awareness' in its connection with sensory objects. [This usage] results in the generation of a multitude of pristine awarenesses, but [despite] such designations the pristine awareness is one. To define as object what is [actually] the subject, i.e. the holistic nature of the objects (*yul cig rang bzhin*) apparent in their particularity, {p. 147} this is a definition of error and only a definitive one.

My self-originated pristine awareness is not the all-creating, but My own being is the only all-creating one. Different names are given to it in accord with the retinues' wishes: some call [My own being] mind of perfect purity; some call it dimension of Reality; some call it the vastness of the sky; some call it self-originated pristine awareness; some call it manifestation of truth; some call it manifestation of consummate joy; some call it corporeal manifestation; some call it divine form, utterance, and spirit (*sku gsung thugs*); some call it the omniscient; some call it the all-encompassing; some call it the three or four wisdoms; some call it the fivefold pristine awareness; some call it dimension and pristine awareness. But the only name given by those who confess that they have seen the self-originated is self-originated mind of perfect purity."

Such She spoke.

This is the fiftieth chapter of *The All-Creating Sovereign, Mind of Perfect Purity,* in which the self-originated pristine awareness is explained.

51

Then the All-Creating Sovereign, mind of perfect purity, taught that there is no progress on a path [leading to] the Great Perfection.

"Oh great bodhisattva listen! I, the All-Creating Sovereign, am the mind of perfect purity. {p.148} This mind of perfect purity is the great universal path. The Buddha's abode [of existence], the world of objects, and the levels [of spiritual achievement] exist in nothing else but in [this mind's] own being. Also the dimension of Reality and Reality [itself] abide therein. The vastness of the sky and the divine mansion exist therein. The Buddha's abode of existence and the world of objects are the mind of perfect purity. Beside [this mind of perfect purity] there is neither a path to make progress on nor a place to exist in. No one ever walked the path of the sky by progressing.

Oh great bodhisattva, listen! Who teach that there is a path of progress are the teachers' three manifestations who emanate from Me. They teach five or three paths of progress. Who desire to arrive [at the goal] by progressing [on these paths] wish to obtain a result in accord with its cause. But this is not in accord with the Great Perfection where there is no progress. [These people] are defeated by the duality of subject and object when they attempt to achieve the two accumulations [of wisdom and merit] by means of the five [paths such as] that of accumulation, practice, meditation, vision and that of realization. But the only result they achieve through their consideration of a doctrine of religious practice is that they will never encounter the path of no-progress. Not even by name [will they be able to achieve] what is beyond striving and achieving, i.e. the great bliss.

The three paths which secretly teach [how to achieve] the result are 'suchness' (*de bzhin nyid*), 'universal appearance' (*kun tu snang*), etc., which are known as the paths of the three forms of [the teachers'] manifestations. Who reflect [upon such systems] by meditating on them, and who want to progress by means of the four religious practices, which turn the self-originated Reality into cause and result, they will never reach a state which is beyond striving and achieving. But those who abide in the dimension of Reality, which is their own mind, free of conceptualization, they dwell as all Buddhas in this [state of] non-conceptualization. For this reason do not try to progress on a path. Your own mind is lucid in its stainless sky-like expanse. {p. 149} Therein all Buddhas of the three times abide. For this reason do not try to progress on a path. Who [understand] their own mind in its non-conceptual Reality, in its actual existence they are spontaneously perfected as the Buddhas of the three times. For this reason do not try to progress on a path.

If ignorance makes them progress on a path, then there will be no time of completed progress, nor will there be time when intuition is achieved. By means of such progress these people will never achieve the state of buddhahood. The Buddha of one's own mind is beyond cognitive perception. But nobody can go by means of spiritual progress to one's own mind which is not [an object of] cognitive perception. By reflecting upon doctrinal views these people are bound to meditation as an object. Through this meditation they are not in balance with that which is beyond cognitive perception. Through observance of their vows they have taken to practice. Through being caught by what cannot be practised they are not in balance with that which is beyond cognitive perception. Through striving after salutary acts they perform a success-oriented meditation. Because of this success-oriented meditation they are not in balance with what is beyond cognitive perception. Through practising the [bodhisattva] stages they perform a meditation of abiding. Because of this meditation of purifying they are not in balance with what is beyond cognitive perception. Through investigating Reality they perform a meditation of clarity. Because of this meditation of clarity they are not in balance with what is beyond cognitive perception. But those who practise a meditation which lucidly intuits pristine awareness, they [have realized] the imperceptible due to this meditation of lucid intuition.

Oh great bodhisattva, listen! A success-oriented meditation, regardless of how clear it may be, will never realize what is without success. The great bliss which is completely free of any activity can be obtained only by those who do not desire what is not [an object of] cognitive perception. The self-originated pristine awareness does not fall under the control of any deeds because it is not produced through meditation nor through the accumulation of karmic imprints. {p. 150} The self-originated pristine awareness is the central vigour of the truth manifestation which can never be achieved by striving but only by abiding in one's own being. You must rid yourself of purposing any achievements. 'Purpose' is nothing but a word. In terms of the utterly pure, even 'Buddha' is nothing but a word. [If] the word 'Buddha' is applied then such teaching is of disputable and not of definitive meaning.

If the teachers' three manifestations, who emanate from Me, use such words as 'teaching, Buddha, sangha, these three jewels do exist' they act like a ferryman telling all sentient beings, who emanated as My retinues from Me, 'be happy, be lucky, bliss is nothing else than giving up this suffering here'. Thereby they are teaching a doctrine [promising] achievements through following various doctrinal views and religious practices. But this is not the deedless lore of Me, the All-Creating One."

Such She spoke.

This is the fifty-first chapter of *The All-Creating Sovereign, Mind of Perfect Purity,* in which is covered 'no progress on the path'.

52

{cont'd p. 150} Then the All-Creating Sovereign, mind of perfect purity, expounded that the deedless Great Perfection is unagitated.[139]

"Oh great bodhisattva, with regard to the desire for achieving all things, do not try to achieve the goal of your desires! The mind which is engaged in desiring gives up all which is unobtainable. Because [the unobtainable mind of perfect purity] is beyond cause and result, the cause will not be achieved if the result is desired. Those who abide in nature, which is beyond cognitive perception, will achieve [all things]. But a meditation [driven by a] desire [for achievements] will make you abandon everything. To be without any desires [for spiritual progress] lets you acquire everything. {p.151} The performance of meditation gets you seized by desire, and this desire is not pure. It is impossible to be seized by the pure. A performance which must be done is to seek after no single thing; this will let you become spontaneously perfected. This unsought spontaneous perfection is not realized through any acts, but is uncreated, timeless, and spontaneously perfected.

It is a great impediment in one's pursuit of realization to give up all in the desire [to obtain] everything. These karmic imprints [produced by] a meditation desiring [results] seize the mind. Because of this seizing, these [practioners] are forced to give up bliss. If they are not seized [by such desires] they will gain all the bliss. This is the innate being of suchness. Unconceptualized suchness is one with the intention of all Buddhas. Where, except for the great bliss, could desire and seizing exist? The non-existent cannot be perceived. What cannot be thought of cannot be contemplated. The central meaning of this negation is that through not desiring [anything, everything] will be obtained. The non-existence of wishing to seize anything is the best [way of] seizing meditation.[140] Those who seize the whole will be accomplished from the primordial, and they will master the accomplishment of being in a state of balance which is beyond cognitive perception.

Oh great bodhisattva, different meditations will not elucidate the one. There does not exist a single [form of] meditation which could make meditation be lucid. In this context there is no meditation. With regard to the one, i.e. suchness, there is no difference between the Buddhas and the sentient beings. To distinguish between bliss and suffering, to teach that one should strive after bliss, and to teach that one should throw off the evil deeds {p. 152} contradicts My lore and is of non-definitive [meaning].

Oh great bodhisattva, do not distinguish as two what is one! Bliss and suffering are one in their perfect purity. Buddhas and sentient beings are one in terms of the mind. Being and the existence of the animated and inanimated world are one in terms of their Reality. Even truth and falseness are equal in terms of Reality. Do not attempt to obtain bliss nor to reject suffering. By abiding in nature all is accomplished. Being attached to bliss constitutes suffering. By not conceptualizing the bliss of the totally lucid [you] are the self-originated pristine awareness. As this [self-originated] pristine awareness is untainted by any karmic imprints, from where then could such karmic imprints of the deeds come?

Understanding pristine awareness and meditation as cause and result leads the cognitive meditation to be affected by karmic imprints. A pristine awareness under the power of karmic imprints is unable to function as discriminative awareness (*rtog pa'i ye shes*). Those who meditate upon the discriminative awareness will be separated from the imperceptible sameness. They are captured by the disease of striving after meditation.

Oh great bodhisattva, I, the All-Creating One, the mind of perfect purity, am the mind of perfect purity of everything. Nothing is outside of the mind of perfect purity. The multiplicity of things emanates from the mind. The multiplicity of emanated things appears in individuality.

It is worthwhile to rejoice in the way the sentient beings appear as to their form, appearance, and color. This rejoicing reveals the affection [innate in all] things which is declared to be a manifestation of the compassionate [nature] of the pristine awareness. [This rejoicing] is unaffected by such things as [the things'] own being and unaffected by the such things as the Buddhas' own being. Therefore it is identical with the Reality of the Buddhas of the three times. {p. 153} Outside of Reality no Buddhas exist; outside of the Buddhas no sentient beings exist. The sentient beings are the imperceptible intention of the Buddhas. Until the mind of perfect purity is realized, neither Buddhas nor sentient beings exist. Therefore the mind itself is more praised than the Buddhas. The mind in itself is immutable and has been immutable from the primordial. The arising of Reality does not stir up an iota of agitation. With regard to the one, the teachers teaching the nine levels (*rim pa dgu*) or the 8[4],000 doctrines do not understand the meaning of the one. If one does not understand the one, one cannot understand the meaning of all. Thus it is truly difficult [to understand] the meaning of the mind as the one."

Such She spoke.

This is the fifty-second chapter of *The All-Creating Sovereign, Mind of Perfect Purity,* in which is covered "no agitation" and "no desire."

53

{cont'd p. 153} Then the All-Creating Sovereign, mind of perfect purity, spoke on [the topic] that all things are unagitated.

"Oh great bodhisattva, you ought to intuit Me! If you intuit Me, you will intuit that all things are unagitated. I Myself am the All-Creating Sovereign, the supreme teacher,[141] who is unagitated with regard to the mind of perfect purity. By virtue of the mind of perfect purity everything is unagitated—peace! The self-originated pristine awareness is without cause and condition, thus it is the supreme master of all causes and results. But this should be kept absolutely secret from the followers of the vehicle of causation. The mastery of the unborn and diamond-like dimension of Reality should not be spoken of but kept secret from the followers of the vehicle of causation. The mastery of the unceasing mind itself, which is like the vastness of the sky, {p. 154} should not be spoken of but kept secret from the followers of the vehicle of causation. That all that appears and exists as animated and inanimated world is totally mastered in its Reality should not be spoken of but kept secret from the followers of the vehicle of causation. That the appearance of five [great elements such as] sky, wind, water, earth, and fire is truly mastered in the actuation (*ngo bo*) of the mind of perfect purity should not be spoken of but kept secret from the followers of the vehicle of causation. That the three existential realms (*khams gsum*) and the three poisons are mastered by the pristine awareness in one's mind should not be spoken of but kept secret from the followers of the vehicle of causation.

With regard to the own being of the mind of perfect purity, the All Creating One, there is neither vanishing nor ceasing as the nature is without ceasing. The dimension of Reality, i.e. nature, is non-conceptual; this blissful peace[142] does not vanish nor cease as nature is non-conceptual. The lucidity of the stainless self-originated pristine awareness is in its vastness neither vanishing nor ceasing; it is ceaseless. The own being of of the dimension of Reality, i.e. what appears and exists as animated and inanimated, is neither vanishing nor ceasing; the own being is ceaseless. All things neither vanish nor cease.

The true being is lucid, and its actuation unagitated. Attempting to bring about causes and result of things which [by their own being] are unagitated, this is not My lore; it is a lore of desire. I am all-accomplished because I am without desire. The nature is non-desiring and undesirable and thus accomplished. But I do not say 'accomplished' because it is just a word [spoken] by those who desire to bring about causes and results. I am a great opponent of praise and dispraise.

'Existing' and 'non existing', 'accomplishing' and 'not accomplishing', 'praising' and 'dispraising', all these designations exist because of their non-conceptual [character] in sameness. I, the progenitor of all Buddhas, do not teach any other thinking (*dgongs pa*) than that of the sameness [of all things]. This undeclared sameness is not taught by any of the Buddhas. The entire teaching is taught as My actuation. The actuation of My true nature {p. 155} is the entirety of all things. Who masters the sameness, which is in its nature pure, will be totally dissociated from desiring the immutable nature. [This mastery of sameness] cannot be seized as an object, thus there is no place for the mind. Those who desire to directly obtain [this state] will remain attached by desiring it. Due to this situation they do not have the thought of non-conceptual sameness.

Reality exists by its nature beyond time. Those who are made to strive after [Reality] or who attempt to desire it are searching for something other than their own mind. They damage all things which exist in this threefold world, and which are the sky-like vastness of the dimension of Reality. They will never find their own mind or abide in their own being. One's own mind is in its nature vast as the sky whose limitations cannot be found, is in its dimension without decrease; but they will be unable to find their own mind in its sky-like nature. The whole nature of things should be seen in this way.

Suchness is in its entirety unadulterated. Whatever one may contemplate is a play of Reality, yet suchness in its actuation is immutable. If it were mutable so that it could increase its vigor then a single [attempt of] meditation could empty the perishable world. Suchness is immutable, although they say otherwise, and its own being is an object of the own being of greatness. 'Own being' is another name of the unadulterated, and 'greatness' is said because as greatness it is unadulterated.

I do not say that there is any difference in terms of size or quality between the Buddhas' form, utterance, and spirit, and the sentient beings' body, speech, and mind. The non-conceptual Reality is identical with sameness. {p. 156} With regard to sameness there is not a single existing or non-existing thing. [Consequently] the sentient beings are not the cause, and the Buddhas are not the result. A teaching of causation is the lore of a teacher who is wrong. For this reason, the things emanating from Me are the same [in their actual being]. What emanates from Me is neither good nor bad but one in sameness."

Such She spoke.

This is the fifty-third chapter of *The All-Creating Sovereign, Mind of Perfect Purity,* on the theme that all things are in their own being unagitated.

54

Then the All-Creating Sovereign, mind of perfect purity, [taught] that Her own being is the self-originated pristine awareness and that this self-originated pristine awareness is associated with five actuations (*ngo bo*). How is this?

(1) It is the central vigor from which all things emanate;
(2) it is actuating definitive and unerring [truth];
(3) it is actuating the overcoming of causation;
(4) it is actuating deedlessness;
(5) it is actuating the decisiveness of all things.

Five essential tractates summarize the self-originated pristine awareness in this context. But the detailed lore is proclaimed in fifty-seven [tractates].[143]

"Oh great bodhisattva, hear these essential points! I, the All-Creating Sovereign, mind of perfect purity, am one with the great self-originated pristine awareness. This self-originated pristine awareness is summarized in the five [tractates] from which the fifty-seven detailed ones come. My actuation is in these fifty-seven tractates. How is it that My actuating being [is revealed this way]? Ten tractates teach that the nature of all things is the actuating being of pristine awareness. Ten tractates, unerring and definitive, teach the actuation of the non-erring and definitve pristine awareness. Ten tractates, beyond causation, teach the actuation of pristine awareness which is non-erring and definitve. {p. 157} Ten tractates, consummate in their deedlessness, teach the actuation of the deedless pristine awareness. Ten decisive tractates teach the actuation of the pristine awareness' decisiveness. From the five actuations of pristine awareness as mind itself come the five sets of ten tractates. As actuations of [My] own being I am teaching five [forms of] confidence. As to [the remaining] seven tractates (i.e. chapters of the KBG) one of these seven definitive chapters teaches about the ground, another about sacred instructions, and five on different necessities.

The detailed teaching of its meaning: first, ten revealing tractates are taught in order to let them see the Reality. [Secondly,] ten more tractates, unerring and definitive, are taught so that confidence in being and non-being and its conceptualization are cleared away. [Thirdly,] ten more tractates, beyond causation, are taught so that [they understand that] the All-Creating Sovereign's own being, which is the pristine awareness, does not depend on causes and conditions. [Fourthly,] ten more tractates, consummate in their deedlessness, are taught so that [they understand that] there is no necessity for striving to achieve the deedless which is the All-Creating Sovereign's own being, i.e. the pristine awareness. [Fifthly,] ten more tractates on decisiveness are taught so that [they can understand that] because of the All-Creating Sovereign's self-originated pristine awareness one's very own being is decisive.

With regard to its meaning there are five reasons. In the tractate 'Reality becoming apparent', the reason is given for seeing Reality in an apparent manner. Those who see Reality in an unerring direct manner {p. 158} have no reason to follow a path of doctrinal views, religious practice, and vows. In the tractate which teaches a non-erring definitive [truth], the reason for a non-erring confidence is given. Because of an apparent confidence in the mind's own non-erring [nature] there is no reason for accomplishing buddhahood. In the tractate [which teaches that] there is no dependence on causes and conditions, it is [said] to be a good quality that there is no reason for engaging in striving and achieving. There the reason exists to abide in the bliss of non-striving because there is no reason for striving and achieving. In the tractate which teaches the consummate deedlessness, the reason for the consummate nature which is deedless is given. Because of the reason for the consummate and deedless nature there is a reason for spontaneous self-perfection since the primordial. In the tractate which teaches decisiveness it is decided that it is in accord with the five [basic] tractates [to say that] the Buddhas of the three times and the sentient beings of the threefold world, all that appears and exists as animated and inanimated world, is without cause, definitive, self-originated, and deedless.

The teaching of the root tractate on decisiveness was first taught by the Buddhas of the three times. Reality's own, sky-like being is seen by the sentient beings as future and past of the three times. [You] see that they do not understand the sky-like Reality because the future is of no concern and the karmic imprints of the past have ceased.

Now the definition of 'Buddha, Buddha'(Tib. *sangs rgyas*): *sangs* is the lucid character of the fields of the sensory faculties, i.e. the dimension of the non-conceptual, with regard to Reality, the nature of the mind of perfect purity. *rGyas* is the all-encompassing [quality] which is like the sky. {p. 159} But I do not apply the name 'Buddha'.

The definition of *khams* (field [of sensory activity]) is taught as follows: it has the characteristics of plenitude and vastness, and is called field because not a single living being of this threefold world can fathom it with his or her sense faculties. But I do not apply the name in a pure and definitive [connotation].

'Mind' is definitively taught as self-originated pristine awareness which is without causes and conditions, but which unceasingly illumines the five sensory faculties of all. Thus what is called 'mind' is explained to be lucid.

Altogether what appears and exists in the form of the animated and inanimated world appears as a wonder because of its lack of origin. Because it exists in diversity it is called appearing and existing.[144]

Inanimated (*snod,* lit. vessel) and animated (*bcud,* lit. juice, sap) are explained as follows: because within the vessel (*snod*) of the five elements are the six categories [of living beings] as sap; thus it is said 'inanimated' and 'animated'.

'All' is summarizing [the meaning of] everything without remainder. For this reason the five aspects of the mind of perfect purity, the All-Creating Sovereign's own being, emerge in a condensed form from the fifty-seven tractates. In short, I am teaching the All-Creating's fivefold own being as (1) Her own being as the previously generated central vigor [of all things]; (2) Her own being as a non-erring and decisive teaching; (3) Her own being transcending cause and result as it is self-originated; (4) Her own being transcending striving and achieving as it is deedless; and (5) Her own being of decisive sameness."

Such She spoke.

[Great bodhisattva:]

"Oh teacher, All-Creating Sovereign, in the oneness of my own intelligence as Sems-dpa' rdo-rje, {p. 160} and the pristine awareness which constitutes the All-Creating's own being, the five fulfillments of necessary reasons arise. Because of the potency (*nus pa*) to appear from what is non-apparent, [inherent to] all things, which exist in the way they appear from the things' [own] central vigor, i.e. the self-originated pristine awareness, one may be confident that this central vigor of things does exist.

Because of the non-erring and definitive teaching of the mind of perfect purity, as to being the sole actuation of the self-originated pristine awareness in its non-duality of ultimate and conventional, and of truth and lies, one may be confident that there are no doubts or uncertainties.

Because of nature being the sole actuation of the self-originated pristine awareness, and being not dependent on anything else as it does not rely on causes nor is accomplished through conditions, one may be confident that the self-originated pristine awareness does exist.

Because of the spontaneous perfection, free of causes and conditions, as sole actuation of the self-originated pristine awareness, which makes it superfluous to strive after the deedless through salutary acts, one may be confident that the spontaneous perfection, which cannot be sought, does exist.

Because of the primordial faultlessness of the self-originated pristine awareness as the sole actuation of the self-originated pristine awareness, and because all things being decisive as to their lucidity in the way they appear, one may be confident that [this lore] is the teaching's lamp."

Such he spoke.

This is fifty-fourth chapter of *The All-Creating Sovereign, Mind of Perfect Purity,* in which is given a summary of the All-Creating Sovereign's own being [as found in] all tractates.

55

{cont'd p. 160} Then the All-Creating Sovereign, mind of perfect purity, proclaimed this tractate that there is nothing else than all things as the mind of perfect purity {p. 161}.

"Oh great bodhisattva, listen! That all that exists in the way it appears as animated and inanimated, and all that can be vocalized in terms of words and their meaning is the mind of perfect purity, this is as follows. It is not my teaching that anything else than the non-conceptual, unobscured mind of perfect purity, which is the dimension of Reality, the expanse of the sky, does exist. I teach that the actuation of the mind of perfect purity is given the form of that which appears as sky, wind, water, earth, and fire. The actuation of the mind of perfect purity appears in three ways as the realm of desire (*kâmaloka*), the realm of forms (*rûpaloka*), and the realm of formlessness (*arûpaloka*). The perfect and pure mind's own being unfolds in the teaching of the teachers' three forms of manifestation. The mind in itself as unceasing pristine awareness appears as the realm of desire. The actuation of the mind itself appears as the realm of forms, while the mind's own unborn being [manifests] as realm of formlessness. The unborn own being [of the mind] is non-conceptual and the manifestation of truth. The mind itself as manifestation of joy rejoices itself in itself. The mind as manifestation of the mind fulfills as corporeal manifestation the mind's purpose.

Because the six categories of sentient beings, such as the denizens of hell, etc. who have fallen into [the suffering of] heat, cold, hunger, thirst, idiocy, and dumbness, are equal in terms of the non-conceptual, therefore they are liberated in the Reality of suchness. Because the self-originated pristine awareness cannot be conceptualized as an object [the sentient beings] are free of karmic imprints and of all faults. Because no good qualities can be acquired, nor any faults be given up, no happiness is to be achieved nor any suffering to be abandoned. {p.162}

Suchness is primordially unagitated. Not one thing is that changes by changing its suchness. Also, not one thing can be acquired by appropriating it with desire. The characteristic of the arising of things' own being is its similarity with the arising of the self-originated pristine awareness from the mind. The term 'similarity' means that [the things' own being] is the self-originated pristine awareness.

Those who see anything else but the self-originated pristine awareness which is Reality as its sole object, they have given up the pristine awareness and will be unable to encounter the self-originated pristine awareness. The names of those who hold that objects are to be given up and terminated are unknown. For seven lifetimes they have forsaken the self-originated pristine awareness after it took them three eons to practise in accord with the two truths, i.e. the ultimate and the conventional truth, and after they have entered the door of signlessness and performed the three purifications, after they have entered the door to all limbs of enlightenment, and after they have performed the stages of *samâdhi* complemented with rituals. After they have entered the door to the non-duality of wisdom and skill-in-means, after they have lived in accord with the unoriginated wisdom and skill-in-means, after they have contemplated themselves as being without inherent nature (*rang bzhin*) in their appearance, and after they have striven hard after [the realization of] the five rituals (*cho ga lnga*) along with their ingredients and peripherals, and the way of the vows, they still will remain for 600,000 years at the level of a wisdom-holder (*vidyâdhara*) and perform without any distraction a meditation aiming at [achieving] the manifestation of joy. But even when they have reached the manifestation of joy they will yearn anew for their own mind. Only after a thousand [eons (?)] will they for the first time[145] find the sameness [of all things] in the non-conceptual [nature].

Oh great Sems-dpa' rdo-rje now you yourself should teach My unerring lore! Oh, the sentient beings, such as gods and humans, are of coarse intelligence. {p. 163} Due to their nature which draws their senses towards the objects, these ignorant beings are content with whatever they are taught. If [you] don't teach them the great unerring and definitive lore they will be satisfied with knowing that truth and falseness are two, after they were instructed in the ultimate and conventional truth which is a teaching about causes and results, and in need of interpretation. For eons they will remain [in a state where they believe] in the duality of truth and falseness. For this reason you must first teach about one's own mind as being without error. When they have been introduced through your teaching to this path of no-error and no-striving they will immediately abide in a state of no-striving. They will meet the path of no-striving. They will meet the meditation that does not need meditating. By abiding in bliss without striving for it, they will acquire it. They abide in their own mind in a non-erring and definitive [manner].[146]

The ability (*yon tan*) of spontaneous self-perfection which cannot be sought [stipulates] that there is no need for developing *bodhicitta,* following the path, practising the bodhisattva stage, contemplating doctrinal views, observing the vows and morality.

Oh great bodhisattva, teach this lore! Those who want to accomplish this teaching which is a defining characteristic of this world must not meditate on deities as an act of bodily performance, nor must they utter mantras and words as acts of their voice, nor must they contemplate the lucid [character] of meditation as an act of their mind."

Such She spoke.

This is the fifty-fifth chapter of *The All-Creating Sovereign, Mind of Perfect Purity,* which explains that all existing things are nothing but the mind of perfect purity.

56

{p. 164} Then Sems-dpa' rdo-rje addressed Her retinues saying that the All-Creating Sovereign, mind of perfect purity, is actuating all things and that She is their creator. He (Sems-dpa' rdo-rje) submitted his understanding as follows:

"Oh teacher of the teachers, All-Creating Sovereign, I understand Your own being to be one with all existent things. In the palace of the dimension of Reality, i.e. Reality, is the All-Creating Sovereign, this is well known. Also in the celestial mansion, which is the expanse of the sky is the All-Creating Sovereign, this is well known. Oh, You, teacher of the unborn manifestations of truth, You are the All-Creating Sovereign; this is well known. Also the all wish-fulfilling manifestations of joy are the All-Creating Sovereign, this is well known. Also the corporeal manifestations of compassion and pristine awareness are the All-Creating Sovereign, this is well known. Also the dimension of passions in this realm of desire is the All-Creating Sovereign, this is well known. Also the dimension of pride in this realm of form is the All-Creating Sovereign, this is well known.[147] Also the organic structure (*lus*) of the mind in the realm of formlessness is the All-Creating Sovereign, this is well known. Also the previously existing Buddhas themselves are the All-Creating Sovereign, this is well known. Also the presently abiding Buddhas in fulfilling their purpose are the All-Creating Sovereign, this is well known. {p. 165} Also the [Buddhas] emerging from Her in the future are the AllCreating Sovereign, this is well known. The four yogas although a doctrinal view about Her, are the All-Creating Sovereign, this is well known. What appears and exists as animated and inanimated, in short what arises due to the five elements, is the All-Creating Sovereign, this is well known. Outside and except for the All-Creating Sovereign nothing exists. Neither Buddhas nor sentient beings, neither an animated nor inanimated world, nor anything which is in short known as a phenomenon appears except the All-Creating Sovereign."

Such spoke Sems-dpa' rdo-rje.

This is the fifty-sixth chapter of *The All-Creating Sovereign, Mind of Perfect Purity,* in which Sems-dpa' rdo-rje expounds his understanding of the All-Creating Sovereign's own being.

57

{cont'd p. 165} Then the All-Creating Sovereign, mind of perfect purity, expounded this chapter on entrusting this teaching to Sems-dpa' rdo-rje.

"Oh Sems-dpa' rdo-rje, capture this! You as self-originated pristine awareness, you originated as the central vigor of Me. Therefore, you ought to grasp My own being. From the three aspects of My own being, the teacher's three forms of manifestation also originate. Therefore, you ought to grasp their own being. You will be the teacher [issuing] the lion's roar of the threefold teaching.[148] You will be teaching the retinues [existent] in time and place that I have made them. Grasp My own being according to My nature as the All-Creating [potential] and according to My name 'All-Creating [Sovereign]'. {p. 166}

As I am the Buddhas' progenitor you will be the progenitor of all Buddhas. I Myself, the All-Creating Sovereign, am father and mother of the teacher's three forms of manifestation, therefore you will be father and mother of the teacher's three forms of manifestation. As progenitor of the Buddhas of the three times you will be the progenitor of all sentient beings. When you will issue the lion's roar you must not say anything else but 'all and everything in the way it exists, and myself,' oh great bodhisattva, 'are nothing else than the All-Creating Sovereign Herself'.

To give such designations as sentient beings and Buddhas in a desire for [gaining] the result after its causes were realized and to claim that sentient [beings][149] will achieve the result of buddhahood, such is not My teaching. My own being, All-Creating, transcends the duality of cause and result. As sentient beings and Buddhas are not two [different entities], buddhahood cannot be achieved through the sentient [beings]. I Myself am the All-Creating Sovereign, the self-originated pristine awareness of the mind itself."

Such She spoke.

This completes the fifty-seventh chapter of *The All-Creating Sovereign, Mind of Perfect Purity,* on the entrusting of the teaching.

NOTES

1. The English translation of *byang chub kyi sems* follows the literal meaning as given in the exegetical literature of Tibet, and not the usual translation of the corresponding Sanskrit *bodhicitta* ("enlightened mind" or "mind of enlightenment").

2. The Tibetan term *gnas* is used throughout the KBG in a modified meaning. The term certainly maintains the general meaning of place, but adds the connotation of existence. It is not too different from the Latin word *existere,* "standing out," from a homogeneous and non-specified form of *esse,*

being. The English word "to exist" has not preserved this connotation, and it is the only verb which can be used for describing the unqualified fact of being. The distinction made between Latin *esse* and Latin *existere*, which roughly corresponds to the use of Tibetan *yod* and Tibetan *gnas* in the KBG, is difficult to preserve in English. Where I felt the distinction was paramount, I rephrased the entire sentence.

3. The Tibetan text repeats the first part of this sentence every time. I replaced this sentence with an ellipsis to avoid cumbersome repetition.

4. The term "method" (Skr. *upâya*, Tib. *thabs*) refers to the Buddha's method of rescuing the sentient beings from the endless abyss of samsara. Its most crucial component is his "great compassion" which enables the Buddha to see all things as essentially one. Sometimes the term is also translated as "skill-in-means". In this text, the term "method" is—as most other terms of the sutra literature—loaded with a different meaning. As shall become clear later on, method in this text means "no-method" as reality is, since beginningless time, in the state of consummation.

5. The Tibetan expression *dus dang gnas* defines the parameter of our individual existence, but also the parameter within which the teaching and the Buddha's existence are revealed to the retinues. In the latter context it could also be translated as "the right time and right place" for the dissemination of the doctrine.

6. This term is here synonymous with *gnas* (mKhan-po Rig-'dzin).

7. "Cause of adornment" (*rgyan gyi rgyu*) is a rNying-ma term indicating that the universe is to the absolute what jewelry is to a prince. Jigs-med gling-pa said once that the universe is an adornment like the seven royal things offered during the normal *pûja*, i.e. elephant, minister, horse, etc.

8. Tibetan *lus* has here the meaning of Tibetan *gzugs* (mKhan-po Rig-'dzin).

9. The Tibetan text has "Her mind" which is in contrast to the direct speech mode of this paragraph.

10. These three reasons are: 1. the self-arising pristine awareness, 2. the five awarenesses, and 3. the five elements.

11. The Tibetan text uses here the personal pronoun of the first person, *nga* = I, where the pronoun of the third person would be more suitable.

12. In the KBG, the term *ye nas* identifies a realm or situation which is not determined by the space/time coordinates. The described situation does not happen within the web of time, but outside of it. The term means that things happen in the eternal now where there is neither a past nor a beginning. The term identifies an atemporal context.

13. Read *nga yis rang byung* for *nga yi rang byung*.

14. The Tibetan word *byung* has numerous connotations, all deriving from the basic meaning "to become, to unfold, to come forth," etc. Here the definition of the term determines to some extent the present connotation. Therefore, the same word *byung* was translated in two ways: "revelation" when it was defined as the nine vehicles and as "manifestation" when it was defined as the totality of the visible world.

15. In the Indo-Tibetan tradition, the letter A, the first in the Indian alphabet, stands for the consummation of wisdom and knowledge. For instance, the meaning of the entire Perfection of Wisdom Sutras (*Prajñâpâramitâ*) is symbolicly condensed to the letter A. In a figurative way, the alphabet is the entrance to the realm of learning and knowing. Therefore, the alphabet's first letter epitomizes this function more than any other letter.

16. I read *khyod kyis ston pa dang bstan pa* for *khyod kyi ston pa'i bstan pa.*

17. Bh reads *nga ni thams cad 'byung ba'i snying po bas* which I consider to be better than Kh "I am the friend of all things."

18. The phrase *snang srid* is the same as *chos thams cad,* i.e. all things, or the entirety of what exists.

19. This sentence refers to the result of the noble eightfold path, i.e. nirvana, which usually is called the "fruit", as the end to the arising of "thirst." By denying nirvana, the need for stopping the arising or origination of thirst (and in its consequence, that of suffering) is also denied. With this statement one of the core tenets of common Buddhism is rejected.

20. Read *bden gnyis kyis* for *bden gnyis kyi.*

21. This result is the intrinsic awareness of the *Atiyoga* stage which views the entire universe as being in a state of consummation.

22. I abbreviated the translation of this sentence which otherwise would read: "Because the mind's own being is endowed with five faculties, these five [faculties of the mind's] own being are called the five great [elements]."

23. It is possible that the ten instructions are identical with or related to the ten aspects of true being (*rang bzhin bcu*).

24. *La dor* is a condensation of the phrase *la dgu lung dgu* plus the verb *dor*. Consequently the meaning is that these ten instructions give up or avoid a path which takes one—in a figurative sense—over nine passes and through nine valleys; thus it is the path without deviations. For similar phrases see the last verse in chapter ten, but also chapter nine has similar wordings.

25. The Tibetan text uses the expression *bdag nyid dbyings* which is unusual as Buddhism in general negates the concept of *bdag nyid,* i.e. "self". mKhan-po Rig-'dzin sees this term as equivalent to *rang bzhin dbyings,* "dimension of own being."

26. This translation follows the Bh reading, which differs significantly from Kh in this sentence.

27. These are three classes of beings: (1) *ye shes sems dpa'*, i.e. the deities visualized in meditation; (2) *dam tshig sems dpa'*, i.e. the person who undertook the vows, or the yogi, who is sometimes also called (3) *ting nge 'dzin sems dpa'*, "the person absorbed in meditation" (see also KBG p. 86.4).

28. Tibetan *drag dal* is glossed as *rtsub po dang lhod dal* in *Bod rgya tshig mdzod chen mo*.

29. The Tibetan term is *byang chub lnga dang cho 'phrul rnam pa bzhi* as it occurs in chapter eight (p.27), or *chang chub lnga dang cho 'phrul chen po bzhi* as in chapter thirty-seven (p. 109). Here it is rendered as *byang chub lnga dang cho 'phrul yan lag*.

30. The *ting nge 'dzin gsum*, or three *samâdhi*, are frequently mentioned in our text. bDud-'joms Rin-po-che, late hierarch of the rNying-ma-pa, explained that term as a *samâdhi* on suchness (*de bzhin nyid kyi ting nge 'dzin*), a *samâdhi* on the totality of existence (*kun snang gyi ting nge 'dzin*), and a *samâdhi* on the cause (*rgyu'i ting nge 'dzin*) in his work *rNying bstan* p. 159a.1ff.

31. Here follows the first mentioning of the ten statements regarding the nature of the Sovereign Mind, or as the Tibetan text calls them "the ten characteristics." This topic reoccurs throughout this text. For more information s. Klong-chen's *Don khrid* p. 169.

32. Both versions of the text read here *nga yi spyod yul kun las 'das*, but a few lines further down in the text it is said *nga ni spyod yul kun las 'das*, which I consider the better reading. For this reason I suggest to read here: *nga ni* for *nga yi*.

33. From here on the text uses the verb *bzlas* frequently. In general, the verb means "to utter mantras or charms." In rNying-ma literature, however, the verb is used in a modified connotation. In the *La zlos gsang ba'i 'khor lo zhes bya ba'i rgyud* (NGB vol. 1, pp.343–365) this verb (sometimes in the form *zlos*) is paraphrased with *blo thag bcad pa* (to determine in one's mind) or *brjod pa* (to declare).

34. The text reads here *sems dpa'* which is usually understood as equivalent to Skr. *sattva*, i.e. living being. But the given context stipulates an emendation. Thus, I suggest to read *sems pa*, mind, for *sems dpa'*, living being.

35. In the context of Mahâyâna literature, the word "disciplining" has the meaning of making sentient beings disciples of the teaching, and not to impose a rigorous disciplinary act, or chastisement on them. The Tibetan uses the word *'dul ba*, which means "to control, to educate, to subjugate, to discipline, to make someone a disciple."

36. The term *gzhi* (modification of the more common term *kun gzhi*, i.e. *âlayavijñâna*) is the subject of another lengthy Atiyoga text found in NGB vol. 6 (cha): the *sPros bral don gsal chen po'i rgyud* (The Tantra of the Great Undistorted Clear Meaning), which is being translated by Christopher Wilkin-

son. In that text the ground is the existential ground of undefined potential, which our text prefers to call "mind of perfect purity." Like the term *bodhicitta*, which in our text gained a new meaning, the term *âlaya[vijñâna]* is not understood by the same meaning which is used in other Mahâyâna writings. .

37. *Byang chub sems gsum;* this statement is in conflict with the rest of the text. Conjecture to *byang chub sems su* for *byang chub sems gsum.*

38. These are the three sections of the Nine Stages (*theg pa rim pa dgu*) characteristic of the rNying-ma teaching: the external stages of the *Kriyâyoga-*, *Caryâyoga-*, and *Yoga-tantras*, the internal stages of *Mahâyoga-* and *Anuyoga-tantras*, while the *Atiyoga-tantras* are the secret teachings.

39. This passage refers to certain practices performed during the stage of *Kriyâyoga*, culminating in the rite of the three purifications (*dag pa gsum*). First, there is the purification of the yogi's own body, speech, and mind (*lus, ngag, yid*), and its subsequent transformation into the deity's form, speech, and mind (*sku, gsung, thugs*). Secondly, the outer realm, consisting of the inanimated world (the "vessel," *snod*), the inner realm, consisting of the animated world (the "sap," *bcud*), and the conceptual realm of ideas (*rtogs pa*, or *kun rtogs*) are purified.

40. Tib. *mos spyod bzhi:* (1) *snang ba thob pa*, attainment of light; (2) *snang ba mched pa*, increase of light; (3) *de kho na na'i don gyi phyogs gcig la rjes su zhugs pa*, entrance into the essential truth; (4) *bar chad med pa'i ting nge 'dzin*, uninterrupted meditation. (Das, S. Ch. *Tibetan-English Dictionary.*)

41. This list of followers of non-Buddhist beliefs consists of two well-known names (*tîrthika* and *lokâyata*) and two unidentified ones. The term *tîrthika* identifies those who follow the general Hindu customs of performing ablutions in sacred rivers, seeing pilgrimages as a salutary act, etc. The term *lokâyata* identifies an ancient philosophical school of materialists who flourished during the early time of Buddhism. Both beliefs were discredited as irrational and meaningless by the Buddhists.

42. This is a reference to the Nine Stages of the Buddhist path as taught by the Old School.

43. The Tibetan text here is obviously disturbed for the following reasons: 1. If "body, speech, and mind" should refer to the All-Creating Sovereign's body, speech, and mind, the Tibetan text has to use the honorific forms (*sku gsung thugs*) instead of the ordinary forms (*lus ngag yid*); 2. The All-Creating One creates all the Buddhas who in turn are endowed with *sku*, *gsung*, and *thugs*, but She herself is beyond any specification. Consequently, it is incorrect to speak of the All-Creating's "body, speech, and mind." Due to these considerations I presented a translation which reads the way I think the text should be understood.

44. In this chapter the word *dgos* is used in combination with the word *don*. Usually the word *dgos* means need, necessity, etc., but in this combina-

tion it rather indicates the goal and destination of a necessary development. The *Bod rgya tshig mdzod chen mo* gives this definition of *dgos don: dmigs yul* (perceived object or goal), *bsam pa'i don* (destination of one's thinking); and for *dgos pa: don snying* (essential meaning or purpose), *dmigs yul gyi dgos pa ci zhig yod* (whatever needs to be perceived). Thus I translate *dgos* here as destination, intended aim, etc.

45. It seems that there are two sets of explantion of the "five meanings." One may opine that the text is disturbed here and that perhaps two manuscripts were compiled into the present text without reconciling the differences.

46. Bh om. *nga yi rang bzhin sku gsum ston pa la.*

47. Khy inserts here the phrase *rang sems de bzhin nyid la rtog ma byed.*

48. The Tibetan makes a pun by using the word *bsgrubs/sgrub* in two different connotations: (1) sâdhana, the ritual and meditational evocation of a Buddha or a deity, and (2) the action of accomplishing or realizing religious or philosophical things.

49. Bh reads *tshi chad,* which the *Bod rgya tshig mdzod chen mo* explains as *sems re thag chad pa,* or *yid thang chad pa,* which denotes a form of exhausted, fatigued mind.

50. This term corresponds to Skr. *niravasheshah dharmah,* a technical term of the Vinaya literature (Mvy #9250).

51. This sentence gives a word-by-word commentary of the Tibetan term for suchness (*de bzhin nyid*).

52. Bh reads *dus* for *du* (Khy).

53. According to Bh which reads *'dul ba rnam pa sna tshogs ston.*

54. The five systems of explanation are covered in chapter thirteen.

55. Read *rgyu 'bras 'das pas* (Bh).

56. This chapter is from here on identical with the *Khung chen ldings pa,* a text which is incorporated in Vairocana's "early translations" (*snga 'gyur*) which constitute the first section of the eighteen texts known as *sems sde bco brgyad*. The *Khyung chen ldings pa* is found in the NGB vol. Ka pp.419–423 (Khy edition) and in the *Vairocana rgyud 'bum* vol. 5, pp.308–314. There are minor differences between the text of the *Khyung chen ldings pa* and that of the twenty-second chapter of the KBG. Several short quotations from this text are found in the SMG.

57. Translated according to *Khyung chen ldings pa* whose wording differs from the one in the KBG as follows: *chos dang chos nyid rtags tu 'dres shing dbyer med la.*

58. Tr. acc. to Bh which reads *'khrul dang ma 'khrul byang chub lam la de rtogs pas thob pa'ang* which I consider superior to the Kh edition. The Khych version adopts the same reading as Bh does.

59. Acc. to Khych.

60. Acc. to Khych.

61. Kh reads *gza' ba'i yul* which I suggest to correct to: *bza' ba'i yul*. This proposed emendation is based on SMG p. 318, l.2: *gza' gtad ni dmigs pa ste | 'dir bza' gtad med pa mi dmigs pa'i don*. . . .

62. Tr. acc. to KBG. The text reads *drang srong* which usually identifies the vedic *rishi*, but the present context warrants a freer translation. mKhan-po Rig-'dzin understood the term as referring to the early disciples of Buddha Shâkyamuni.

63. S. Namkhai Norbu, *rGum chung* p. 195, for further explanation.

64. "To enjoy," Tib. *bza'*, is literally "to eat." As in Latin and other ancient languages, the Tibetan verb used for describing the physical consumption of food is also used for the process of a "mental consumption," i.e. cognition.

65. This part is particularly mysterious. mKhan-po Rig-'dzin would not comment on it.

66. Tr. acc. to Bh and Khych.

67. Another unclear sentence.

68. This advice is given many times in this text. The Tibetan word *rtog pa* implies mentally examining a thing, or speculating on it. In the Buddhist context it refers to the analytical process of examining the mental process as recommended in the Abhidharma literature. But the present text condemns such an attitude as being obstructive to the state of balance and stillness.

69. Kh reads *rang gi sems*, while Bh has *rang bzhin*, which I consider the better reading.

70. This sentence except for the appositional clause is quoted from the *Kun la 'jugs* in SMG p. 29, l. 2.

71. This rDzogs chen term is explained by Namkhai Norbu in *sBas pa'i rgum chung* p. 284 (Tib. text p. 277) as *ye nas lhun gyis grub pa'am | yongs su rdzogs zin pa* "the achievement by eternal self-perfection or the completion of total perfection."

72. Tib. *nag tshur* = *la tshva'i sman gyi rigs shig ste | ro skyur | zhur rjes snyoms | nus pas rma rul gso | skra dkar nag por 'gyur | so rnyil dang kha'i nad sel* (*Bod rgya tshig mdzod chen mo*). This word identifies a certain chemical component added to medications used in embalming and in the treatment of wounds; further it is used for coloring hair, and cleaning teeth.

73. This sentence is quoted in a slightly different wording in the SMG (p.30.6) where it is attributed to a work with the title *rTsal chen*.

74. Bh reads *chu zla med pas* which I prefer over *chu zla med ltar* in Kh.

75. *ye shes sems dpa'*, lit. "beings of pristine awareness," is a rNying-ma term defining the deities seen during contemplative evocations. In contrast, the person who performs the meditation is known as *dam tshig sems dpa'*, "beings of vows;" here the equivalent term *ting 'dzin sems dpa'* is used.

76. The four seals (*phyag rgya bzhi*) are: the seals of rituals (*las kyi phyag rgya*), the seal of resolve (*dam tshig gi phyag rgya*), the seal of Reality (*chos kyi phyag rgya*), and the great seal (*phyag rgya chen po*), s. *Bod rgya tshig mdzod chen mo* vol. 3, 1733.

77. This refers to the general practice of tantric meditation, that is to make the letters of mantras radiate with light and to condense them later into one letter which dissolves into one's own heart.

78. *'dren pa'i lung*, "a teaching of guiding," versus a teaching of certainty which does not need any interpretation. The context implies that such a doctrine is a misleading one; in other words the guiding ends in error.

79. Bh reads *bcos pas rnal du 'byor med pas | rnal du ma 'byor mi 'gyur |*.

80. With this sentence a quotation from the *rDo rje sems dpa' mi nub pa'i rgyal mtshan* begins (s. NGB I, p. 424). The same texts is also known as *Nam mkha' che;* under this title it is preserved in the Vairocana Tantras (the quotation is found in VGB I, p. 350, lines 3–5).

81. The Tibetan expression *Kun-tu bzang-po* is the usual name the rNying-ma-pas give to the primordial Buddha, but it can also be an adjectival phrase describing the nature of the absolute. It is not always clear which usage is intended by the text. In the present case I was inclined to understand the expression as an adjectival phrase till I came across a passage which paraphrases the one which we discuss here, and in this latter passage Kun-tu bzang-po is used as a name (s. NGB vol. 1, p. 376).

82. Up to here, this sentence corresponds with the *Nam mkha che* VGB I, p. 343, l.4, where the sentence is part of a longer discussion of Atiyoga and how to merge skill-in-means (*thabs*) with wisdom (*shes rab*).

83. Each of the three last of the nine vehicles of the rNying-ma tradition (*theg pa rim pa dgu*) are subdivided into three levels. Thus there is Ati-atiyoga, Anu-atiyoga, Mahâ-atiyoga; Ati-anuyoga, Anu-anuyoga, Mahâ-anuyoga; and Ati-mahâyoga, Anu-mahâyoga, and Mahâ-mahâyoga. Up to here the Ati-atiyoga is discussed. In the present chapter, this structure can be identified only in parts.

84. This sentence corresponds to the *Nam mkha che* VGB I, p. 348, l.2.

85. The last three sentences correspond with SMG p. 434, l.4, which presents them as quotes from the *Nam mkha che.*

86. This passage refers to the Ati-Mahâyoga.

87. The term self-fulfillment (*rang don*) identifies one part of being transfigured into the state of a Buddha. It is the realization of being a manifestation

of truth and reality (*chos sku, dharmakâya*) which is the fulfillment of one's own being. The other part of buddhahood is the realization of the purpose of others (*gzhan don*), that is to teach them the path to enlightenment out of compassion for them.

88. Part of this sentence is found in the *Nam mkha che* VGB I, p. 367.l.7f.

89. This paragraph refers to the tantric practice of using vowels and consonants as symbols of more esoteric meaning. According to gNubs-chen, author of the SMG, the vowel "A" represents primeval pure awareness, while the consonants "PA" and "TA" represent two different forms of skill-in-means (*upâya*): *rten pa'i thabs*, a method of relying on support, and *bya med pa'i thabs*, the deedless method. This practice involves, among other things, the participation of a consecrated woman as embodiment of pristine awareness. The paragraph is quoted from the *Nam mkha che* in the SMG p. 24,4; in the *Nam mkha che* (VGB I, p. 367, l.1 f.) this passage (*'di ni . . . 'byung*) is given with a slightly different wording (in the second phrase the syllable "PA" is replaced with "TA").

90. This passage uses a mystifying language with several demonstrative pronouns in each phrase, but with no noun as clear reference. Such style is not uncommon in Indian religious texts; it occurs, for instance, in some vedic hymns, but also in early Buddhist sutras (*Cullasuññatâ sutta*). The idea underlying such style is that any noun is inappropriate to designate the ultimate. For this reason, I chose the pronoun "that" to refer to the ultimate; in order to distinguish this use of the pronoun from its common use, I capitalize it. The pronoun "it" was treated in the same way, when the English required such change.

91. This means the *bîja* mantra is visualized in a moon disc.

92. The Tibetan sentence has a double negation which, under normal circumstances, means an affirmation; however, the present context suggests a true negation of the statement. In other words, the double negation here is emphasizing the negation.

93. The content of this phrase corresponds to *Nam mkha che* VGB I, p. 357,l.1 (vol. 1 of *Vairo rgyud 'bum*). I was told by present rNying-ma scholars that this passage refers to a common Buddhist saying found in the *vinaya* texts. This interpretation is substantiated by the following passage found in the *Theg pa yas 'bubs kyi mdo dang don gyi 'grel pa dgu pa* (NGB I,321.3: "According to the *vinaya* system, the non-observing of the vows (read *sdom* for *sdem*), i.e. their violation, is like cutting the tip of the palm tree whereby the tree cannot anymore grow. While according to the Vajrayâna, the violation of vows is like the burning of seeds in the fire . . . " Nevertheless one could understand the passage as an allusion to certain yogic practices which are, for instance, mentioned in *Caryâgîti* 45 (Kvaerne, Per. 1977, p.248). The symbolism of tree as used by some of the tantrics of the Sahâja movement is briefly discussed by Kvaerne (op. cit., p. 41f).

94. This phrase corresponds in its meaning with *Nam mkha che* VGB I, p. 355, l.5, where it reads *me tog* for *mi rtog* (as does Bh of the KBG).

95. Tib. *kleng = gleng.*

96. The yogis do not aspire anymore to this bliss, but in a natural, detached manner they dwell in such state, but to call it a goal is an illusion.

97. This sentence remains mystifying.

98. The latter part of this chapter compares the individual components of a *pûja*, perhaps a *ganacakra*, with the stillness of the Atiyoga practitioner.

99. The bulk of chapter thirty of the KBG also exists as an independent text with the title *rDo rje sems dpa'i lta ba/ rDo rje sems dpa' nam mkha' che* (Skr. is given as *âryapad vadzra sadtra*) in NGB I, pp. 424–430. In its colophon the text has the title *Byang chub sems mi nub pa'i rgyal mtshan lta ba nam mkha' che* which resembles somehow the title of chapter thirty of the KBG. This independent text is attributed to dGa'-rab rdo-rje. In the VGB (vol. I, pp.291–381) is the *rDo rje sems dpa' nam mkha' che rtsa ba'i rgyud skye ba med pa* transmitted. Parts of this text correspond to the above-mentioned.

100. The text given in this short chapter is also preserved as an independent text among those discovered in the Tun-huang caves and is known as Stein 647 of the India Office Library Collection. (La Vallée Poussin, Louis de. *Catalogue of the Tibetan Manuscripts from Tun-huang in the India Office Library.* London: Oxford University Press, 1962, p. 206). There, the text has the title *Rig pa'i khu byug,* "The Cuckoo of Intuitive Knowing." A commentary is added to the Tun-huang text wherein it is said that the title "The Cuckoo of Intuitive Knowing" is applied as a simile, while the title used in our text, "Six Diamond Verses," is used as it refers to the number of *shloka* of this short text (the third title used for it is *Rig byed snang ba'i rgyan,* "The Ornament of Apparent [Reality] which brings forth Intuitive Knowing." (Karmay, Samten. "The rDzogs-chen in Its Earliest Text: A Manuscript from Tun-huang," *Soundings in Tibetan Civilization,* ed. by B.N. Aziz and M. Kapstein. New Delhi: Manohar, 1985, p. 280ff. On p. 279 Karmay gives Stein 746 as the number of the Tun-huang document which is incorrect). In our text another introductory phrase was added, and the six lines are rendered as the teaching of the All-Creating Sovereign. The same text occurs again as an independent one in NGB vol. 1, p. 419.

101. This sentence could also be translated: "Although they may not understand [things] in their suchness, they ought to give up this sickness of striving because Vairocana and Samantabhadra are consummate (*zin pa*)." Several rNying-ma scholars whom I asked about this phrase insisted that the latter version is the correct one, while others pointed out that both translations mean the same. The contextual evidence and the nature of the KBG with its outspoken criticism of deity-yoga caused me to translate the Tibetan words according to their meaning and not treat them as names. The indepen-

dent text (mentioned in the previous note) supports the interpretation of the rNying-ma scholars as it starts by venerating Samantabhadra. In translating *zin pa* with "consummate", and not with the common "grasped," I followed the advice given by the same scholars, but also Namkhai Norbu suggests the translation of "perfected" for *zin pa* (Namkhai Norbu. *sBas pa'i rgum chung.* Arcidosso, Italy: Shang-Shung Edizioni, 1984, p. 284).

102. I adopt Bh as the better reading: *khyod las byung ba yi sku gsum* vs. *khyod las byung nga yi sku gsum.*

103. This sentence makes it quite clear that the Tibetan term *lhun gyis grub* has also the connotation of spontaneous self-perfection, and not only that of spontaneity (s. also Namkhai Norbu. *sBas pa'i rgum chung,* p. 13).

104. For a philosophical discussion of *gsal ba* s. Guenther. *Matrix of Mystery,* p.62f.

105. This way of explaining things as to *dpe,* simile, *don,* finite meaning or purpose, and *rtags,* characteristics, is frequently found within rDzogs-chen texts, for instance, the text of KBG chapter thirty-one is preserved under three different titles whereby the title *Rig pa'i khu byug* (The Cuckoo of Intuitive Knowing) represents the *dpe* category, the title *Rig byed snang ba'i rgyan* (The Ornament of Apparent [Reality] which Brings Forth Intuitive Knowing) represents the *don* category, while the third title *rDo rje tshig drug* (The Six Diamond Verses) represents the *rtags* category (Samten Karmay. "The Rdzogs-chen in its Earliest Text" p. 280).

106. Bh adds this sentence.

107. Acc. to Bh which reads *sa* for *gnas.*

108. The Indian concept of *lîla,* literally play, sport, defines the way in which the supreme being(s) perceives the world. For instance, Shiva perceives the universe through and in his dance, and so do other Hindu gods. In Buddhism this concept is less common, but it does occur in Mahâyâna context. In most cases the term is used to describe the intimate joy experienced in the union of wisdom and skill-in-means, or of bliss and emptiness. Our text is different as it puts the metaphor of a supreme being at the ground of the universe, and the emanation of this supreme being, i.e. Samantabhadra as the embodiment of the totally good nature of the universe, perceives the universe like a spectator enjoys a theatrical performance. This idea is aptly expressed in the last line of the final chapter of the KBG.

109. The double negation of the Tibetan has to be taken as an enhanced negation.

110. This is a metaphor referring to the sheer endless path and enormous difficulties before reaching one's goal. In a slightly different sense it is used in the donor chronicles of Zanskar, Ladakh. There the phrase is used to describe the distance between Bodhgaya, the world's centre in Buddhist cosmography, and the remote valley of Zanskar.

111. The Tibetan text says "and so on" for "you others."

112. The English has no verb to express the fact of mere being like other European languages do. But the Tibetan verb *yin* means exactly that: to be, but without any activity, without "standing out" (Lat. existere) from the anonymous. In our text, "nature" is by virtue of its own being without doing anything or achieving anything; in a strict sense, it is not even existent. Due to this situation I try to transcribe the sense of the Tibetan sentence by using different phrases, such as "is in itself," "is as such," etc.

113. According to Bh version.

114. Bh adds the last sentence which is missing in Kh.

115. According to Bh.

116. Acc. to Bh.

117. Kh adds here four more phrases which duplicate the last four ones, thus they have to be considered as a scribe's error.

118. This passage is corrupt in Kh.

119. Acc. to Bh.

120. Bh reads *ston pa rang byung ye shes 'gag med yin,* which I consider to be in conflict with the following sentence which is rendered in identical wording in both versions. Therefore I see Kh as preferable.

121. The Prajñâpâramitâ literature knows of seven limbs of enlightenment: mindfulness, investigation into things, vigor, joyous zest, tranquility, concentration, and even-mindedness (s. Conze, Edward. *The Large Sutra on Perfect Wisdom*, p. 668).

122. *Phyal ba* s. *phyal dpyad* as a rNying-ma term in the *Bod rgya tshig mdzod* = *mnyam nyid* stillness, balance.

123. This refers to the debate about the logical absurdity of such statements as "goer", "going", etc., as made in the *Madhyamaka kârikâ* chap. 2; s. Streng, Frederick. *Emptiness—A Study in Religious Meaning*, p. 184.

124. This sentence deviates from the pattern of the two previous ones. One would expect a sentence starting with "the mind-related vow" instead, the text talks about this issue in a more liberal manner.

125. *ta na 'ga' na* = *sbyor dang sgrol* (*Bod rgya tshig mdzod chen mo*), refers to the tantric practices of *yuganaddha,* and to freeing the mind of a person who is engaged in evil acts. These activities were always controversial as to whether or not they constitute a genuine part of Vajrayâna ethics.

126. In the Caryâyoga it is taught that in order to overcome any form of bias, even the most repulsive things have to be accepted as "pure". To this end, the yogi consumes faeces, human flesh, etc. in a ritual context. At the Atiyoga level such practices are rejected.

127. *dpa' bo*, Skr. *vîra*, is a name for the heroic fighter for liberation, i.e. the yogi or yoginî in their apotheosis.

128. The Tibetan text reads *btsal bas med pa'i 'bras bu* ("not generating a no-result through striving") which I think should be amended to *btsal ba'i med pa'i 'bras bu*.

129. In rDzogs-chen there are five greatnesses (*che ba rnam pa lnga*) mentioned. They refer to the greatness of certain teachings, s. Namkhai Norbu, *rGum chung* p. 129, and 209. In this case the *che ba lnga* are identical with the *don lgna*. In the present case of the KBG "greatness" has the meaning of total superiority to everything which exists as particulars, and as such it is synonymous with infinity (s. H.V. Guenther. *Matrix*, p. 260 n. 52).

130. These eighteen characteristics define a Buddha in the Mahâyâna, s. E. Conze. *The Large Sutra on Perfect Wisdom*, p. 159 f.

131. The Tibetan text of these sentences varies in its wording, although they are meant to be partial repetitions. The translation follows what I consider the best version. Consequently, the translation does not always strictly follow the wording as found in the individual sentences.

132. The Tibetan text omits this important part of the sentence which I restored from the context.

133. Translation follows Bh.

134. Acc. to Bh.

135. The Tibetan term *sa* means earth, place, etc., but also *bhûmi*, a Sanskrit term denoting the ten stages on which the bodhisattvas progress till they reach buddhahood. The KBG uses the word *sa* in an ambiguous manner: in the connotation of *bhûmi* when it criticizes the causation vehicle, and in the connotation of an ontological place in which the existing world rests. In order to make the meaning of the text in its translation transparent, I rendered the word *sa* as "place" or "ground" when I felt that this was the intended meaning, and as *bhûmi* when this was the stipulated meaning.

136. The Tibetan plays with the ambiguous meaning of the verb *grub pa* which means to achieve, realize, accomplish, etc. In Buddhist writings of tantric provenance the verb has the meaning of evoking deities before one's inner eye, and to realize the results coming from this practice. Thus, this sentence wants to tell us that by engaging in these evocations and related practices one will achieve nothing.

137. Some background information on these themes is available in H.V. Guenther. *Matrix*, chap. 4,1 and related notes.

138. These six "places" (*sa*) are again covered in chapter sixty-five where Sems-dpa' rdo-rje juxtaposes them with the ten "places." More information on this subject is found in *Shes bya kun khyab* by Kong sprul Yon-tan rgyamtsho (vol.3, p. 587).

139. Bh reads *ma g-yos pa* for *'dod pa med pa*. That version is preferable because it re-occurs at the end of chapter fifty-two in both versions.

140. The Tibetan uses the syllable *'dzin* as verb ("seize") and as part of the technical term *ting nge 'dzin* ("meditation"). This ambiguity is impossible to preserve in English.

141. Bh adds here two more lines which, in my opinion, are a scribe's error.

142. As so often before, the text uses the same word in opposite meanings. Here the word *zhi ba* is on the one hand used as a verb identical with *yal ba* (both meaning "to cease, end, vanish, disappear"), while on the other hand it is used as a noun synonymous with *bde ba* ("bliss, peace, etc.").

143. This is a reference to the KBG itself whose root sutra contains fifty-seven chapters.

144. The Tibetan sentence *sna tshogs srid pas snang srid zhes su btags* attempts to explain the term *snang srid*, here translated as "appearing and existing" in terms of its assumed etymological affiliation with the word *sna* in *sna tshogs* (diversity).

145. Bh reads *gzod [ma]* for the non-sensical *bzod*.

146. Kh inserts here four more lines which are a repetition of the previous ones. Thus I consider them a scribe's error.

147. The dimension of pride refers to the practice of deity yoga where a natural and not self-centered pride arises at the moment a certain degree of proficiency is accomplished. For further details s. Tsong-kha-pa. *The Yoga of Tibet, the Great Exposition of Secret Mantra-2 and 3*. Intr. by H.H. the XIVth Dalai Lama, tr. and ed. by Jeffrey Hopkins. Wisdom of Tibet Series 4. London: George Allen & Unwin, 1981, p. 12.

148. Bh reads *ston pa smra ba'i seng ge khyod kyis bgyi*, which I consider superior to Kh.

149. The Tibetan text has only *sems*, mind, here, but the context and the following line makes it clear that sentient beings cannot achieve something, i.e. buddhahood, because they are already in this state.

THEMATIC ANALYSIS BY CHAPTERS

I. *Introductory Chapter*

A. The place where the lore is proclaimed: the Mind as the seat of Reality is characterized by a symbolic setting of

1. a palace, indicating the pristine awareness
2. retinues, indicating the Sovereign's three natures, i.e. own being, actuating essence, and compassion
   a. the retinue of truth manifestation (*dharmakâya*)
   b. the retinue of actuating essence, the manifestation of consummate joy (*sambhogakâya*)
      (1) retinue [of the element] earth
      (2) retinue [of the element] water
      (3) retinue [of the element] fire
      (4) retinue [of the element] wind
      (5) retinue [of the element] sky
   c. retinues [in form] of corporeal manifestations (*nirmâna*)
      (1) sentient beings of the realm of desire (*kâmaloka*)
      (2) sentient beings of the realm of form (*rûpaloka*)
      (3) sentient beings of the realm of formlessness (*arûpaloka*)
   d. (as a note on item a. above) retinues equal to the own being corresponding to the four yogas:
      (1) retinue of Atiyoga (*shin tu rnal 'byor*)
      (2) retinue of Anuyoga (*yongs su rnal 'byor*)
      (3) retinue of Mahâyoga (*rnal 'byor chen po*)
      (4) retinue of the bodhisattva yoga (*sems dpa' rnal 'byor*)
   e. (as a further elaboration of the topic "retinues") the retinues cognizing the Sovereign's own being:
      (1) retinue resting in the Sovereign, i.e. the Buddhas of the past
      (2) retinue realizing the Sovereign's objective, i.e. the present Buddhas

(3) retinue that brings forth the Sovereign's deeds, i.e. the Buddhas to come later

3. All retinues are one despite the different aspects, which stipulates that there is only one method

B. The Sovereign rests in Herself
   1. absorbs the retinues into Her mind
   2. blesses them with Her own being
   3. endows all things with Reality

C. The Sovereign rests in the void focus (*bindu*)

D. Sems-dpa' rdo-rje arises from the void focus and asks the following questions:
   1. Is the void focus of the non-conceptual (*spros med*) also the teacher Herself?
   2. Is the void focus of the non-conceptual also the entirety of retinues?
   3. Is the void focus of the non-conceptual also the entirety of teachings?
   4. Is the void focus also time and place?
   5. How does the teacher of the teachers teach if everything abides in the nature of this void focus?
   6. For what purpose do the retinues circulate as Her retinues?
   7. Why is a teaching taught to the retinues?
   8. How can it be that time and place are one?

E. Sovereign's answer:
   1. Mind-as-such, i.e. the Sovereign, is the central vigor (*snying po*) of all things: non-conceptual, the primordial void focus
   2. Teacher, the teachings, the retinues, time and place emerged from the primordial void focus
   3. The Sovereign's own being is known as the void focus

II. Chapter: How Reality has become apparent

A. Question: what is the objective of existence (*'tshal*)

B. Answer:
   1. five self-originated awarenesses bring forth the five great [elements] as cause of adornment
   2. the self-originated awareness of hatred, that of the awareness of attachment, of ignorance, of jealousy, and of pride are identical with the beautiful appearance of the forms of the "families"

C. Question: reason for the five self-originated awarenesses adopting five different forms

D. Answer: the Sovereign Mind as universal maker of all of existence

III. Chapter: The origin of all things as deeds of the All-Creating Sovereign

A. The All-Creating Sovereign predates existence
B. Question: How does the creation of diversity happen; are there one or many teachers, teachings, and retinues
C. Answer:
 1. the oneness of the Sovereign Mind
 2. three forms of teachers emananting from Her
 3. these three forms teach the three teachings
D. Question: Path towards the stage of the Sovereign Mind
E. Answer:
 1. No-path towards the stage of the Sovereign Mind,
 2. but the emanated teachers teach a universal path (*kun gyi lam*) in five stages
  a. these five paths, associated with the five self-originated pristine awarenesses, are attachment, hatred, ignorance, pride, and jealousy
F. Question: Five paths in accordance with the self-originated pristine awareness
G. Answer:
 1. literal explanation of the terms
 2. five paths of the self-originated pristine awareness as origin of everything
 3. self-originated pristine awareness is
  a. living beings
b. progenitor of all Buddhas
 4. the three realms of formlessness, form and desire in correlation with the manifestation of the Sovereign Mind's nature

IV. Chapter: Explaining the Sovereign Mind's names
A. A bodhisattva ought to understand these names which will lead to a comprehensive understanding of everything
 1. central vigor: because Sovereign Mind is the vigor of everything
 2. self-originated: because She is totally beyond [the scope of] striving and achieving and as central vigor She is free of causes and conditions
 3. pristine awareness: because by virtue of this ceaseless and stainless [awareness] She is the teacher of all things
 4. mind of perfect purity
B. central or inner vigor as source of everything
C. purity is the central vigor of the mind of perfect purity
D. definition of the mind's abilities
E. summary of the main topic, i.e. the Mind is source of all

V. Chapter: On meaning
A. The intrinsic being (*yod*) is nothing but one
B. The teaching (*bstan*) is given in two aspects

1. Its origin (*byung*) is revealed in the nine vehicles
2. Its integration (*'dus*) is integral to the Great Perfection
3. Its explicit being (*yin*) is the mind of perfect purity
4. Its existence (*gnas*) abides in the dimension of Reality (*chos nyid dbyings*)
5. Its luminosity illuminates the space of intuitive wisdom (*rig pa'i mkha*)
6. Its pervasiveness (*khyab*) covers the entire animated and inanimated world
7. Its manifestation (*byung*) manifests as the entirety of what appears and exists.

C. To comprehend the essential oneness *vs.* the diversity of the visible world, one has to take the sky as a simile

VI. Chapter: The perfection of all things rests in the Sovereign Mind's own being:

A. Topic of this chapter: the Sovereign Mind's own being will be explained as to its meaning in words, and sounds; more accurately the chapter deals with the immanence and transcendence of the Sovereign Mind
   1. The own being as the letter A
   2. Speaking these words will result in perceiving the meaning

B. Q: If all is encompassed in the Sovereign Mind what constitutes then the teachers, teachings, and retinues

C. A: Things exist in the realm of Reality in total integration with the Sovereign Mind
   1. All existent things are nothing but the form, utterance and spirit of the Sovereign Mind
   2. The unborn, non-conceptual actuating essence does not exist (*mi gnas*), but transcends all areas of perception
   3. The Sovereign Mind's own being is revealed in the diversity of the existent world
   4. This lore is not taught to the followers of the vehicle of causation (i.e. Mahâyâna)
   5. Excursus oncause, result, simile, objective, and definition in conjunction with the emanation of the world
   6. The Sovereign Mind as source of existence
      a. unthinkable in itself, but
      b. to be recognized in the things the Sovereign Mind creates.
   7. Rejection of Buddhist concepts such as:
      a. two truths
      b. purification
      c. meditation
   8. The Sovereign Mind creates the elements (sky, wind, wa-

ter, earth, and fire), which constitute the Buddhas, the threefold world, the five paths, and the six [categories of] sentient beings
9. Non-duality of Buddha and sentient beings
10. Relationship of the Sovereign Mind as the true nature of Reality with its three aspects
11. The true teaching cannot be reified in any form
12. The Sovereign Mind as origin of the universe

VII. Chapter: fathoming Reality in terms of the diversity of creation *vs.* the oneness of the Sovereign Mind
A. Q: the oneness of the Sovereign Mind *vs.* the particularity of existence
B. A: the Sovereign Mind exists in three aspects:
1. spontaneously self-perfected which corresponds to its own being,
2. which becomes manifest as "vigor," symbolically present in the Buddhas, and
3. as actuating potency, tangible as compassion
a. the actuating potency in the form of compassion creates all
b. although the particulars of the creation may be counted and fathomed,
c. in its true being creation remains inexplicable
4. the six sensory objects and their related sense organs should not be considered under the perspective of subject/object dichotomy
5. further elaborations on the oneness of being *vs.* the diversity of existence
6. failing to understand that the diversity is identical with the essential oneness results in fundamental errors regarding the spiritual life
7. the essential cause (ontological cause) is responsible for diamond (vajra) nature, which is realized in two ways:
a. the outer one: desire to achieve results by means of acts
b. the inner one : free of performing any acts or abandoning any other ones
8. deedlessness as the only appropriate action
9. the Sovereign Mind is consummation
10. but also the creation is in a state of consummation

VIII. Chapter: how all things are set up in the Reality as objects due to the own being of the things
A. Suchness is present in:
1. all things, and

2. the Sovereign Mind's own being
B. Suchness becomes tangible in the three aspects of being (i.e. own being, actuating essence, and compassion)
C. Suchness also becomes tangible in the teacher's three forms of manifestation (*sku gsum*):
   1. teachers of causation
   2. teachers of interdependence
   3. teachers of result

These teachers teach conventional Buddhism
D. Definition of Suchness as constituting existence
E. Suchness is one but is experienced through the four yogas:
   1. Bodhisattva-yoga: perception of object/subject dichotomy, deity-yoga, five forms of enlightenment; deficiency in the understanding of stillness, central vigor, and non-conceptual thinking
   2. Mahâyoga: the deedlessness of stillness is recognized, mastery of the deity-yoga, the mandala of the deities is understood as an allegory of one's own mind; deficiency in intuiting stillness
   3. Anuyoga: understanding of stillness as cause and pristine awareness as its result, the oneness of cause and result; deficiency in not understanding that stillness transcends causality
   4. Atiyoga: intuition of stillness, i.e. the non-contrived essence (*don*). Views, salutary acts, and vows ought to be considered in this perspective which will lead to appropriating suchness
F. Each stage of the four yogas is subdivided into four sections:
   1. Bodhisattva-yoga:
      a. Bodhisattva-Bodhisattva-yoga: the mind does not reflect upon sensory objects
      b. Mahâyoga-Bodhisattva: wonderful blessings
      c. Anuyoga-Bodhisattva: four great seals
      d. Atiyoga-Bodhisattva: understanding the own being of the vows, lacking in understanding that the [four] yogas are free of acquiring and rejecting
   2. Mahâyoga:
      a. Bodhisattva-yoga-Mahâyoga: acquiry of the three *samâdhis*
      b. Mahâyoga-Mahâyoga: seeing one's own pure mind as pristine awareness
      c. Anuyoga-Mahâyoga: perfecting the four services (*bsnyen sgrub*)
      d. Atiyoga-Mahâyoga: everything is seen as the "great self"
   3. Anuyoga:

a. Bodhisattva-Anuyoga: deity-yoga as a natural outflow of dwelling in Reality
b. Mahâyoga-Anuyoga: the gender-relatedness of tantric practice is irrelevant
c. Anuyoga-Anuyoga: dwelling in being as apparent in existence
d. Atiyoga-Anuyoga: existence appear as it is; the dimension of reality is considered as the cause of pristine awareness

4. Atiyoga:
a. Bodhisattva-Atiyoga: the consummate, primordially pure mind free of striving and rejecting
b. Mahâyoga-Atiyoga: the consummate, pure mind transcending striving and rejecting
c. Anuyoga-Atiyoga: the consummate, pure mind is transcending cause and result
d. Atiyoga-Atiyoga: being is beyond praise and dispraise, existing and non-existing

G. The stages Bodhisattva-yoga up to Anuyoga are considered as the bodhisattva's stages (*bhûmi*)

H. Characteristics of the Atiyoga lore:
1. no progress on the path
2. no practice of the bodhisattva stages (*bhûmi*)
3. no observing of the vows
4. no contemplation of doctrinal views

I. This lore is not part of the vehicle of causation

IX. Chapter: Removal of faulty errors and obscurations

A. Nature of the mind of perfect purity
1. central vigor of absolutely all things
2. stainless because it is pure and unborn
3. free of error because without a path to proceed on
4. effortless as totally perfect from the primordial
5. the mind of perfect purity, i.e. the essential vigor of all things, is existent

B. Consequences of common Buddhist practices:
1. pursuing the ten perfections (*pâramitâ*) by striving for the ten bodhisattva stages (*bhûmi*) will result in a state of ignorance for three eons
2. to observe vows and pledges for the purpose of purification results in obscuration by error for seven lifespans
3. striving for spiritual progress by relying on the concept of causality by considering doctrinal views and religious practice in a dual fashion will result be in a state of error and obscuration for three lifespans

4. to strive for spiritual progress by means of pursuit and abandoning results in a state of being clouded by duality

C. Six desires for a result that does not exist
1. two truths as cause for spiritual progress
2. performing the three purifications
3. distinguishing between doctrinal views and the religious practice
4. practice of pursuit and abandoning
5. meditation
6. seeing the dimension [of Reality] and pristine awareness as cause and result

D. The ten characteristics of the Sovereign Mind:
1. no doctrine is to be contemplated
2. no vows to be observed
3. the salutary acts (*phrin laṣ*) are without effort
4. pristine awareness is without obscuration
5. no practising of the [ten] bodhisattva stages (*bhûmi*)
6. no path to proceed on
7. things are neither subtle (*phra ba chos med*)
8. nor dual, nor dependent
9. no accurate sacred instruction firmly established except for that about the mind
10. no definition of the instructions except that they are beyond praise and dispraise

E. The consequences if these ten characteristics are disregarded

F. The true nature of the Sovereign Mind is oneness despite the ten characteristics
1. theorizing this oneness is doomed from the beginning like a person attempting to walk over the dome of the sky
2. the ten characteristics are brought into relationship with the Sovereign Mind's own being

G. Because of the ten characteristics the Sovereign Mind encompasses and permeates the totality of existence
1. the Sovereign Mind is the sole focus of spiritual existence
2. to identify the world of objects with the Sovereign Mind is wrong
3. the right attitude is to see their sameness (i.e. to avoid a reifying thinking)

H. Admonition to teach the Atiyoga lore

X. Chapter: the all-perfected structure [of the universe] is explained

A. The consummation of the teachers
1. in their three forms of manifestation (*trikâya*):
a. manifestation of truth (*dharmakâya*)

b. manifestation of joy (*samyaksambhogakâya*)
c. corporeal manifestation (*nirmânakâya*)

B. Teaching of the three manifestations of the teacher:
1. outer teaching of the joy manifestation:
a. three outer sections of the rituals
b. three purifications
c. blessing through meditation
2. inner teaching of the corporeal manifestation:
a. three *pitaka*:
(1) hearers
(2) solitary awakened ones
(3) Mahâyâna sutras
(a) 21,000 precepts of the *vinaya*
(b) 21,000 sermons of the *sûtra pitaka*
(c) 21,000 tractates of the *abhidharma pitaka*
(4) the vehicle of causation (Mahâyâna):
(a) three poisons and their remedies
3. secret teaching of the truth manifestation:
a. secret generation
b. secret perfection
c. great secret perfection

C. The three retinues of the teacher's three manifestations:
1. retinues of the teacher's truth manifestation
a. consist in the Sovereign Mind's own being
b. manifest as inanimated and animated [world]
2. retinues of the teacher's manifestation of joy:
a. the bodhisattvas of the first to tenth *bhûmi*
3. retinues of the teacher's corporeal manifestation:
a. monks and nuns
b. lay men and women

D. The realms ("Buddha lands") of each of the three manifestations:
1. manifestation of truth: the palace of Akanishtha
2. manifestation of joy: a divine mansion in the Akanishtha realm, above the boundaries of this world
3. corporeal manifestation: Gridhrakûta, the place where Shâkyamuni, the seventh Buddha, became manifest

E. The realms of the respective disciples of each manifestation of the teacher:
1. disciples of the truth manifestation are found in the limitless dimension of Reality
2. disciples of the teacher's joy manifestation are found where there is enjoyment sought in form, sound, smell, taste, and touch
3. disciples of the teacher's corporeal manifestation consist of

the six categories of sentient beings in all 100,000 millions of worlds

F. The inherent oneness of all the teacher's manifestations:
  1. cause: mind of perfect purity,
  2. result: the buddha[hood], is also one with everything

G. The ways of promulgation
  1. truth manifestation by means of blessings
  2. manifestations of perfect joy by means of their own actuating being
  3. corporeal manifestations by integrating the word with the meaning.

H. The Sovereign Mind is actuating the three forms of manifestation

I. The All-Creating One: the progenitor of everything
  1. one, but known in three aspects (*rnam pa gsum*)
  2. ten characteristics
  3. the Sovereign Mind perfectly fulfills all needs and desires

J. Three aspects of the Sovereign Mind's own nature:
  1. manifestation of the truth
  2. manifestations of pristine awareness
  3. manifestations of compassion

K. The nature of teaching:
  1. the truth manifestation teaches the non-conceptual mind of perfect purity
  2. the manifestationsof enjoyment explain the mind of perfect purity by means of their manifestation and their wisdom
  3. undefined Buddha-manifestations teach a variety of methods

L. The nine teachings of the rNying-ma tradition
  1. external
  2. internal
  3. secret

XI. Chapter: the intrinsic self of the Sovereign Mind encompasses the root of all things

A. All is encompassed by the Sovereign Mind's own being
  1. the teachers' three forms of manifestations
  2. Buddhas of the three times
  3. bodhisattvas
  4. the four yogas
  5. the threefold world
     a. the realm of desire
     b. the realm of form
     c. the realm of formlessness
  6. the five great elements
  7. six categories of sentient beings
  8. all that appears

9. all that exists
10. the entirety of the animated and inanimated world

B. The Sovereign Mind's own being unfolds in three aspects
   1. the unborn, corresponding to the truth manifestation
   2. the miracle of genesis, corresponding to the manifestations of joy,
   3. compassion, corresponding to the corporeal manifestations

C. The four yogas the means to experience the oneness of the Sovereign Mind

D. The Sovereign Mind's own being is of fivefold aspect:
   1. as actuation it manifests as the five elements: sky, wind, water, earth, and fire
   2. as compassion it manifests as the five forms of the self-originated pristine awareness

E. Summary and Repetition of the basic theme of this chapter.

XII. Chapter: Explanation about the source of the lore of certainty (i.e. Atiyoga)

A. The Sovereign Mind is source of all sacred instructions
   1. the original teaching is the Mind
   2. tantras and sutras are only comments by the teachers

a. characterized by striving and achieving despite their origin in the Sovereign Mind

B. The Sovereign Mind the quintessence of the one vehicle which epitomizes the three vehicles proclaimed by the three forms of manifestation

C. The great wisdom dispells the darkness
   1. this darkness does not understand that all things are encomapssed in the primary purity
   2. pristine awareness will arise after the darkness is dissipated

D. In contrast, followers of the vehicle of causation hold that
   1. all things which exist are "poison"
   2. therefore they ought to be abandoned

   or:

   3. that the things constitute the objects for the mind's attachment
   4. in that case, they recommend to counteract the trend towards attachment through the two truths

   or:

   5. that the things ought to be seen as objects of purification

E. But the followers of Atiyoga know about the intrinsic oneness of the Sovereign Mind
   1. they have cut the chain of obscurations
   2. they gave up such thinking that there is anything else but the mind

F. Sovereign Mind admonition to teach
   1. that all that exists does so in the Sovereign Mind
   2. this will result in the transfiguration of all who capture this message
G. The adepts will reject
   1. the two truths
   2. practices such as giving up and obstructing things considered disadvantageous
   3. to bless things by means of the three purifications
   4. to achieve or strive for the contemplation on bodhicitta

XIII. Chapter: The ways of explanation pertinent to the mind
A. five ways of explanation
   1. the meaning of accounts of transmission (*lo rgyus*)
   2. the meaning of "root"
   3. the meaning of yoga
   4. the meaning of the intended aim
   5. the meaning of the word

XIV. Chapter: the All-Creating One remains secret to those of deficient talent
A. The Sovereign Mind is all-permeating
B. Its own being however remains obscrued
   1. If it does not remain obscured
   2. the three forms of manifestation cannot arise
   3. with the consequence that no teacher, no teaching, no host of disciples will exist
C. The secrecy of the Sovereign Mind's own being is the fundament for the existence of the Buddha, the teaching, and the community
D. Therefore only the Sovereign Mind teaches this lore and none of the teachers

XV. Chapter: the evidence as to the three aspects of the Sovereign Mind's own being is explained
A. The meaning of what constitutes the "teacher"
   1. truth manifestation
   2. joy manifestation
   3. corporeal manifestation
B. The Sovereign Mind's own nature becomes evident in
   1. its nature free of subject/object dichotomy
   2. actuating essence
   3. compassion
C. The followers will see
   1. that the own being engenders the Buddhas and sentient beings

2. thus the Buddhas and sentient beings are the Sovereign Mind's retinues giving evidence to its existence
3. the Sovereign Mind's actuating force becomes evident as
    a. teacher and retinues
    b. to the bodhisatvas of the tenth *bhûmi*
    c. to the newly converted ones as teacher of causality
    d. becomes evident in itself
    e. although the followers of causality see it in their own diversified manner
4. Sovereign Mind actuates the person
    a. this constitutes a revelation of own being
    b. which comes forth as the person's own being
    c. the Sovereign Mind's actuating force is the actuation of the individual

D. Sems-dpa' rdo-rje gives an instruction:
1. Sovereign Mind as the consummation of all
2. Sovereign Mind has to be understood as one's own being
3. also the world of objects has to be understood as one's own self

E. Sovereign Mind declares:
1. evident Reality is one's own mind
2. this lore is not like the Mahâyâna teaching of causality
3. the great bliss is not realized through desiring it
4. Reality is the Buddha, and *vice versa*
5. striving for spiritual progress is the true obscuration
6. the Mahâyâna teaching as fraud
7. genuine, i.e. unmanipulated, Reality is
    a. one's own mind
    b. the Buddha as manifestation of truth
8. the three forms of manifestation in their correlation with retinues, "vehicles," and teachings
9. the Sovereign Mind's own being as matrix of the world
10. in this capacity it gives testimony of itself
11. the oneness of the Sovereign Mind's own being is
    a. the source from which the perceivable objects arise
    b. these perceivable objects constitute the world as we know it
12. the Sovereign Mind's own being is evident and present as such in all things which exist
    a. this evidence of being is present in the physical elements which lends them a divine nature (called "Buddha" in the text)
    b. it is evident in the actuating force
    c. the evidence of being is the "revealed Buddha"
    d. this evidence of being is the "great self" of every thing which is identical with the "great Buddha"

13. simile, meaning, and investigation
    a. sky is a simile indicating Reality
    b. (the other two topics are not commented upon)

XVI. Chapter: Instructions given to Sems-dpa' rdo-rje
A. Sovereign Mind created
1. the teacher
2. the teachings
3. the retinues
4. the time (and locale) suited for their instruction
5. the teacher of the teachers
B. Sems-dpa' rdo-rje's self is the Sovereign Mind's own being
C. the world as a creation of the Sovereign Mind is in a state of consummation
1. thus striving for growth or change is "sickness" attacking the pristine awareness
2. everything is encompassed in this state of consummation

XVII. Chapter: The bones of manifestation
A. Question: what constitutes relics or "bones"
B. Answer: the three forms of the teacher's manifestations
1. they will be appropriately worshiped by contemplating the mind as all the Buddhas

XVIII. Chapter: No achievement by means of striving
A. The world originates from the Sovereign Mind's actuation
B. The nature of all things is immaculate and perfect
C. Thus no striving is purposeful

XIX. Chapter: Self-perfection through non-striving
A. The three teachers do not teach a lore of not-striving
B. But the All-Creating One teaches the one vehicle, i.e. that of non-striving
1. because the spontaneously self-perfected nature is free of striving
2. the Sovereign Mind's own being is brought into relation with the three forms of manifestation

XX. Chapter: The All-Creating One, as origin of all things
A. The All-Creating Sovereign, mind of perfect purity, is
1. the central vigor of all things
2. the seed of all things
3. also the cause of all things
4. the stem of all things
5. the ground (*gzhi ma*) of all things
6. the root of all things

B. The three manifestations originate only in a nominal way from the Sovereign Mind's own being
C. In essence all Buddhist teaching is on the own nature of the Sovereign Mind

XXI. Chapter: The systems of explanation as to the firm statements
The Sovereign Mind is the source of non-erring accurate statements
A. Two different systems of explanation:
B. the explanation of transcending cause and result (i.e. Atiyoga)
1. given in five ways
2. the explanation system given by the teacher in Her three manifestations (i.e. common Buddhism)
a. three systems of explanation
C. Reasons why the inexplicable mind is talked about

XXII. Chapter: *The Ten Teachings on the Deedless Perfection*, in which the non-existent no-objects [are treated]
A. Great origin of the deedless (*bya med*) teaching of perfection
1. non-existent, i.e. the goal of the deedless
2. the eye which sees the no-object, sees the wonder
3. apparent existence of the true self and the eternal Buddha ought to be understood like the simile of body and its shadow
B. Abiding in stillness
1. is not an object of gain
2. nor does it arise from the threefold world
C. Truly acute awareness is free of all thinking
1. the selfless compassion
2. exists from the primordial
D. No Buddha exists
E. No teaching exists
1. from the perspective of the consummate acts loose their ethical distinctiveness

XXIII. Chapter: From *The Ten Teachings on the Deedless Perfection*, in which is explained the sky-like thinking which is not an object of doctrinal views
A. The main point of not thinking (*bsam du med pa*) is to abide from the primordial in a sky-like [state]

XXIV. Chapter: From *The Ten Teachings on the Deedless Perfection*, in which an instruction is given on the deedless perfection, the seal of non-becoming
A. Abiding in All-Good means:
1. only abide in the mind of perfect purity

2. you abide in the central vigor of all things
3. this topic is applied to the concept of the three manifestations

XXV. Chapter: From *The Ten Teachings on the Deedless Perfection* the emergence of one's own mind as teacher

A. Saying that one's own mind is the teacher of the world will result in the opposite effect
B. Thus the Sovereign Mind is present in the mind as teacher
C. The Sovereign Mind is the cause of everything
   1. as the mind's actuation the five great elements come forth
   2. from the five elements the five teachers (i.e. the pentade of Buddhas (*pañcatathâgata*) emerge
   3. reflections upon the teacher's manifestations
      a. pristine awareness as teacher manifest as element 'earth'
      b. manifest as the element 'water'
      c. manifest as the element 'fire'
      d. manifest as the element 'wind'
      e. manifest as the element 'sky'
D. Sovereign Mind is the creator and therfore all sentient beings are her children and equal to herself; Sovereign Mind as source of existence

XXVI. Chapter: From *The Ten Teachings on the Deedless Perfection*, about the deedless perfection not to be contemplated

A. The mind of perfect purity:
   1. beyond thinking and inexplicable
   2. a lamp for the teacher
   3. the central vigor of all things
   4. Manjushrî himself
   5. dwells in the self-perfected bliss
   6. the ground of an ocean of diverse religious practices
   7. the mother of the *tathâgata*
   8. the path of all *tathâgata* is
      a. subtle and difficult to understand
      b. non-speculative and beyond thinking
      c. non-existent (*mi gnas*), imperceptible, and non-conceptual (*spros med*), it is free of all thinking
      d. cannot be captured in words, free of form and color, it is not an object of the sense faculties
      e. firm, difficult to comprehend, and totally inexplicable
   9. the conventional path of Buddhism in contrast to the Atiyoga path
      a. the pure and the impure are not two different entities but like an amalgam

b. pristine awareness and ignorance are not to be distinguished
10. the paradox of intuiting the Sovereign Mind engenders its "clouding" as soon as one reflects upon the intuition
a. the eye seeing directly
b. the mastery of balance
11. the truly pure path consists of the five obscurations (*klesha*) and the five limitless offenses

XXVII. Chapter: From *The Ten Teachings on the Deedless Perfection* about the lore of the dimension of deedless purity
A. The consummate nature of all precludes spiritual striving
B. The wholeness of being cannot be fathomed by reckoning the particularities of existence

XXVIII. Chapter: The deedless perfection as immutable
A. Immutability as the main trait of the Sovereign Mind's own nature
1. except for the three forms of manifestation
a. their followers are not taught Reality
b. nor the identity of the five obscurations with the five pristine awarenesses
c. the futility of changing or purifying the mind
d. the futility of deity-yoga
e. the futility of higher tantric practices (*anuttara yoga*)
2. the teachings of the three forms of manifestations are in need of interpretation

XXIX. Chapter: The mind in balance
A. Balance is the main aspect of the Sovereign Mind's own being
B. In its five aspects (*rang bzhin rnam pa lnga*) it is poised:
1. teacher
2. teaching
3. retinue
4. place
5. time
C. Balance as the consummation of existence, contrasted by falsifying attempts to change, better, or purify oneself
1. Hearers and Solitary Buddhas do not understand this subtle lore
2. Mahâyâna followers do not appreciate the lore of balance
3. nor will the followers of the four lower yoga sections
4. followers of the Mahâyoga will aspire to achieve something new which will result in the creation of major obstacles
5. followers of the Anuyoga will equally fail to rest in balance

6. followers of the Atiyoga alone will realize that they are already in a state of deedless great bliss, i.e. buddhahood

D. Good reason for teaching this lore

XXX. Chapter: The indestructible nature of rDo-rje sems-dpa' as a banner of victory

A. the interlocutor's own being is the Sovereign Mind's own being
1. the Sovereign Mind as deedless liberation
2. world and buddhahood are indistinguishable and inseparable
3. Reality is intuited not by striving for it but by leaving it as it is
4. understanding the sentient beings' suffering as the consummate Sovereign Mind results in joy
5. elaborations on the "sky" as metaphor for the deedless liberation

B. Passage on tantric meditation of seed syllables
C. Futility of meditating on "Buddha fields"
D. "That" as indicator of the Sovereign Mind permeating and encompassing all
E. no particularities can be discerned
F. the Sovereign Mind is gender-unrelated
G. insertion of another paragraph on syllable meditation
H. rejection of common Buddhist meditation practice
I. the Atiyoga practioners are free in every aspect as they do not engage in any discriminative activity
J. "That" as the epitome of the depth of being
K. a paragraph about the universe and its interwovenness with "It" and "That"

XXXI. Chapter: The Six Vajra Verses

A. The Sovereign Mind's own being is one even in its manifest forms
B. The apparent existence is consummate and therefore striving for achievements is "a sickness"

XXXII. Chapter: The four definitive statements about the lore of the deedless as realization of the quintessence

A. Whatever appears is one in its suchness

XXXIII. Chapter: The definitive teaching and the teaching that needs interpretation

A. The intelligibility of the world is due to the self-originated pristine awareness
B. The Sovereign Mind asks Sems-dpa' rdo-rje about these issues:
1. what is the meaning of the word "dimension"
2. what is the meaning of the word "sky"

3. what is the meaning of the word "apparent"
4. what is the meaning of the expression "sentient beings"

C. Sems-dpa' rdo-rje answers:
1. "dimension" means the non-diversified own being of the Sovereign Mind
2. "sky" means it is not obscured
3. "element" (in the afore-going paragraph "apparent") means it is the central vigor of all things
4. "sentient beings" means to be the quintessence of all things
5. these statements amount to acknowledging the Sovereign Mind as origin of all

D. Sovereign Mind confirms the accuracy of this statement

E. Sems-dpa' rdo-rje claims that the Sovereign Mind's own nature is synonymous with
1. Reality
2. mind
3. primordial awareness
4. the intelligibility of Reality

F. Affirmation by the Sovereign Mind of the previous statements

G. Sovereign Mind poses the following questions to Sems-dpa' rdo-rje:
1. how is it that the vehicles come forth in three aspects?
2. how is it that people striving for results can achieve the three results?

H. Sems-dpa' rdo-rje answers:
1. the three teachings are taught due to the mind being of discriminative intelligence

I. Sovereign Mind proclaims:
1. the ultimate is taught to be of a definitve meaning
2. without understanding this, there is no point in teaching
3. the ultimate is in a state of as-it-is
4. everything as being in an intrinsic sense of buddha-nature, is beyond praise and dispraise

XXXIV. Chapter: The lore of integrating the Buddhas' intention

A. Main theme: the Sovereign Mind as integrating the intention of all Buddhas
1. with regard to simile (*dpe*)
2. to quintessence (*don*) and
3. characteristics (*rtags*)

B. A discussion of how unbelievers see the "sky"

XXXV. Chapter: The lore of the Great Perfection

A. Eight topics characterizing the Great Perfection
1. 'Entrance': one enters through the door of non-striving
2. 'Doctrinal views': are not to be contemplated

3. 'Vows': not to be observed
4. 'Salutary deeds': not to be sought
5. 'Path': no path to be proceeded on
6. 'Stages of accomplishment' (*bhûmi*):not to practice them
7. 'Pristine awareness': non-speculative (*mi rtogs*) and immovable
8. 'Reality': the state of as-it-is which is un-altered

B. These topics cannot be understood by the followers of the vehicle of causation

XXXVI. Chapter: the All-Creating Sovereign's form, utterance, and spirit
A. the Sovereign Mind's form, utterance, and spirit are the source of existence
1. Sems-dpa' rdo-rje is admonished to teach about these three aspects
a. by integrating the word with its meaning
2. without this teaching nobody will generate genuine understanding; this is true with regard to all sentient beings regardless of their stage on the Buddhist path

XXXVII. Chapter: The lore and sutra on no-meditation
A. Intuiting Reality
B. But no meditation upon the mind
1. traditional Buddhist teaching, such as the evil forms of rebirth and the ten perfections, obstruct the intuition of Reality
2. transfiguring one's mind into a deity during the practice of deity-yoga is a degradation of one's own mind
C. To dwell upon "nature" leads to the insight that the mind is the actuation of suchness
D. The imperceptible stillness of the mind is the Reality of the now and here

XXXVIII. Chapter: Errors and faults as to doctrinal views and religious practice
A. The vehicles and sutras are faulty
1. because they do not transcend theoretical examination by applying the two truths
B. Kriyâyoga is faulty
1. because of subject/object dichotomy
C. Upayoga is faulty
1. because of lack of intuiting non-duality
D. Yoga is faulty
1. because of lack of overcoming acquiring and rejecting
E. Mahâyoga is faulty
1. because it does not transcend striving and achieving
F. Anuyoga is faulty
1. because it does not transcend a thinking in accord with

cause and result
G. The mind of perfect purity is like the sky which cannot be captured by dualistic and conceptual thinking
H. Each vehicle is wrong with regard to its
1. doctrinal views
2. vows
3. salutary acts
4. stages of spiritual progress
I. The Great Perfection transcends all vehicles

XXXIX. Chapter: The Sovereign Mind is the central vigor of the Buddhas, and that in its totality it is without errors
A. The nature of the Sovereign Mind encompasses all that exists
1. the three kinds of Buddha-manifestation come from the Sovereign Mind
2. deficiency of the Buddhas to fully intuit the mind of perfect purity
B. Self-originated pristine awareness illuminates the sensory faculties and the sense objects
C. The Sovereign Mind excels everything, even the Buddhas
D. The charactersitics of the definitive teaching

XL. Chapter: The nature of the mind of perfect purity
A. The mind of perfect purity as the own being of the All-Creating Sovereign
1. Sovereign Mind instructs all living beings that they are in the state of buddhahood from the primordial
B. Question by Sems-dpa' rdo-rje: if this is so why do the living beings continue to migrate through the cycle of life and death
C. Answer: all things bespeak of Reality. Therefore to repudiate the five sensory objects depreciates Reality

XLI. Chapter: Sovereign Mind is the nature of all things
A. The Sovereign Mind is described as
1. a lamp for the teachers
2. the mind of perfect purity
3. the central vigor of all the Buddhas of the three times
4. father and mother to all sentient beings
a. exemplified as "primordial Buddha"
5. the cause for all that exists as animated and inanimated
6. actuation of whatever exists as animated or inanimated
a. the five allegoric Buddhas are correlated with the five great elements

XLII. Chapter: All existent things are enlightened
A. The Sovereign Mind as the true Buddha manifest in the three forms

1. not altering the mind is the true teaching
2. despite this fact the Buddha-manifestations teach a system of altering the mind

XLIII. Chapter: All things are the teacher herself
- A. Sovereign Mind as the source of
  1. three forms of manifestation
  2. three kinds of teaching
     - a. teach the nature of the things
     - b. the actuation of things
     - c. the meaning of words
  3. three forms of retinues
  4. more questions about the nature of the three kinds of teachings proclaimed by the three forms of manifestation

XLIV. Chapter: The Deedless in connection with the nature of the Sovereign Mind (the topic given in the chapter title added at the end does not agree with the content nor with the opening statement)
- A. The consummate nature of the Sovereign Mind is creative yet deedless
- B. Warning to the followers of conventional Buddhism not to alter in any way the consummate nature of the mind of perfect purity
- C. The consummate nature and balance will be received by not considering it as one's goal
- D. Religious practices are superfluous and meaningless
  1. the teaching of the Great Perfection surpasses that of all preceding Buddhist teachings
  2. it is beyond striving and achieving

XLV. Chapter: Rejecting the contemplation of doctrinal views
- A. The non-contemplation of doctrinal views is equated with the Sovereign Mind
  1. this amounts to criticizing the conventional Buddhas for not instructing their disciples in the unalterable nature of the Sovereign Mind
  2. therefore conventional Buddhist practice is like a child's play
  3. criticism of tantric deity-yoga
- B. By contrast, the Great Perfection is a "good quality" of the Sovereign Mind
  1. this makes striving in itself superfluous
  2. even meditating upon the Sovereign Mind is wrong
  3. purifying or cleansing one's mind or the external world are mistakes
  4. all religious striving is futile like chasing the sky
- C. The vehicle of causation (i.e. Mahâyâna) results from the needs

of people not open to the lore of the deedless

D. The lore of the Sovereign Mind transcends all conceptual thinking
   1. meditating is a "sickness"

XLVI. Chapter: No vows pertinent to the Great Perfection

A. The nature of the Sovereign Mind is unborn and nonconceptual
   1. from it the objects originate as "wonders"
   2. understanding this will dissociate oneself from vows and their applications

B. Criticism of the followers of common Buddhism

C. The practice of "vows" in accord with the Great Perfection is neither to observe them nor to damage them

D. Criticism of practising the vows correlated with "form", "utterance", and "spirit"

E. Criticism of tantric licentiousness regarding the "five vows"

F. No vows pertinent to the Great Perfection
   1. but rejecting the concept of "substances" establishes the person in stillness

G. To perceive Reality in its particularity and diversity is to betray the own nature of the Sovereign Mind
   1. only by intuiting self-originated pristine awareness as permeating the totality of existence leads to its own realization
   2. unsuitedness of the "two truths" of Mahâyâna Buddhism (i.e. conventional and absolute truth)

XLVII. Chapter: No salutary acts pertinent to the Great Perfection

A. The Great Perfection is primordially perfected
   1. thus no salutary acts possible

B. The Buddha manifestations teach meditation practices and the ten perfections; these are rejected as futile
   1. inadequacy of the *dharma* theory
   2. meditation and the evoking of deities is inadequate
   3. grounded in one's self makes all religious practices superfluous

XLVIII. Chapter: The ground of all things is the Sovereign Mind itself

A. The Sovereign Mind is present as mind of perfect purity in all things
   1. thus the Sovereign Mind is the ground of all

B. Three aspects of the Sovereign Mind's own nature
   1. unborn
   2. without termination
   3. source for the wonder of ceaseless creation

C. Six bases
   1. doctrinal view a basis for cognizing Reality

2. vows a base for purging one's own faults
3. rites a base for spiritual realization
4. the path a base for progress by means of proceeding
5. making the bodhisattva stages a base for abiding in them
6. making the pristine awareness a base for understanding

D. The objects are intrinsicly interrelated with the observing self. This point is demonstrated by reference to six of the ten characteristics of the Sovereign Mind:
1. thus the isolation of the objects from the self and their examination within the parameters of "doctrinal views" is rejected
2. "no observance of vows"
3. "no striving after salutary acts"
4. "no proceeding on the path"
5. "no practice of the bodhisattva stages"
6. "no understanding of the pristine awareness as object"

XLIX. Chapter: The Sovereign Mind is the place (*sa*) in which all existing things abide (the chapter title identifies the topic as "the Great Perfection is not a place of practice")

A. The Sovereign Mind as the place of being and total integration

B. By contrast, the Buddhas in their three manifestations teach the bodhisattva stages in three aspects:
1. the bodhisattva stage of generation
2. the bodhisattva stage of practice
3. the bodhisattva stage of realization
4. these three aspects are a teaching in need of interpretation

C. The definitive teaching is given by intuiting point A.

D. Six bodhisattva stages are juxtaposed to six stages of the mind sharing the same names

E. The place where buddhahood is achieved is a place of no-practice

L. Chapter: The Sovereign Mind is faultless

A. The self-originated pristine awareness is aware of all but remains imperceptible in itself
1. thus it is not an object
2. but present in all objects
3. free of karmic imprints

B. Subject/object fully integrated in being

C. List of synonyms for the Sovereign Mind's own being

LI. Chapter: No progress on a path towrds the Great Perfection

A. The mind's own nature encompasses
1. buddhahood

2. the world of objects
3. levels of spiritual achievement

B. The manifest Buddhas teach various "paths"

C. Critique of success-oriented meditation

LII. Chapter: No agitation and no desire

A. Desire is selective and targeted, therefore
1. spiritual striving, such as meditation, is ill-conceived
2. but abiding in "nature" connects the individual with the whole

B. But to give up all to obtain everything is equally wrong

C. Abiding in non-conceptualized suchness connects one with the whole

D. No meditation is capable of illuminating the One, i.e. suchness

E. In nature all pairs of opposites collide

F. To see meditation as a means for realizing pristine awareness is wrong

G. The mind of perfect purity in its oneness comprises multiplicity as well as individuality

H. Reality as the holistic One gives rise to joy

I. The Mind as sole Reality

LIII. Chapter: All things are in their own being unagitated

A. The essentials of the Atiyoga lore should be kept secret from the followers of the vehicle of causation

B. Mind is ceaseless

C. True being is lucid and beyond the reach of desire

D. Mastery of sameness

E. The expanse of the sky as symbol of the Mind

F. Suchness is immutable, but Reality is its "play"

G. Sameness of all existing things precludes the teaching of causation

LIV. Chapter: Survey of the structure of the KBG text

A. The five actuations:
1. the central vigor from which all things emanate
2. definitive and unerring [truth]
3. overcoming of causation
4. deedlessness
5. decisiveness of all things

B. The Atiyoga lore is given in a condensed form of five tractates, but in a detailed form of fifty-seven chapters (i.e. the KBG)
1. the first condensed tractate, corresponding to the first ten detailed chapters, deals with the nature of all things as the actuating being of pristine awareness (*ye shes ngo bo chos kyi ngo bo las mngon du phyung*)

2. the second condensed tractate, and chapters 10–20 of the KBG deal with the actuation of the non-erring and definitve pristine awareness
3. the 3rd condensed tractate, and chapter 20–30 of the KBG teach the actuation of pristine awareness which is non-erring and definitve
4. the 4th condensed tractate, and chapter 30–40 of the KBG teach the actuation of the deedless pristine awareness
5. the 5th condensed tractate, and chapters 40–50 of the KBG teach the actuation of the pristine awareness' decisiveness
   a. the remaining seven chapters teach about:
      (1) the ground,
      (2) sacred instructions,
      (3) five on different necessities

C. Definitions of:
   1. Buddha
   2. field of sensory activity (*khams*)
   3. Mind
   4. Inanimated (*snod*, lit. vessel) and animated (*bcud*, lit. juice, central vigor)
   5. All

D. Sems-dpa' rdo-rje repeats the basic statements of this chapter

LV. Chapter: All existing things are nothing but the mind of perfect purity
   A. The mind of perfect purity constitutes
      1. the inanimate
      2. the animate
      3. the world of knowing and articulation
   B. This stipulates that all distinctions are irrelevant with regard to the Mind
   C. Reality is the sole "object" to be sensed
   D. This renders all religious striving obsolete and places its practitioners in error
   E. Sems-dpa' rdo-rje is advised to teach the sentient beings the Atiyoga lore

LVI. Chapter: Sems-dpa' rdo-rje expounds his understanding of the All-Creating Sovereign's own being
   A. The All-Creating Sovereign encompasses all

LVII. Chapter: Entrusting this teaching to Sems-dpa' rdo-rje

TIBETAN TEXTS

Bod rgya tshig mdzod chen mo. Beijing: Mi-rigs dpe-skrun-khang, 1984, 3 vols.

Byang chub sems mi nub pa'i rgyal mtshan lta ba nam mkha' che, see *rDo rje sems dpa'i lta ba / rDo rje sems dpa' nam mkha' che*

Don-grub rgyal-po of Nyang. *Rig 'dzin chen po Ratna gling-pa'i rnam thar skyes rabs 'bring po tshigs su bcad pa*, in *Selected Works of Ratna gling-pa*, reproduced from a manuscript from the library of Ri-bo-che Rje-drung of Padma-bkod by Tseten Dorji. Tezu, Dist. Lohit (India): n.p., 1973

Dudjom Rinpoche. *Gangs ljongs rgyal bstan yongs rdzogs kyi phyi mo snga 'gyur rdo rje theg pa'i bstan pa rin po che ji ltar byung ba'i tshul dag cing gsal bar brjod pa lha dbang g-yul las rgyal ba'i rnga bo che'i sgra dbangs* (short: *rNying bstan*). Kalimpong: n.p., 1967

Khung chen ldings pa, in NGB vol. 1, pp.419–423 (Khy edition), and in *Vairocana rgyud 'bum* vol. 5, pp.308–314

Klong-chen rab-'byams-pa Dri-med 'od-zer. *Lo rgyus chen mo* in *sNying thig ya bzhi* vol. 9

Klong-chen-rab-'byams-pa Dri-med 'od-zer. *Byang chub kyi sems kun byed rgyal po'i don khrid rin chen gru bo* (short *Don khrid*) in *gDams ngag mdzod* ed. by 'Jam-mgon Kong-sprul. Delhi: n.p., 1971, vol. 1, pp.159–184; tr. by Lipman, K. and M. Peterson. *You are the Eyes of the World*. Novato, California: Lotsawa, 1987

Kong sprul Yon-tan rgya-mtsho (Blo-gros mtha'-yas). *Shes bya kun khyab*, 3 vols. Peking: Mi rigs dpe skrun khang, 1982

Kong sprul Yon-tan rgya-mtsho (Blo-gros mtha'-yas) (ed.). *gDams ngag mdzod*. Delhi: n.p., 1971, 12 vols.

La zlos gsang ba'i 'khor lo zhes bya ba'i rgyud in NGB (Kh) vol. 1, pp.343–365

Nam mkha' che, see *rDo rje sems dpa' nam mkha' che*

Namkhai Norbu. *sBas pa'i rgum chung*. Arcidosso, Italy: Shang-Shung Edizioni, 1984

Ratna-gling-pa. *The Nyingmapa Apology of Rin-chen dpal-bzang-po, Chos 'byung bstan pa'i sgron me rtsod zlog seng ge'i nga ro*. Repr. by Kham-sprul Don-brgyud nyi-ma. Tashijong, Palampur (India): n.p. 1972

rDo rje sems dpa' nam mkha' che rtsa ba'i rgyud skye ba med pa, in VGB vol. 1, pp.291–381

rDo rje sems dpa'i lta ba/ rDo rje sems dpa' nam mkha' che (Skr.*âryapad vadzra sadtra*) in NGB 1, pp.424–430

Rig byed snang ba'i rgyan, s. *Rig pa'i khu byug*

Rig pa'i khu byug, in KBG chap. 31, NGB vol. 1, p.419

rNying ma'i rgyud 'bum, A Collection of Treasured Tantras Translated During the Period of First Propagation of Buddhism in Tibet, (1) ed. by Dingo Khyentse Rinpoche. Thimphu, Bhutan: n.p. 1973 (Kh edition); (2) *The mTshan-brag Manuscript of the rNying ma rgyud 'bum*. Thimphu, Bhutan: National Library, Royal Government of Bhutan, 1982 (Bh edition)

rTsal chen [sprugs pa] in NGB (Kh) 1, pp.465–475

Sa-skya bka' 'bum: The Complete Works of the Great Masters of the Sa-skya Sect of the (sic) Tibetan Buddhism. Tokyo: The Toyo Bunko, 1968

Selected Writings of Padmasambhava, ed. 'Chi-med Rig-'dzin bla-ma. Leh: n.p., 1974

sPros bral don gsal chen po'i rgyud (The Tantra of the Great Undistorted Clear Meaning) in NGB (Bh edition) 1982, vol 13, pp.1–296, (Kh) vol. 6, pp.374–608

Stein, R.A. (ed.). *Une chronique ancienne de bSam-yas: sBa-bzed* (Publications de l'Insitut des Hautes Etudes Chinoises, textes et documents I). Paris: Adrien Maisonneuve, 1961

Theg pa yas 'bubs kyi mdo dang don gyi 'grel pa dgu pa in NGB 1, pp.315.3–321.6

Bai ro'i rgyud 'bum (*Vairocana rgyud 'bum*). Leh: n.p., 1971, 8 vols.

INDIAN TEXTS

Abhidammattha Sangaha, ed. by T.W. Rhys Davids in *Journal of the Pali Text Society* 1884, pp.1–46; tr. by S.Z. Aung and C.A.F. Rhys Davids. *Compendium of Philosophy*. London: Pali Text Society, 1910

Buddhaghosa. *Atthasâlinî* VIII, iii, tr. by Pe Maung Tin. *The Expositor (Atthasâlinî), Buddhaghosa's Commentary on the Dhammasanganî, the First Book of the Abhidhamma Pitaka*. Ed. and rev. by Rhys Davids. London: Pali Text Society, 1921

Caryâgîti, tr. by Kvaerne, Per. *An Anthology of Buddhist Tantric Songs*. Oslo: Norske videnskaps akademi II.14, 1977

Cullasuññatâ sutta, in *Majjhimanikâya*, ed. by Bhikkhu J. Kashyap. Bihar: Pâli Publication Board, 1958, vol. 3, pp.168–73

Kashyap, Bhikshu J. (ed.). *Dhammasanganî* (Abhidhamma Pitaka vol. 1). Bihar: Pâli Publication Board (Bihar Government), 1960

Kashyap, Bhikshu J. *Kuddakapâtha—Dhammapda—Udâna—Itivuttaka—Suttanipâta (Khuddakanikâya I)* (Nâlanda Devanâgari Pâli Series). Bihar: Pâli Publication Board (Bihar Government), 1959

Mâdhyamaka kârikâ, s.F. Streng, *Emptiness*

BIBLIOGRAPHY

Bechert, Heinz (ed.) *Zur Schulzugehörigkeit von Werken der Hînayâna-Literatur* (Abhandlungen der Akademie der Wissenschaften in Göttingen). Göttingen: Vandenhoeck & Ruprecht, 1985

Bethlenfalvy, Géza. *A Hand-list of the Ulan Bator Manuscript of the Kanjur Rgyal-rtse Them spangs ma*. Budapest: Akadémiai Kiado, 1982

Bohm, David and Weber, Renée. "Implizite und explizite Ordnung: zwei Aspekte des Universums" in *Das holographische Weltbild*, ed. by Ken Wilber. Munich/Bern: Scherz Verlag, 1986

Broido, Michael. "Sa-skya Pandita, the White Panacea and the Hva-Shang Doctrine" *The Journal of the International Association of Buddhist Studies* vol. 10, no.2, 1987, pp.27–68

Capra, Fritjof. *The Physics of Tao*. Boston: New Science Library, 1975

Capra, Fritjof. *Wendezeit*. Bern: Scherz Verlag, 1987

Chan, Wing-tsit (tr. and ed.). *A Source Book in Chinese Philosophy*. Princeton: Princeton University Press, 1963

Chatterji, J.C. *Kashmirian Shaivism*. 1914, rpt. Albany, NY: State University of New York Press, 1986

Conze, E. *Buddhist Thought in India* (Ann Arbor Paperbacks). Ann Arbor: The University of Michigan Press, 1967

Conze, E. *The Prajñâpâramitâ Literature*, 2nd rev. and enlarged ed. (Bibliographia Philologica Buddhica, Series Maior 1). Tokyo: The Reiyukai, 1978

Conze, Edward. *The Large Sutra on Perfect Wisdom*. Berkeley, Los Angeles, London: University of California Press, 1975

Conze, Edward. *Buddhist Scriptures* (Penguin Classics). Harmondsworth, UK: Penguin Books, 1984

Coward, Harold. *Sacred Word—Sacred Text*. Maryknoll: Orbis Books, 1988

Dargyay, E. *The Rise of Esoteric Buddhism*. Delhi: Motilal Banarsidass, 2nd ed. 1979

Dargyay, Eva K. "A Rnying-ma Text: The *Kun byed rgyal po'i mdo*" *Soundings in Tibetan Civilization*, ed. by Aziz, Barbara N. and M. Kapstein. New Delhi: Manohar Publications, 1985, pp. 283–293

Dargyay, Eva K. "The Concept of a 'Creator God' in Tantric Buddhism," in *Journal of the International Association of Buddhist Studies* 1985, 8, pp.31–47

Detweiler, Robert. "What is a Sacred Text?" in *Reader Response Approaches to Biblical and Secular Texts* (Semeia 31), ed. by Robert Detweiler. Decatur, GA: Society of Biblical Literature, 1985

Dürr, Hans Peter (ed.). *Physik und Transzendenz*. Bern/Munich/Vienna: Scherz Verlag, 1986

Dyczkowski, Mark S.G. *The Doctrine of Vibration. An Analysis of the Doctrines and Practices of Kashmirian Shaivism*. Albany, NY: State University of New York Press, 1987

Eimer, Helmut. "Some Results of Recent Kanjur Research" *Archiv für zentralasiatische Geschichtsforschung*, ed. by Schuh, Dieter and M. Weiers. Sankt Augustin, West Germany: VGH Wissenschaftsverlag, 1983, fasc. 1

Encyclopaedia of Buddhism ed. by Malalasekera, George P. Colombo: Government of Sri Lanka, 1961

Frye, Northrop. *The Great Code*. San Diego: Harcourt Brace Jovanovich, Publishers, 1982

Giles, Herbert A. (tr.) *Chuang Tzu, Taoist Philosopher and Chinese Mystic*. 1889, rpt. London: Allen and Unwin, 1980

Gonda, Jan. "The Creator and his Spirit (*Manas* and *Prajâpati*)" in *Wiener Zeitschrift für die Kunde Südasiens* vol. 27, 1983, pp.5–42

Granoff, Phyllis. "The Yogavâsistha: the Continuing Search for a Context" in *Silver Jubilee Volume*, Poona University, Centre for Advanced Studies of Sanskrit (forthcoming)

Grönbold, Günter. *Der Buddhistische Kanon, eine Bibliographie*. Wiesbaden: Otto Harrassowitz, 1984

Guenther, Herbert V. *The Tantric View of Life*. Berkeley, London: Shambala Publications, 1972

Guenther. *Matrix of Mystery* Boulder: Shambhala, 1984

Imaeda, Yoshiro. *Catalogue du Kanjur Tibetain de l'edition de 'Jang Sa-tham* (Bibliographia Philologica Buddhica Series Maior IIa) Tokyo: The International Institute for Buddhist Studies, 1982

Kalupahana, David J. *A Path of Righteousness—Dhammapada*. Lanham/New York/London: University Press of America, 1986

Karmay, Samten G. "An Open Letter by Pho-brang Zhi-ba-'od to the Buddhists in Tibet" *The Tibet Journal* vol. 5, no. 3, 1980, pp.3–28

Karmay, Samten G. "The rDzogs-chen in Its Earliest Text: A Manuscript from Tun-huang", *Soundings in Tibetan Civilization*, ed. by B.N. Aziz and M. Kapstein. New Delhi: Manohar, 1985, pp.272–282

Karmay, Samten G. *The Great Perfection. A Philosophical and Meditative Teaching of Tibetan Buddhism*. Leiden: E.J. Brill, 1988 (I could not make use of the book to the extent I had wished.)

Klein, Anne C. "Primordial Purity and Everyday Life: Exalted Female Symbols and the Women of Tibet" in *Immaculate and Powerful* ed. by Atkinson, Buchanan, and Miles. Boston: Beacon Press, 1985

Klein, Anne C. "Non-Dualism and the Great Bliss Queen" in *Journal of Feminist Studies in Religion*, vol. I, 1, 1984

Klein, Anne C. "Gain or Drain? Buddhist and Feminist Views on Compassion" in *Women and Buddhism* (*Spring Wind—Buddhist Cultural Forum* vol. 6, 1–3,) 1986, pp.105–116

Kristeva, J. *Le texte du roman. Approche sémiologique d'une structure discursive transformationelle*. The Hague: Mouton, 1970

Lai, Whalen and Lewis R. Lancaster (eds.) *Early Ch'an in China and Tibet* (Berkeley Buddhist Studies Series 5). Berkeley: Asian Humanities Press, 1983

La Vallee Poussin, Louis de. *Catalogue of the Tibetan Manuscripts from Tun-huang in the India Office Library*. London: Oxford University Press, 1962

Lalou, Marcelle. "Documents Tibétain sur l'expansion du dhyâna Chinois" *Journal Asiatique* 1939, 505

Lamotte, Etienne. *Histoire du Bouddhisme Indien des Origines à l'ère Saka*. Bibliothèque du Muséon. Leuven: Université de Louvain, 1958, rpt. 1967

Lancaster, Lewis. "Buddhist Literature: Its Canons, Scribes, and Editors" in *The Critical Study of Sacred Texts*, ed. by Wendy D. O'Flaherty. Berkeley: Graduate Theological Union, 1979, pp.215–229

Lanigan, Richard L. *Speaking and Semiology. Maurice Merleau-Ponty's Phenomenological Theory of Existential Communication*. The Hague: Mouton, 1972

Loseries, Ulrich. *Guru Padmasambhavas "Instruktion 'Die Kette der Anschauungen'"* (Inaugural-Dissertation Friedrich-Wilhelm Universität, Bonn). Bonn: n.p., 1989

Mainkar, T.G. *The Yogâvasistha Râmâyana: A Study*. Sangli: Prabha Press, 1955

Moi, Toril. *Sexual/Textual Politics: Feminist Literary Theory*. London and New York: Methuen, 1985

Muller-Ortega, Paul Eduardo. *The Triadic Heart of Shiva. Kaula Tantricism of Abhinavagupta in the Non-dual Shaivism of Kashmir*. Albany, NY: State University of New York, 1989

Müller, F. Max. *The Dhammapada—a Collection of Verses* (Sacred Books of the East X). Rpt. Delhi: Motilal Banarsidass 1968

Osaki, Akiko. "What is meant by destroying the âlayavijñâna?" *Indogaku Bukkyôgaku Kenkyû* (Journal of Indian and Buddhist Studies: Univ. of Tokyo) XXVI.2

Prigogine, Ilya/Isabelle Stengers. *Order out of Chaos, Man's Dialogue with Nature*. New York: Bantam Books, 1984

Ritter, Joachim (ed.). *Historisches Wörterbuch der Philosophie*. Darmstadt: Wissenschaftliche Buchgesellschaft, 1974

Roerich, George (ed. and tr.). *Biography of Dharmasvâmin (Chag lo-tsa-ba Chos-rje-dpal) a Tibetan Monk Pilgrim*. Patna: K.P. Jayaswal Research Insitute, 1959

Ruegg, D.S. *The Life of Bu ston Rin po che* (Serie Orientale Roma 34). Rome: Istituto Italiano per il Medio ed Estremo Oriente, 1966

Schmithausen, Lambert. *Alayavijñâna. On the Origin and the Early Development of a Central Concept of Yogâcâra Philosophy* (Studia Philologica Buddhica, Monograph Series IV). Tokyo: The International Institute for Buddhist Studies, 1987

Schopen, Greg. "The Inscription on the Kusân Image of Amitâbha and the Character of the Early Mahayana in India", in *Journal of the International Association of Buddhist Studies* vol. 10,2, 1987, pp.99–137

Seizan, Yanagida in "The *Li-tai Fa-pao Chi* and the Ch'an Doctrine of Sudden Awakening" in Lai, Whalen and L. Lancaster, 1983, 13–49.

Streng, F.J. *Emptiness—A Study in Religious Meaning*. Nashville, Tenn.: Abingdon Press, 1967

Suzuki, Daisetz Teitaro. *The Zen Doctrine of No-Mind*, ed. by Chr. Humphreys. New York: Samuel Weiser, 1973

Takasaki, Jikido. *A Study on the Ratnagotravibhâga (Uttaratantra) Being a Treatise on the Tathâgatagarbha Theory of Mahâyâna Buddhism* (Serie Orientale Roma 33). Rome: Istituto Italiano per il Medio ed Estremo Oriente, 1966

Thomi, Peter (tr.). *Cûdâlâ. Eine Episode aus dem Yogavasistha*. Wichtrach: Institut für Indologie, 1980

Thomi, Peter (tr.). *Yogavasistha. Die Lehren des Weisen Vasistha*. Interlaken: Ansata Verlag, 1988

Tsong-kha-pa. *The Yoga of Tibet, the Great Exposition of Secret Mantra—2 and 3*. Intr. by H.H. the XIVth Dalai Lama, tr. and ed. by Jeffrey Hopkins. Wisdom of Tibet Series 4. London: George Allen & Unwin, 1981

Tucci, Giuseppe *Minor Buddhist Texts* (Serie Orientale Roma IX). Rome: Istituto Italiano per il Medio ed Estremo Oriente, 1956

Tucci, Giuseppe. *Tibetan Painted Scrolls*. Rome: La Libreria dello Stato, 1949

Visvader, John and William C. Doub. "The Problem of Desire and Emotions in Taoism and Ch'an," in Lai, Wahlen and L.R. Lancaster 1983, pp.281–297

Wilber, Ken (ed.). *The Holographic Paradigm and Other Paradoxes*. Boston: Shambhala, 1982

Yampolsky, Philip. "New Japanese Studies in Early Ch'an History" in W. Lai and Lewis R. Lancaster 1983, pp.1–11

GENERAL INDEX

INDEX OF TIBETAN TERMS AND NAMES